ANTHONY J. PAYNE

POLITICS IN JAMAICA

C. HURST & COMPANY, LONDON
HEINEMANN EDUCATIONAL BOOKS (CARIBBEAN)

First published in the United Kingdom by
C. Hurst & Co. (Publishers) Ltd.,
38 King Street, London WC2E 8JT,
in association with
Heinemann Educational Books (Caribbean) Ltd.,
175 Mountain View Road, Kingston 6, Jamaica,

Printed in England on long-life paper

ISBN: 1-85065-046-2

POLITICS IN JAMAICA

PREFACE AND ACKNOWLEDGEMENTS

I first visited Jamaica in September 1974. Young and naive, I came as a research student attached to the Department of Government at the Mona campus of the University of the West Indies. My arrival was a vivid introduction to the ways of the Third World. 'Immigration' held me for several hours, suspicious of anyone who seemed intent on studying politics at the University; by the time I emerged, anyone who might have been meeting me off the flight had long since left the airport; all the phone lines into Kingston were down as a result of heavy rains over the previous two days; the bank was closed, and I clambered, exhausted, into a taxi to take that first exciting drive along the Palisadoes, around the bay and into the sounds and sights of Kingston. From that moment onwards I never really looked back. I stayed the year, did my research and fell for Jamaica.

Since then I have returned to the island at every opportunity, followed its politics consistently, and responded positively to every request made by academic colleagues to write or talk about Jamaica. The result was the production of a number of articles and conference papers, some published, some not, most not easily accessible to the general reader interested in the political fortunes of Jamaica. I did not set out to write a book, and owe the idea of gathering together what I had written and shaping it into a commentary on the post-independence experience of Jamaica to several friends who persuaded me that such a survey of politics in the most important island territory in the Commonwealth Caribbean would be of interest to students of Third World politics generally.

It is therefore necessary to acknowledge where some of the following chapters were published in their original versions. Chapters 1 and 2 derive from *The Journal of Commonwealth and Comparative Politics*, XXI, 2, and XIV, 1, respectively; Chapter 4 appeared in *Dependency under Challenge: The Political Economy of the Commonwealth Caribbean*, a work edited by myself and Paul Sutton (Manchester University Press, 1984); Chapter 5 was published in an earlier form in *The World Today*, 37, 11; Chapters 7 and 9 first saw the light of day in *The Round Table*, 295 and 302 respectively; Chapter 8 appeared in *Third World Quarterly*, 9, 3; and Chapter 10 was adapted, in part, from my book, *The Politics of the Caribbean Community 1961–79: Regional Integration amongst New States* (Manchester University Press, 1980). In preparing this book I have, where necessary, edited the original versions of the argument, but I must still thank all the editors and publishers referred to above for the permission they granted me to use the substance of the material I had already published under their auspices.

Other colleagues who have helped me to understand politics in Jamaica and other parts of the Caribbean are genuinely too numerous to mention by name, but they receive my thanks. Two debts, however, must be personally acknowledged. One is to Dennis Austin, my former professor at the University of Manchester, who was responsible for sending me to Jamaica in the first place. Still a valued friend, he read the entire manuscript and, as always, made many suggestions for its improvement. The other is to Charles Mills, Professor of Government in the University of the West Indies, who looked after me in my first anxious days in Jamaica and has also remained a friend ever since. A great Jamaican, I hope that he will read the book with interest and, at least, a small sense of responsibility for its existence! Finally, I hope that other Jamaicans will not be offended by the appearance of a book about their affairs written by an outsider. I ask them to receive it as a critical tribute to their country by someone who feels great warmth and affection for all things Jamaican.

Sheffield,
November 1987

ANTHONY J. PAYNE

CONTENTS

BASIC DATA

Population	1,848,512 (census of 7 April 1970). 2,095,878 (census of 8 June 1982).
Population density	493 per sq. mile (1982).
Economically active	925,800 (1982).
Life expectancy	71.2 years (1981).
Infant mortality	16.2 per 1,000 live births (1978).
Ethnic composition	76% African descent; 15% Afro-European; 9% Chinese, Afro-Chinese, East Indian and European.
Capital	Kingston (population of metropolitan area, 643,809 [1977]).
Area	4,243 sq. miles (10,991 sq. km.).
Language	English (official). A creole *patois* is also widely spoken.
Religion	Predominantly Christian: the Anglican, Roman Catholic and Presbyterian Churches are the principal denominations. Also a growing community of Rastafarians.
International affiliations	CARICOM and the Caribbean Development Bank, the African, Caribbean and Pacific Group in association with the EEC, the World Bank and IMF, the Inter-American Development Bank, the OAS, the Commonwealth and the UN.
Governmental structure	Parliamentary Democracy.
Head of State	Queen Elizabeth II.
Governor-General	Sir Florizel A. Glasspole.
Legislature	Bicameral, composed of a Senate of 21 appointed members and a House of Representatives of 60 elected members.
Executive	Cabinet, led by the Prime Minister, who is responsible to Parliament.
Judicature	Supreme Court, Court of Appeal and Resident Magistrates' Courts, with right of final appeal to the Judicial Committee of the Privy Council in the United Kingdom.
Defence	Total defence force in July 1984: 9,720, comprising a paramilitary force of 6,000, army of 3,500, navy of 140 and air force of 80.
Political parties	1. **Jamaica Labour Party**. *Leader*: Edward Seaga; *Chair*: Bruce Golding; *Gen. Sec.*: Ryan Peralto.

2. **People's National Party**. *President*: Michael Manley; *Chair*: P.J. Patterson; *Gen. Sec.*: Dr Paul Robertson.

3. **Workers' Party of Jamaica**. *Gen. Sec.*: Dr Trevor Munroe.

Communications media

Daily newspapers	2— est. daily circulation, 84,091.
Televisions	160,000 in use (1983).
Radios	856,960 in use (1983).
Telephones	119,000 in use (1980).

Transport

Railways	205 miles of standard-gauge track.
Roads	6,986 miles, of which 4,720 are paved.
Ports	Principally Kingston, Montego Bay and Montego Freeport.
Airports	Norman Manley International Airport, Kingston, and Donald Sangster International Airport, Montego Bay.

Education

Primary	Free and compulsory at ages 6–11, involving 359,488 children in 894 schools (1980)
Secondary	Competitive entry, involving 56% of children aged 12–18 (1980).
Higher	College of Arts, Science and Technology, the School of Agriculture, and the Mona campus of the University of the West Indies.
Adult literacy rate	96.1% (1970).
Government expenditure	13.1% of total (1980).

Economy

Gross National Product	J$5,512.4 million (1982).
Budget expenditure	Recurrent J$1,677.9 million; capital J$687.7 million (1980–1).
Imports	J$2,840.9 million (1983).
Exports	J$1,392.0 million (1983).
Main imports	Mineral fuels and lubricants; machinery and transport equipment; basic manufactures; food and livestock; chemicals.
Main exports	Crude materials except fuels; food and livestock.
Import sources	United States 39%; Venezuela 11%; Netherlands Antilles 11%; United Kingdom 7%; Canada 4%; and Japan 4%(1983).
Export destinations	United States 33%; United Kingdom 20%; Canada 12%; Trinidad and Tobago 9%; and Norway 8%(1983).
Foreign debt	J$10,095 million.

THE CARIBBEAN AREA
GULF OF MEXICO
UNITED STATES
Florida
Grand Bahama I.
Gt Abaco I.
New Providence
Eleuthera I.
Cat I.
Andros I.
S.Salvador or Watlings I.
Long I.
BAHAMA ISLANDS
Mayaguana I.
Caicos I.
Turks I.
Gt.Inagua I.
ATLANTIC OCEAN
CUBA
Grand Cayman I.
JAMAICA
HAITI
DOMINICAN REP
Puerto Rico
Virgin Is.
ANGUILLA
St Martin
BARBUDA
ST KITTS
NEVIS
ANTIGUA
MONTSERRAT
Guadeloupe
DOMINICA
Martinique
ST LUCIA
ST VINCENT
BARBADOS
GRENADA
TOBAGO
TRINIDAD
MEXICO
BELIZE
GUATEMALA
HONDURAS
EL SALVADOR
NICARAGUA
COSTA RICA
PANAMA
CARIBBEAN SEA
Aruba
Curacao
Bonaire
Margarita
VENEZUELA
GUYANA
SURINAM
BRAZIL
COLOMBIA
PACIFIC OCEAN
N
Statute miles
0
200
400
0
300
600
Kilometres

JAMAICA

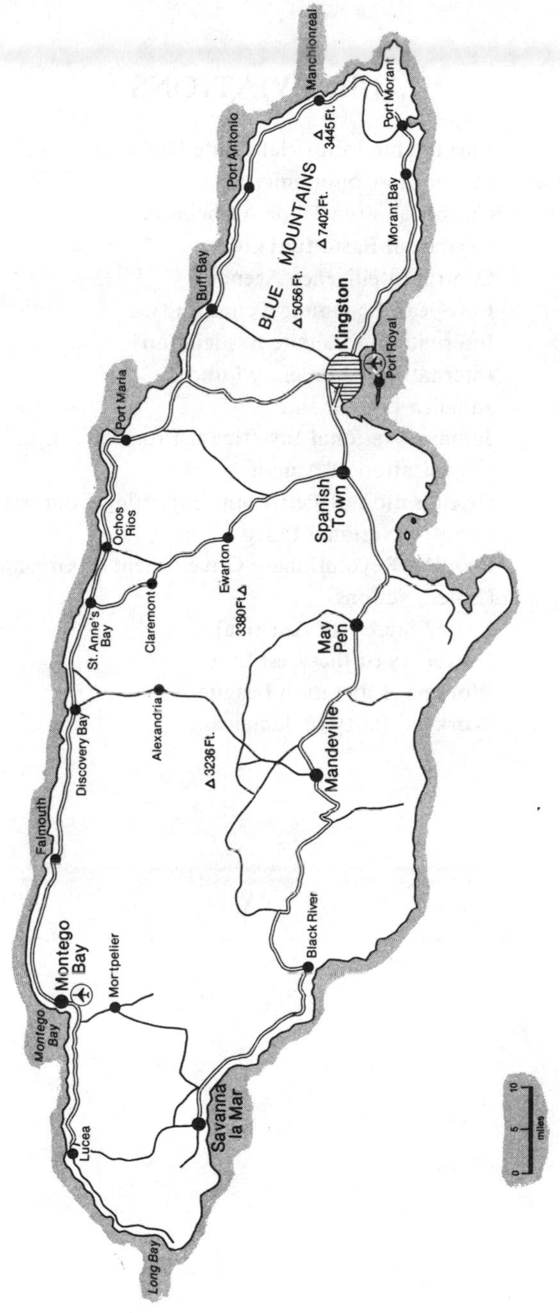

Long Bay
Lucea
Montego Bay
Montego Bay
Montpelier
Savanna la Mar
Black River
Falmouth
Discovery Bay
Alexandria
Δ 3236 Ft.
Mandeville
St. Anne's Bay
Claremont
Ewarton
3380 Ft. Δ
May Pen
Ochos Rios
Spanish Town
Port Maria
Kingston
Port Royal
Buff Bay
BLUE MOUNTAINS
Δ 5056 Ft.
Δ 7402 Ft.
Port Antonio
Morant Bay
Δ 3445 Ft.
Port Morant
Manchionreal
0 5 10
miles

ABBREVIATIONS

BITU	Bustamante Industrial Trade Union
CARICOM	Caribbean Community
CARIFTA	Caribbean Free Trade Association
CBI	Caribbean Basin Initiative
CIA	Central Intelligence Agency
EEC	European Economic Community
IBA	International Bauxite Association
IMF	International Monetary Fund
JLP	Jamaica Labour Party
JNIP	Jamaica National Investment Promotion Ltd.
OAS	Organisation of American States
OPEC	Organisation of Petroleum Exporting Countries
PNP	People's National Party
PRG	People's Revolutionary Government of Grenada
UN	United Nations
US(A)	United States (of America)
UWI	University of the West Indies
WLL	Workers' Liberation League
WPJ	Workers' Party of Jamaica

INTRODUCTION

JAMAICA SINCE INDEPENDENCE

Jamaica is one of the many new states created by Britain's retreat from empire since the end of the Second World War. It gained its political independence on 6 August 1962 and has just completed and survived its first quarter-century of statehood. Its experience during those twenty-five years has been extraordinarily vivid. Despite being only a small island of some 2 million people, Jamaica has contrived to make itself a big place whose affairs illuminate many of the post-colonial dilemmas of the Third World as a whole. The chapters that follow review different aspects of the political experience of the island since 1962. They begin their story, as any account of the modern history of Jamaica must, with the Rodney riots of 1968 – the moment when nationalism in the island was forced to embrace economics as well as politics – and end with an analysis of the prospects of the main political parties at a moment when they look forward to a general election. This introduction does not prejudge the subsequent discussion: it seeks only to lay out the agenda by considering what it is about Jamaican politics that is worthy of attention.

The answer falls into four parts. First, Jamaica is one of the relatively few recently independent states in the Third World to have maintained a working democratic system; secondly, it is one of the few such states to have successfully generated a sense of nationhood among its people; thirdly, it has experimented more than most with a variety of different strategies of economic development ranging from left to right across the ideological spectrum; and, fourthly, it has sought actively to find a role for itself in international politics. In short, Jamaica has not taken independence lying down. Its politics express a diversity of themes about which some general observations can be made before turning to the detail of the argument.

The maintenance of democracy

The maintenance of democracy in Jamaica is a real achievement, made the more impressive by the failure of so many other new states in this respect. Consider some of the norms of political life in Jamaica. Competitive elections take place: five have been held since independence. At least three major political parties presently exist, two of them having fought each other for control of the state over a period of more than forty years. Freedom of thought, expression and assembly is well established. Parliament survives and functions. Political leaders voluntarily relinquish office in the face of electoral defeat. The bureaucracy and the judiciary are not subject to excessive or unreasonable political interference. Indeed many honourable and dedicated public servants work long and hard in the service of the state. There is no torture or a secret police, nor has there been a military coup. In all of these ways Jamaica is unlike much of the rest of the developing world.

Nevertheless, one should not become too lyrical: nearly all of these points need to be qualified in some way. For example, Jamaican politics *are* violent. In all, some 750 people died in political conflicts in the months leading up to the 1980 election, including a minister in the government who was shot by a gunman. Although such an event was exceptional, it is the case that both the major political parties, the Jamaica Labour Party (JLP) and the People's National Party (PNP), have long organised their own political gangs as the means to defend their supporters' access to state patronage. The implements of violence were confined to the knife and *machete* until the growing involvement of Jamaicans in the illegal export of marijuana ('*ganja*') to the United States in the 1960s brought the gun to the island and made it a part of the political process.

Other features of the democratic apparatus of the country have also been strained on many occasions during the post-independence era. A list of political offences is easily assembled. There was gerrymandering of constituency boundaries by governments of both parties during the 1960s and 1970s; an extraordinary Gun Court Law was passed by the PNP government in 1974, permitting indefinite detention without right of appeal of persons found guilty of using firearms; both the JLP and the island's leading newspaper, *The Daily Gleaner*, overstepped the usual boundaries of legitimate opposition in the late 1970s in their zeal to unseat the government; a coup was planned by some officers in the Jamaica Defence Force, only to be discovered and stopped by the army's own command in June 1980; the election of 1983 was boycotted by the PNP following a dispute with the JLP government over the voters' register; and the House of Representatives since that time has been, in effect, a single-party assembly. None of these occurrences has *broken* Jamaican democracy, but they show that the system has its rough edges.

More generally, there are grounds for doubting the extent or depth of the political participation which is actually achieved within the framework of the institutions of democracy in the island. Jamaican politics and indeed Jamaican society are both élitist and authoritarian in their fundamental values. The parties are not mass organisations in any full sense. They are led by the educated middle class, funded by local businessmen, and only involve the masses as voters, cheerleaders and recipients of patronage. A strong personalist tradition – the 'hero' and his 'crowd'[1] – dominates the political culture, as evinced by the flamboyant style of all Jamaica's leading politicians, including Edward Seaga and Michael Manley in the present era. Although the potential excesses of this tendency have been kept in check by the other parts of the democratic system, the dangers of what West Indians sometimes call 'onemanism' remain. Jamaica is a society with a liking for populist and messianic rhetoric, something which is cultivated by its long-standing religiosity and tradition of respect for the figure of the 'preacher'.

Put together in this way, then, the evidence is more mixed. The quality of democracy in Jamaica leaves much to be desired and, even as it stands, needs to be constantly protected from unscrupulous leaders, trigger-happy gunmen and ambitious soldiers. The maintenance of democracy is hard work, but, by and large, Jamaica has toiled effectively in its cause. Powerful forces favouring democracy exist in the country, not least a people who have become attached to their own electoral tradition. Jamaica can still count as a democracy, especially when discussed in a Third World context. Elections have not been grotesquely rigged, as in Nigeria; former leaders have not been hanged by successor-regimes, as in Pakistan; prime ministers – to take a nearby Caribbean example – have not been put up against a wall and murdered, as in Grenada. All in all, given the pressures, it has been quite an heroic performance.

How is this to be explained? Theories of democracy range widely and often do not make clear where definition ends and theorising begins. Those theories that emphasise 'regime performance', satisfaction of popular demands and economic well-being do not shed much light on the Jamaican post-independence experience, much of which has revolved around the crisis of the economy and the containment of dissatisfaction. On stronger ground are theories which draw attention to the capacity of cross-cutting social cleavages to contribute to democratic stability by moderating the intensity of politics. Jamaicans generally possess a number of politically relevant affiliations (class, race, generation, party) which pull them in conflicting directions and reduce the zero-sum character of political conflict. The decline of a local plantocracy by the time of independence also removed from the Jamaican scene one of the most powerful

1. A.W. Singham, *The Hero and the Crowd in a Colonial Polity* (New Haven, 1968).

anti-democratic forces at work in other parts of the Third World. Even so, it is hard to be persuaded that socio-economic factors predetermine the nature of Jamaica's democracy.

Political factors must constitute the bulk of the explanation of the emergence of a democratic system. In this context the crucial consideration was Jamaica's experience of British colonialism. In a recent analysis of the prospects of further democratisation in the world, Samuel Huntington quoted the observation that 'every single country in the Third World that emerged from colonial rule since the second world war with a population of at least one million . . . with a continuous democratic experience is a former British colony'.[2] As he further noted, the effectiveness of British rule in encouraging democratic development appears to depend on the duration of that rule before independence. Whereas in most of Africa British colonialism lasted less than a century, Jamaica was part of the British Empire for over 300 years. The colonial legacy was long and deep: it left behind a respect for authoritarianism, but also an awareness of the possibilities of democracy. The preparation for democratic self-government was also more elaborate and sustained in Jamaica than in many other British colonies where independence came with great haste. Universal suffrage was first established in 1944 and was followed by a series of constitutional advances which crept closer and closer to full self-government until complete independence was granted.

The importance of all this is not to say that Britain left Jamaica with a perfect set of democratic institutions – the illusion of 'Westminster in the sun'. Similar inheritances collapsed quickly enough in other ex-British colonies. Rather, it is to suggest that Britain socialised a generation of Jamaicans into broadly democratic values. English-speaking, colonially educated, the recipients of élite scholarships from Jamaica College to Oxford, Cambridge and London, the beneficiaries of other training programmes in Britain – what else could the Jamaican élite become but would-be parliamentary democrats, especially since they grasped the fact that political independence granted on these terms would not bring them down from the top of the tree socially and economically? The result was that, at independence, local leaders who genuinely believed in democracy took responsibility for its preservation and continued the process of education and dissemination into the next generation.

It is this élite, incorporating politicians, civil servants, judges,

2. See Samuel Huntington, 'Will More Countries Become Democratic?', *Political Science Quarterly*, 99, 2 (1984), p. 26.

army officers, journalists, university teachers and others, which has been mainly responsible for the maintenance of that degree of openness and competitiveness which the Jamaican political system still possesses. The political crisis of 1980 was its greatest test. The democratic system was under genuine threat in a situation where preoccupation with politics was intense. Yet Manley did not rig the election in order to stay in power; the JLP stopped just short of inciting a complete breakdown of law and order; the Jamaica Defence Force caught the conspirators in its midst; and a team of honourable public servants was established to preside over the process of voter registration. Democracy came close to collapsing, but it did not do so. What the Jamaican experience reveals, above all, is that the democratic commitment of political leaders does have a significant impact on the prospects for stable democracy. With certain individual exceptions, the post-independence leadership of the Jamaican state has felt the necessary attachment to the democratic system and has displayed an adherence to the rules of the game – even, albeit waveringly, in times of stress and at the expense of sectional political goals. This has been the factor which has made the difference in underpinning the country's formal democratic structures.

The building of a nation

The building of a nation in Jamaica, though less traumatic than in some of the ethnically divided new states of Africa and Asia, has been just as critical to the country's future stability and prospects. What all Jamaicans do at least have in common, notwithstanding the racial and colour divisions of the society, is that they were originally immigrants to the land which they now inhabit. There are no aboriginal inhabitants, no pre-colonial cultures. This did not create a *tabula rasa*: the gulf between the African culture of the bulk of the imported slave population and the British colonial culture of the ruling minority long precluded the emergence of a unified Jamaican identity. The process of building one arguably did not even begin till the 1930s, but it was fostered by the attainment of political independence, and Jamaica today possesses a remarkably confident sense of national identity.

The political leadership must again take some of the credit. It was admittedly aided by the basic homogeneity and small size of the country, which made the construction of a national political life easier. Yet it is important that all Jamaica's post-independence leaders, without exception, have sought to present their politics in nationalist terms. They have, for example, subscribed to and sustained the tradition of Jamaica's official 'national heroes'. These canonised figures represent a revealing racial and class cross-section of Jamaican historical society – the legendary Nanny, a leading figure in the resistance to the British in the eighteenth century by the Maroons (descendants of former slaves of the Spanish); the slave leader Sam Sharpe who led a major revolt in 1831; the coloured gentleman George William Gordon and the black Christian deacon Paul Bogle, heroes of the Morant Bay rebellion of 1865; Marcus Garvey, the voice of black African consciousness; and the near white lower-class moneylender Alexander Bustamante and the brown-skinned lawyer Norman Manley, the founding fathers respectively, of the JLP and the PNP. In practice, too, all governments since 1962 have endeavoured to weld together the racial segments of Jamaican society. Sometimes the effort has been primarily rhetorical, as in the JLP administration's identification of itself in the late 1960s as a 'black power' government; but sometimes it has been more meaningful, as in the PNP government's attempts to establish diplomatic ties with African states and embrace African cultural forms in the 1970s.

Looked at over all the years since independence, the result has been a considerable step towards the full social inclusion of the black masses into the mainstream of society. During the 1970s many black Jamaicans did come to feel for the first time that they were full members of a national community, entitled to be treated as citizens on an equal basis with others of a lighter skin. Despite the economic hardships which have followed, that self-confidence has not been lost. Even the Rastafarian community, vilified and excluded from normal social intercourse in the 1960s, has been legitimised as an accepted part of society. Indeed for a while, the cultural characteristics of the movement, if not all its religious connotations, became a feature of youthful middle-class rebelliousness. Social values have changed and the social structure of the country has been loosened up. Modern Jamaica is far from being a haven of racial tolerance, but it has moved a long way towards forging a sense of national identity which genuinely crosses racial boundaries.

This consciousness is visible, moreover, not only in Jamaica itself but wherever Jamaicans live – in Brixton and Brooklyn as much as in Kingston and Mandeville. Jamaicans are proud of their nationality, often assertively and aggressively so. 'JA', as the country is popularly known, is the homeland to which travellers fondly return and in which many older migrants aspire one day to live again. This feeling is one of the reasons why Jamaicans living in Britain and the United States often find it harder than other immigrant groups to accept the conventions of their new environments and why

Jamaicans have long been suspicious – to the point of disruption – of all attempts to integrate their identity into a wider West Indian framework. In Jamaica, as in other societies, the negative side of nationalism is an intense parochialism.

The positive side, and very much part of the phenomenon, is a vivid cultural nationalism. The popular *reggae* music of Bob Marley has become famous all over the Western world, but Marley is only the most widely known of a large number of Jamaican writers, artists and musicians. For a new state only just finding its feet as an independent entity, Jamaica has made a remarkable contribution to the world of the arts. The novels of Roger Mais, the dialect poetry of Louise Bennett, the sculpture of Edna Manley, the painting of Karl Parboosingh – all attest to the vigour of the cultural tradition in modern Jamaica. Add to their work the reputation of such formal national organisations as the Jamaica Folk Singers and the National Dance Theatre Company, and one can understand that being and feeling Jamaican generates a vivid creativity in many of its people. What is more, the best of Jamaican culture reflects precisely the nationalist fusion – that peculiar and enticing blend of what Rex Nettleford, in a felicitous phrase, called 'the melody of Europe, the rhythm of Africa'.[3] Its political significance is the greater because it is a popular culture that is expressed on the streets as much as on the verandahs of the houses of the élite.

Compared to other Third World states which have experienced civil wars, ethnic riots and communal violence, Jamaica again stands out as a relative success story. The colonial legacy was not as arbitrary in its shaping of the nation as in some other parts of the world where tribal peoples were lassooed together by lines drawn on a map by European governments. The sea has defined who is and who is not a Jamaican, thereby adding that extra sense of 'islandness' to the national identity. However, the racial divisions that do exist in Jamaican society could have been exacerbated by different actions and policies by governments and the people, and it is noteworthy that on the whole the trend has been in another, more creative direction.

The pursuit of development

The pursuit of development has been the greatest burden which Jamaican governments have had to carry in the period since

3. Rex Nettleford, *Mirror Mirror: Identity, Race and Protest in Jamaica* (London, 1970), p. 173.

independence, and here their record has been unimpressive. It is not that Jamaica is a desperately poor country, like Haiti, but rather that the performance of the economy since the 1960s has failed to match the ever-expanding demands of the Jamaican people for material improvements in their standard of living. These aspirations are nurtured by Jamaica's location within the ambit of the developed world. Its people are daily made aware of the consumer expectations of the North American continent via media contact and personal observation of the lifestyle of tourists. This is the context within which it is necessary to measure the historically high rate of unemployment in the island and the truly awful conditions in which the poor of West Kingston habitually live. The reality is that the Jamaican economy ought to have done better. By the standards of other developing countries, Jamaica is not short of natural resources, which range from agricultural land to bauxite and beaches, and it is situated close to the world's largest market in the United States. With these endowments, the country ought to have been able to find a path towards broadly consistent economic growth which would in turn have generated the resources to raise the living standards of the poor substantially. Certainly, every government since 1962 has been publicly committed to this goal.

What is striking in looking at the actual management of the economy since independence is the variety of development strategies which have been espoused by different governments at different times. Jamaica has been a laboratory of economic modelling. The policy of the 1962–72 JLP government was geared towards import-substitution industrialisation; it offered foreign capitalists a protected market and relied upon the establishment, by the state, of incentives to attract them to set up industrial enterprises in the island. Local businessmen were encouraged to play a subordinate role within what was no more than a form of neo-colonial development. The policy of the PNP government which came to power in 1972 envisaged a more assertive role for the state in winning greater independence for Jamaica within the world economy. Foreign capital was permitted to operate, but to an increasing extent only on the state's terms, which included on occasion joint ownership; local capital was equally encouraged but required to distribute more of its profits to its workers in the form of higher wages and improved conditions. This populist model threatened briefly to develop into a form of state socialism which had the effect of frightening off all forms of capital and bringing the economy virtually to the point of collapse. After 1980 the JLP government reverted to the open embrace of foreign capital but shifted the focus of development towards the goal of export-led growth. The apparatus of protection was dismantled, the role of the state downgraded, and local business left to sink or swim in the world market. The story has thus been of a journey from neo-colonialism to contemporary economic liberalism by way of populism and a brief flirtation with Marxist socialism.

At each stage, however, the mix of factors has been flawed in some way. The neo-colonial strategy generated 'growth without development'; it delivered benefits to a narrow section of Jamaican society but could not find a satisfactory way of dispersing the gains widely enough among the people as a whole. The extent of 'trickle-down' was insufficient. The populist strategy put the state in the driving seat and temporarily won substantial new welfare benefits for the poor and dispossessed; but it was allowed to run out of control until it so alarmed capitalist interests that growth ceased. When this happened, neither the state nor the workforce was willing or able to fill the productive gap. The liberal strategy has deflated the economy and squeezed general living standards to the point where a sufficient 'adjustment' is deemed to have taken place to allow for resumed growth, but cannot work out who is to lead that process if foreign capital remains largely uninterested. The state is not acceptable for ideological reasons, and local capital is not able for competitive market reasons.

In the meantime, ordinary Jamaicans have had to live through a long and gloomy period in which they have seen unemployment remain high, prices rise hugely, the country's debts escalate, basic infrastructure visibly deteriorate and the productive sector of the economy weaken substantially and dangerously. Some indeed would say that only the hidden *ganja* economy has kept the country solvent. The fact is that only the rich have been able to stay ahead of the economy's relative decline – either by departing completely to Miami or by retreating higher and higher into protected fortresses in the hills surrounding Kingston. Guarded by their dogs and looking out from behind the bars on their windows, they at least are partly insulated from the growing sense of despair about the future of the economy – *under any conceivable model of development* – which now dominates the public mind.

Is the despair justified? Or are there positive lessons which can be drawn from the very diversity of Jamaica's efforts to generate economic development? The issue of the dependence of the Jamaican economy on external forces which it cannot control is a live one, and although it would be over-simple to claim that every model of development tried in Jamaica has been broken on the back of changes outside the country within the international economy, it would not be wrong. The ebb and flow of the bauxite industry, the price of oil, the state of the sugar markets, the level of activity in the US economy – all these considerations have played a major part in the functioning of the political economy of post-independence Jamaica: they shape and limit the policies which can realistically be pursued. Yet it is too severe to claim that they determine them. Other conclusions also emerge: that the state cannot afford to opt out of the pursuit of development; that the local bourgeoisie in Jamaica, though too weak to lead the growth process, is sufficiently strong to damage it; that foreign capital can be no more dispensed with than relied upon; and that the working people of the country are prepared to accept major sacrifices in their standard of living to bring about economic recovery.

The irony is that Jamaica has still to experiment with the one development model which seems to fit such conclusions best. Widely adopted in other comparable Third World states, Petras has inelegantly labelled it 'national developmentalism'.[4] This strategy is characterised by the deployment of state resources to support the activities of weak national capitalists. Although the precise mix between state and private entrepreneurial leadership of this process can vary, the goal of redefining dependence to favour national class interests at the expense of foreign interests remains the same. Policies typically include selective nationalisations, joint ventures between the state and private capital, the progressive imposition of constraints on the inflow of foreign investment, and the enactment of incomes and wages policies to control the flow of rewards to the workforce. By these means the state takes responsibility for the generation of economic growth but does not seek to bring the economy into its total control or eliminate the need for private capital. Measured in terms of an expanding gross national product, it has proved to be a quite effective mix in a number of diverse settings, such as South Korea and Kenya.

The question is whether such a 'national developmental' model could work in Jamaica. The main problems are threefold. First, there is the matter of whether the civil service machine, which has historically been conservative and generalist, in line with its British origins, could acquire sufficient edge to prime the development process. Secondly, there is doubt as to the capacity of the Jamaican business sector to take advantage of the niche in the productive part of the economy which such a strategy would require it to fill. Thirdly, there is the difficulty of constraining levels of popular

4. James Petras, 'New Perspectives on Imperialism and Social Classes in the Periphery', *Journal of Contemporary Asia*, 5, 3 (1975), p. 298.

consumption while resources are put into investment and production. All are formidable problems, solutions to which would require much energy and political skill, as well as an external economic environment characterised by expansion rather than contraction. Nevertheless, analysis of Jamaica's experience with development policy since independence suggests that this is the only road left, short of socialist revolution.

The search for an international role

The search for a role in international politics has also characterised the post-independence period in Jamaica. As in other states coming to independence, foreign affairs was the one area of policy in which there was no previous experience upon which to draw. A foreign policy machine embracing diplomats, civil servants and intelligence analysts had to be created from scratch, and a body of knowledge of international affairs laboriously built up - none of which is easily done in conditions of resource scarcity. Few new states are therefore able to make a mark in international politics in their early years of independence, and Jamaica was no exception.

Nevertheless, Third World states do have decisions to take on the type of foreign policy they wish to pursue once the inevitable learning phase is past. The literature of international relations broadly identifies two available models of behaviour, which have been described respectively as 'the acquiescent adaptation' approach and the 'uses of foreign policy' approach.[5] The first conceives of the external environment as, at best, providing a limited range of policy options and consequent minimum flexibility for the small developing state as international actor. The second views foreign policy as a means to support the achievement of domestic objectives and regards the international system as capable of manipulation to the advantage even of the smallest states. The Jamaican experience suggests, however, that these two models pose too simple a choice and that, in reality, the line between adaptation and activism is considerably more blurred.

What does the record of Jamaica show? Certainly, the foreign policy adopted by the first JLP government in the 1960s was primarily characterised by acquiescence in the dominant Western view of the world, as encapsulated within Bustamante's bald declaration that Jamaica was 'with the West'. But by the end of the

5. Vaughan Lewis, 'Issues and Trends in Jamaican Foreign Policy 1972–77' in Carl Stone and Aggrey Brown (eds), *Perspectives on Jamaica in the Seventies* (Kingston, 1981), pp. 43–4.

decade, driven by domestic political pressures, there was beginning to be apparent a growing sensitivity to Third World trends towards non-alignment and associated arguments about the assertion of sovereignty over natural resources. The government assumed observer status in the Non-Aligned Movement, engaged in a more active diplomacy at the United Nations on such issues as apartheid and the future of Southern Africa, and, following Britain's application to join the European Economic Community (EEC), was forced to accept the importance of international economic bargaining on such matters as the trading arrangements for protected crops like sugar and bananas. In short, Jamaica was tentatively asserting itself in the outside world, but was still constrained by a desire for its behaviour to be seen as 'respectable'.

From these beginnings the country unquestionably moved out into the full glare of the international system under Michael Manley's leadership in the 1970s. The new activism began with a warm embrace of the process of Commonwealth Caribbean integration, and grew into a search for contacts with other parts of the Caribbean and Latin America and indeed the whole of the Third World. Jamaica took up positions on such issues as the future of Angola, the role of the Palestine Liberation Organisation and the struggles of the Vietnamese people. The world was Manley's stage, and for a while he strode it with panache and conviction. It cannot be denied that positive advantages were won for Jamaica through its active participation in such international matters as the Law of the Sea negotiations and the talks that led to the signing of the Lomé Convention. The problem was that Manley ultimately burnt his fingers through some of the excesses of his activist diplomacy. From Washington's perspective, the close relationship which was developed with Cuba placed Jamaica's foreign policy in an East-West context and eventually brought retaliatory action that was profoundly damaging to the economy. Jamaica had embraced the cause of 'anti-imperialism' at the rhetorical level, but it lacked the means to fight it either politically or economically.

The reaction against the militancy of this phase of Jamaican foreign policy led the country to retreat into the protective arms of the United States. After 1980 Seaga went out of his way to court the US administration and was rewarded with increased aid, an easing of trade barriers, political support in dealing with the International Monetary Fund and endless encomiums from President Reagan. Seaga worked hard to obtain these favourable terms. He was one of the originators of the US Caribbean Basin Initiative (CBI); he was vigorous in his criticism of the revolutionary government in

Grenada; he has repeatedly sought to persuade other Commonwealth Caribbean governments within the Caribbean Community (CARICOM) to extend the organisation to include other pro-US states in the region like the Dominican Republic and Haiti. It is not for nothing that he has been frequently described as 'America's man in the Caribbean'. To adopt the terminology of the models of foreign policy mentioned earlier, Jamaica under Seaga's leadership has been active in its acquiescence in and adaptation to US hegemony in the Caribbean.

The question that arises is whether there is another option. Is it possible for a country like Jamaica to construct a foreign policy in which the mix is the reverse - in which the activism is adapted to geopolitical reality? There are, clearly, limits beyond which a Caribbean state cannot go without incurring the powerful displeasure of the United States. Cuba, Nicaragua and the Soviet Union are all out of bounds except for the most perfunctory of economic dealings. Yet that is not to say that a more assertive 'Third Worldist' approach is inherently unviable. The lesson of post-independence Jamaica in this respect is that there are ways of making the international system work to domestic advantage, but that the task has to be undertaken with a blend of vigour and caution, boldness and *realpolitik*, which no Jamaican government has quite achieved so far. Seaga's vision of the international stage is unnecessarily limited to the American lake in which he sits; Manley's was too expansive and insufficiently aware of the constraints imposed by Jamaica's location. Jamaica unavoidably has to operate in the active presence of an aggressive superpower, but it does not have to be a client-state.

Indeed, the lesson is a general one. What emerges from these introductory remarks about post-independence Jamaica is the existence of options within limits. At root this is what Third World politics is about. There *is* a path between the determinism of structural forces and the voluntarism of free choice, and it is the state which has to find that path. Jamaica has built up a broadly democratic political system, but that was not inevitable; it has developed a strong sense of nationalism, but that was not predetermined either; it has struggled to find a strategy of development that works, but has not yet exhausted all possibilities; and it has groped around for a role in world affairs, and found again that different stances are possible even within relatively narrow geopolitical limits. It is the choice of options which makes the politics of every Third World state different, and it is the fact that Jamaica has used its opportunities since independence in such a peculiarly creative way which makes its politics worthy of general interest.

1
THE RODNEY RIOTS

After two decades the Rodney riots of October 1968 still appear a deeply significant set of events in the post-independence history of Jamaica. They occurred when the government of Jamaica banned from the country Dr Walter Rodney, a lecturer at the University of the West Indies (UWI). The decision provoked anger and resentment among the students on the Jamaican campus of the University, which led them to march in protest into the city of Kingston. Broken up in violence by the police, the demonstration spilled over into an outbreak of rioting and looting by Kingston's unemployed and urban poor. The disorder lasted for a day or so before the authorities brought it under control. Shortly afterwards the University went back to work, Rodney's contract of employment was terminated, and the crisis seemed to have passed, leaving the Jamaican political system more or less intact.

However, the many implications of the affair could not be so quickly dismissed from view. It was not, as many Jamaicans feared, an incipient revolution, but it was without doubt a telling commentary on the state of affairs in the country only a few years after independence. Even at the time there was a realisation that the riots had brought the question of fundamental social and economic change to the centre of the political stage in Jamaica. Since then the country has been prepared to recognise the problem of inequality and has grappled with it openly, albeit without much success. Many therefore see the Rodney riots as a watershed in Jamaican history, denoting the proper beginning of the post-colonial era. This first chapter depicts the economic, social and political background to the riots, describes the dramatic events of October 1968, and assesses their significance for the development of politics in Jamaica.

Background

The origins of the Rodney riots lie ultimately in the plantation history of Jamaica which brought thousands of black slaves to work in the cane fields and left them without adequate means of support when emancipation, free trade and competition destroyed the system of sugar monoculture. Some ex-slaves established themselves as independent peasants, usually on poor land, and grew either food for the domestic market or new primary products for export, such as bananas; others continued to work as wage-labourers on the diminished number of plantations. The economy was not significantly restructured until after the Second World War, when it began to acquire its modern shape. Bauxite production began in 1952 and grew swiftly to an output of 1 million tonnes by 1953 and 6 million by 1958; tourism was developed as a further valuable earner of foreign exchange; and many light industrial plants were established on the island as a result of the policy, adopted by successive governments during the post-war period, of offering a range of incentives to overseas investors. By these various means the Jamaican economy was able to grow throughout the 1960s by an average of nearly 6 per cent annually.[1]

Yet despite this apparently creditable achievement, the economy remained weak and dependent in several ways. Domestic agriculture stagnated and was the source of continuing poverty in rural areas. Income distribution was more uneven than ever, the share of the poorest 40 per cent of the population in personal earned income declining from 7.2 per cent in 1958 to 5.4 per cent in 1968. Illiteracy, poor housing and unemployment remained the lot of vast numbers of Jamaicans. The level of unemployment and underemployment in the society had increased hugely, doubling from 12 per cent to 24 per cent during the very period of fast economic growth. The higher wage rates paid in the new mineral and manufacturing sectors encouraged people to forsake low-paid agricultural employment in the hope of finding work in these industries, even though the capital-intensive character of most of the imported technology meant that few jobs were created there. The expanding sectors generally forged very limited links with other parts of the economy. A substantial amount of sugar was still shipped in a raw state, although it was technically and commercially feasible to refine it on the island; most of the bauxite mined was exported as ore despite the advantages to Jamaica of processing it locally; the manufacturing sector consisted largely of 'screwdriver' operations, heavily dependent on the import of raw materials and partly finished components; and the tourist industry, notorious for its failure to integrate itself with local agriculture, was thus partly responsible for Jamaica's growing imports of foodstuffs. The overall effect was accurately described as 'a form of perverse growth'.[2]

1. For a full discussion, see O. Jefferson, *The Post-war Economic Development of Jamaica* (Kingston, 1972).
2. Ibid., p. 285.

Much of the explanation of the problems inherent in this pattern of growth lay in the nature of the foreign control to which the Jamaican economy was still subject at the end of the 1960s. The island's leading sugar estates were owned by a large British company, the bauxite industry was in the hands of four US and Canadian corporations, and many hotels were parts of foreign businesses. Banks and insurance companies, a large section of the communications network and even a number of basic public utilities (including the electricity and telephone services) were also foreign. Only in the manufacturing sector were most firms in majority local ownership, although the distinction between a family firm and the branch plant of a foreign company was hard to discern in practice. As a Jamaican economist pointed out, 'a family firm may manufacture a metropolitan product under a franchise, the clauses of which are so detailed that the metropolitan enterprise is determining almost all the major managerial decisions – raw and intermediate materials procurement, capital equipment, marketing methods, accounting formats and even employment policy.'[3] What is certain is that in Jamaica, as in so many other parts of the Third World, the generation of economic growth in the 1950s and 1960s was fuelled primarily by the inflow of private foreign capital in the cause of development, but was ultimately lost to the local economy *via* profit repatriation and the various other well-known aspects of intra-company transfer pricing.[4]

The flawed nature of the economic development experienced in Jamaica after the war produced a discordant class system. At the top of the social hierarchy it fostered the emergence of a local capitalist class allied in a subordinate role to foreign capital. This class was initially based on ownership of land and control of the colonial distributive trade through import/export agencies and commission houses, but succeeded in adjusting its role in the economy in the 1960s by moving, somewhat reluctantly, into local manufacturing, generally on behalf of former suppliers. It grew into a tightly-knit clique, not extending much beyond twenty-one family groupings and focused on just five inter-related 'super-groups': the Ashenheims, the Desnoes-Geddes, the Harts, the Henriques and the Matalons, who between them occupied more than one-third of the available directorships in the corporate economy[5] and did extremely

3. Steve de Castro, *Tax Holidays for Industry: Why we have to abolish them and how to do it* (Kingston, 1973), p. 6.
4. See N. Girvan, *Foreign Capital and Economic Underdevelopment in Jamaica* (Kingston, 1971).
5. S. Reid, 'An Introductory Approach to the Concentration of Power in the

well financially out of the post-war growth of the Jamaican economy. Other social groups also benefited, though to a lesser degree. The educated middle class took advantage of the growing numbers of professional and managerial positions being established both in the private and public sector, and the unionised sector of the working class was able to bargain effectively for improvements in wages and working conditions. This latter group comprised craftsmen, technicians and production workers throughout industry and commerce, but also included some unskilled manual and service workers in such key growth industries as bauxite.

Set against the numerically small groups which had gained from the Jamaican economic boom of the 1950s and 1960s were much larger sections of the people who had suffered both relatively and absolutely. Under the dual pressure of modernisation and the market, many peasants were forced off the land, emigrating to Kingston where they swelled the ranks of the urban poor and unemployed. Wage levels for many casual workers and domestic servants within the urban economy were such that even employment did not lead to any escape from poverty. The unemployed lived in appalling conditions, somehow existing below official subsistence levels. By the late 1960s they numbered some 150,000, approximately a quarter of the population of Kingston. Of these, at least one-third can be said to have comprised a *lumpenproletariat*, permanently detached from the labour market. The latter survived mainly through petty and organised crime, gambling, prostitution and trade in illegal commodities such as *ganja*. Many were involved in the Rastafarian movement.

Exacerbating this polarised class structure was the question of race. According to figures derived from census data for 1967, 91.4 per cent of the population were either fully or partly of African ancestry and thus considered black, 1.7 per cent were East Indian, 0.6 per cent Chinese, 0.8 per cent European white and 5.5 per cent some other category.[6] Yet the Jamaican capitalist class was characterised by an almost complete absence of blacks and a preponderance of Jews, local whites, Lebanese, Syrians and Chinese.[7] At the other end of the social spectrum it was almost exclusively blacks who were poor, unemployed and living in the West Kingston ghetto.

Jamaican Corporate Economy and Notes on its Origin' in Carl Stone and Aggrey Brown (eds), *Essays on Power and Change in Jamaica* (Kingston, 1977), pp. 15–44.

6. O.C. Francis, *The People of Modern Jamaica* (Kingston, 1963), pp. 1–5.
7. Reid, op. cit., p. 25.

As Gordon Lewis wrote, the grim reality of Jamaican life in the mid-1960s was 'of a racial separatism, undeclared yet virulent, that infected every nook and cranny of interpersonal and inter-class relationships, based on a social system characterised by strongly entrenched class-colour correlations'.[8] Class conflicts did not run exactly parallel to racial cleavages, but the links were too close for the tensions not to be readily apparent and occasionally felt.

For the first two decades after the introduction of universal suffrage in 1944, Jamaica's political system succeeded so well in containing the explosive implications of this social structure that the country gained something of a reputation in the world for political stability. Party, rather than class or race, was developed as the primary collective frame of reference for the politically conscious in Jamaica.[9] At the centre of the political system were two competing political parties, the JLP and the PNP. Formed as institutional expressions of the contrasting styles of their founding leaders, Alexander Bustamante and Norman Manley,[10] neither sought to build up a distinct class base or to concern itself with serious mass politicisation. Rather, they developed into electoral machines,[11] led and dominated by educated professionals who acted as brokers and bargainers in an attempt to assemble multiple-class coalitions that could contain the divergent interests of all social strata. Thus each party was financed by prominent members of the local capitalist class, serviced by trade unions run primarily as 'vote-catching annexes',[12] and defended in the ghettoes by political gangs drawn from the *lumpenproletariat* itself. At the same time, party leaderships paid homage to the official myth of the multiracialism of Jamaican society, well symbolised by the national motto of 'Out of

8. G.K. Lewis, *The Growth of the Modern West Indies* (New York, 1968), p. 191.
9. For a fuller account, see Carl Stone, *Class, Race and Political Behaviour in Urban Jamaica* (Kingston, 1973).
10. For a discussion of the political ideas of Norman Manley, the founder of the PNP, see R. Nettleford (ed.), *Manley and the New Jamaica* (London, 1971), and for a discussion of the political style of Alexander Bustamante, the founder of the JLP, see K.W.J. Post, 'The Politics of Protest in Jamaica, 1938: Some Problems of Analysis and Conceptualisation', *Social and Economic Studies*, 18 (1969), pp. 374–90.
11. P.D. Robertson, 'Party "Organization" in Jamaica', *Social and Economic Studies*, 21 (1972), pp. 30–43. This firmly rejects the thesis of an earlier article by P. Bradley that Jamaican political parties were genuine mass parties ('Mass Parties in Jamaica: Structure and Organization', *Social and Economic Studies*, 9 (1960), pp. 375–416). He argues that they were rather 'personalist political parties', incapable at that point in time of performing any other role than that of electoral mechanisms.
12. Lewis, op. cit., p. 179.

Many One People'. The resulting system impeded the formation of either class or racial solidarity among the large, massively underprivileged sector of the population. As Stone put it, 'it may seem to be a gross over-simplification to suggest that the alliances reflect grand conspiracies on the part of the privileged strata to manipulate and control the manual classes . . . [yet] . . . the effect of the strategy produces such a result.'[13] Accordingly, the positions of the two parties gradually converged until they differed only on a small range of issues, none of them threatening the common strategy of multiple-class, multiracial electoral appeals. The simple truth was that both parties shared a common stake in the stability of Jamaican political life and worked together to suppress the dissemination of disruptive political messages.

Therefore, despite superficial similarities to the political norms of Western liberal democracy, what emerged in Jamaica in the 1950s and 1960s was a clientelistic style of politics rooted in the particular pattern of economic development experienced in the country. The low level of employment made available by the highly capital-intensive strategy of industrialisation meant that the possibility of working for the state and its various departments, boards and corporations became ever more crucial as a source of livelihood. A patronage tradition developed in which political support was exchanged for the material benefit of a job or even a home.[14] In this way, mass participation in the political system was directly related to the welfare value of party politics. To insure against penetration of the system by a radical third alternative feeding on the material disaffection of the opposition party's clients, the opposition was traditionally allowed unofficial access to a minority portion of the available state largesse.[15] Social discontent was thereby reduced and channelled against the party in office, not against the political system itself, underlining again the role of partisan politics in containing a revolutionary expression of political alienation. In view of the absence of serious discussion of differing socio-economic or ideological alternatives, democratic participation in Jamaica was limited to judging which party élite was most likely to maximise the welfare of each individual and his family.

For all the seeming vitality of Jamaican democracy in this period,

13. Stone, op. cit., p. 46.
14. This explains why every election in Jamaica in which office changes hands is followed by a period of inter-party violence, as men and women are relieved of jobs and evicted from homes they previously enjoyed as a result of support for the defeated party.
15. As much as 40 per cent, according to D. Forsythe, 'The Piecrust Principle', *Tapia* (Trinidad), 1 June 1975.

it is obvious that the quality of mass involvement in politics was very low. The role of the poorer ranks of the party coalitions was simply to act as an accurate mirror of current mass grievances, thereby enabling the political and business leaders to devise more adeptly the techniques of symbolic accommodation which were the basic stuff of political presentation in an élitist society where, as James Mau showed in the mid-1960s, the upper and middle classes were fearful of violent uprisings and rebellious behaviour on the part of the poor and unemployed.[16] The electorate responded on the whole, not to the policy content of contrasting JLP and PNP programmes of development, but to the different styles and attributes of the respective party leaderships – a 'darkened theatre audience that alternatively applauds and hisses the actors on the national stage'.[17] As a system, it was far from fragile, having established firm roots in the hearts and minds of the majority of the urban mass public, and yet the feeling persisted that it was intrinsically vulnerable to the incursion of a form of politics prepared to articulate, rather than mask, the class and racial cleavages of Jamaican society.

Events

Even as Jamaica moved peacefully to independence in 1962 under JLP leadership, some of the strains long contained by its political system had already started to emerge into the open. A succession of incidents during the 1960s revealed the growth of a tendency to political violence in the island. The trend began with the so-called Henry 'rebellion' of 1960, in which a Rastafarian group led by the Reverend Claudius Henry, in league with an armed black militant organisation in New York, planned an insurrection against the Jamaican government. It was poorly organised and ended in failure when Henry was arrested and the guerilla camp located in the Red Hills just outside Kingston was discovered in a large security operation. This rebellion was followed three years later by the Coral Gardens 'uprising' which consisted of an attack by six Rastafarians on a petrol station, and subsequently a party of police, in Montego Bay. Again a vast military-police hunt was set up to catch the small number of men involved. The scale of political violence reached a new level in 1965 when the 'Chinese riots' broke out. They took place after a female employee of a Chinese-owned store on the Spanish Town Road in

16. J.A. Mau, *Social Change and Images of the Future: A Study of the Pursuit of Progress in Jamaica* (Cambridge, Mass., 1968).
17. Lewis, op. cit., p. 190.

Kingston claimed to have been beaten by her employers following a dispute. An angry crowd gathered and a week of violence followed in which numerous Chinese business houses were attacked by mobs, eight people were shot, and some ninety were arrested. The disturbances involved hundreds of people rather than tens, and indicated that West Kingston was becoming a volatile social and political flash-point within Jamaican society. This was amply confirmed when an outbreak of gang warfare between supporters of the PNP and JLP, and clashes between gangs and the security forces, began in that area in February 1966 and lasted for fully twelve months until the 1967 general election was over. Some of the incidents were grave, involving knifings, shootings and bombings, and a state of emergency was declared for a month in October 1966. Much of the political warfare in the area was sponsored by leading politicians of both parties as they fought for control of the ghetto. Their tactics had serious implications for the Jamaican political system as the violence served to arm and, above all, politicise sections of the Kingston *lumpenproletariat* which made up the rival gangs.[18] After the election campaign was over, the violence subsided somewhat, and 1967 remained the peak year in the whole decade for press reports of violent incidents.[19] Everybody had become aware of the propensity to violence in Jamaican political life and, in particular, the re-elected JLP government was left feeling uneasy about the security question.

In January 1968, just as this period of instability was ending, Walter Rodney returned to Jamaica. He was twenty-six years old, a Guyanese, and newly appointed to a lectureship in history at the Mona campus of the University of the West Indies, situated some six miles from the centre of Kingston. After graduating at Mona in 1963 with a first-class honours degree in history, he had gone to England to undertake research and in 1966 been awarded a Ph. D. degree by the University of London for a thesis on the history of the upper Guinea coast of Africa in the seventeenth and eighteenth centuries. He had spent a year in Africa, teaching at the University of Dar es Salaam in Tanzania, before coming back to Jamaica to take up a post which was no more than a just reward for one of the brightest scholars the University had yet produced. Arriving after the start of the academic year, Rodney took up his teaching responsibilities with the Department of History, delivering, in addition, a series of open lectures on African history outside the syllabus. He also gave talks

18. For a full discussion of all these incidents, see T. Lacey, *Violence and Politics in Jamaica 1960–70* (Manchester, 1977), pp. 82–94.
19. Ibid., pp. 67–8.

on the theme of black power, not only to university audiences and middle-class clubs and organisations, but also to the black poor and unemployed of West Kingston. Rodney himself indicated that he spoke wherever it was possible for black brothers to meet together.

> It might be a sports club, it might be in a school room, it might be in a church, it might be in a gully . . . They are dark, dismal places with a black population who have to seek refuge there . . . I have spoken in what people call 'dungle', rubbish dumps, for that is where people live in Jamaica . . . I have sat on a little oil drum, rusty and in the midst of garbage, and some Black Brothers and I have grounded together.[20]

Rodney's message met with a vivid response from all who heard it – students, urban youths, the unemployed and Rastafarians alike – and he began to gather around him the nucleus of a Jamaican black power movement.

The notion of black power was not new in Jamaica. Its roots lay in the movements that followed Bedward and Marcus Garvey early in the twentieth century[21] and in the cult of Rastafarianism which grew in popularity in the 1950s.[22] Rodney revived this tradition of political analysis, but set it more firmly than ever before within an economic framework which recognised imperialism as a key element conditioning the lives and prospects of the Jamaican people. He defined black power as 'a movement and an ideology springing from the reality of oppression of black peoples by whites within the imperialist world as a whole.'[23] The West Indies had always been a part of white capitalist society, oppressed and exploited at each stage of history from slavery to emancipation and beyond. In the contemporary era black power meant 'three closely related things: (i) the break with imperialism which is historically white racist; (ii) the assumption of power by the black masses in the islands; (iii) the cultural reconstruction of the society in the image of the blacks.'[24] In view of the complications introduced by the process of class formation and the variety of racial types and mixtures found in Jamaica, Rodney made it clear that he regarded blacks as people of either African *or* Indian origin and was prepared to 'keep the door

20. W. Rodney, *The Groundings with my Brothers* (London, 1969), p. 64.
21. For the history of these movements, see A.A. Brooks, *History of Bedwardism or the Native Baptist Free Church* (Kingston, 1971); A. Jacques-Garvey, *Garvey and Garveyism* (Kingston, 1963); and E.D. Cronon, *Black Moses: The Story of Marcus Garvey and the Universal Negro Improvement Association* (Madison, 1955).
22. See M.G. Smith, R. Augier and R. Nettleford, *The Rastafari in Kingston, Jamaica* (Kingston, 1960).
23. Rodney, op. cit., p. 24.
24. Ibid., p. 28.

open' to the browns, reds and so-called West Indian whites to allow them to make up their minds where they stood on the issue of black power. In this sense, he argued, black power was not racially intolerant, but merely strove to ensure that the black man had power over his own destiny.

The moment that power is equitably distributed among several ethnic groups, then the very relevance of making the distinction between groups will be lost. What we most object to is the current image of a multi-racial society living in harmony – that is a myth designed to justify the exploitation suffered by the blackest of our population, at the hands of the lighter-skinned groups . . . Black Power must proclaim that Jamaica is a black society – we should fly Garvey's Black Star banner and we will treat all other groups in the society on that understanding – they can have *the basic rights of all individuals* but *no privileges to exploit Africans* as had been the pattern during slavery and ever since.[25]

Rodney alleged that the JLP government was afraid of the potential wrath of the Jamaican masses because it knew that Jamaica was a black man's country and that it was a white man's government committed to the preservation of white power. Only a revolution could bring about change, 'for the first essential is to break the chains which bind us to white imperialists, and that is a very revolutionary step.'[26]

From the government's point of view Rodney was a most dangerous threat. His arguments brought together class and racial issues in precisely the way that the structure of the Jamaican political system had hitherto sought to prevent and to which it was most vulnerable. As Roy McNeill, Minister of Home Affairs, was subsequently to tell the House of Representatives, 'in my term of office and in reading of the records of problems in this country, I have never come across a man who offers a greater threat to the security of this land than does Walter Rodney.'[27] The fear that his message aroused can be gauged by the speed with which the government tried to force him out of the country. In August 1968, when Rodney had only been in Jamaica eight months, McNeill summoned the Vice-Chancellor of the University, Sir Philip Sherlock, to inform him of the government's concern about the activities in which one of his staff members was engaging beyond the campus. Nothing came of this meeting, and on Monday 14 October the Vice-Chancellor was again called to discuss the matter, this time by the Prime Minister,

25. Ibid., pp. 29–30. Rodney's emphasis.
26. Ibid., p. 31.
27. *Jamaica Hansard. Proceedings of House of Representatives*, 1, 1 (1968–9), p. 394.

Hugh Shearer, and the Cabinet as a whole. Asked to terminate Rodney's contract of employment with the University, he replied that there were no professional grounds for taking such a step and that in any case authority on such an issue rested not with him but with the University appointments committee. According to his account of the meeting, Sherlock left with an undertaking that he would consult senior members of the University's academic staff and seek a second interview with the Prime Minister two days later on Wednesday 16 October.[28] In the event, he was given no time to do this, for the government moved swiftly to ban Rodney the day after the first meeting on the grounds that the matter was urgent. It seems likely that, having failed to persuade the University to act on his behalf, Shearer learnt that Rodney was in fact out of the country attending a black writers' conference in Montreal and decided to seize the opportunity to prevent him from returning. Accordingly, when Rodney's aircraft touched down in Kingston at 2.20 p.m. on Tuesday 15 October, he was refused permission to leave the cabin and sent back to Montreal on the return flight.

News of Rodney's exclusion did not reach the campus until it was broadcast at 9 p.m. on the evening of the 15th. The Vice-Chancellor refused to make any comment until he knew more of the facts, but the Guild of Undergraduates - the students' organisation - called an emergency meeting in one of the halls of residence for 11 p.m.[29] Some 900 students gathered and resolved to march the following day on the offices of the Minister of Home Affairs and the Prime Minister in order to deliver two petitions of protest - a promptness of response which has been attributed in part to the example of student agitation in other parts of the world in 1968.[30] At the meeting, some students urged that the demonstration be confined to the issue of the ban on a university lecturer - as distinct from the content of Rodney's politics or indeed the race question as a whole. Probably the vast majority of students were motivated mainly by the first of these considerations, but in practice there proved to be no way of disentangling the various inter-related issues. During the evening the leaders of the student Guild were informed that it was likely that the march would be deemed illegal under Jamaican law, and they took clear steps to urge self-discipline upon the students. A

28. *Daily Gleaner*, 22 Oct. 1968.
29. R. Gonsalves, 'The Rodney Affair and its Aftermath', *Caribbean Quarterly*, 24, 3 (1979), p. 4. Subsequent discussion of the activities of the Guild of Undergraduates in the affair is drawn from this account by the president of the Guild at the time.
30. N. Girvan, 'After Rodney - The Politics of Student Protest in Jamaica', *New World Quarterly*, 4, 3 (1968), p. 60.

pamphlet was hastily printed which stressed that the demonstration 'challenges the Government of this country and consequently places us all in danger'.[31] It therefore advised the students to wear their gowns, obey identifiable marshals, avoid provoking the police, and generally observe order.

On the morning of Wednesday 16 October, buses which had been ordered to take the students to different points in the city from where it had been planned that they would converge on the two ministerial offices did not arrive. The students proceeded on foot along the Mona Road where they were stopped by a cordon of policemen armed with guns, batons and tear gas. The police seemed at first to be uncertain of their orders, and some students were allowed through, only to be stopped again further along the road, at which point the police resorted to violence, beating some students with batons and eventually releasing tear gas. One of the participants has given this vivid account of what then occurred:

> Nothing like this had happened before in comfortable, residential St Andrew. The peaceful, middle-class thoroughfares of shopping centres and graceful, disintegrating old houses were suddenly turned into a battleground. For a brief moment, while the smoke was swirling and swallowing cars, it was difficult to tell who the heroes were. Apologetically, students invaded lawns, asking for the use of water taps for damping gowns and handkerchiefs. Fumes reached them there too, and suddenly, on these carefully tended lawns, as though responding to some supernatural command, students, gardeners, housewives and gentlemen of leisure were bent double, retching and swearing and calling for water. Students jumped over barbed wire fences into open lots and gullies, half-blind, weeping and spitting and dribbling down their fronts like untrained children.[32]

Understandably, in these circumstances the march broke up in disarray, regrouping eventually outside the Ministry of Home Affairs in Duke Street in the centre of Kingston. A public meeting was held at which the Guild President, a left-wing lecturer in economics Dr Norman Girvan, and the pregnant Mrs Rodney all spoke, attacking the breach of academic freedom and human rights which the ban constituted. By this time a large crowd had gathered, including a number of unemployed youths, workers and Rastafarians, in addition to the students.

After a brief meeting with officials of the Ministry, the

31. 'Demonstration by the Students against the Unjust Treatment of Dr Rodney who has been banned from re-entering Jamaica', student pamphlet (mimeo, 1968).
32. *Comment* (published by the Joint Policy Sub-Committee of the Academic Board of the University of the West Indies, Mona), 12 Nov. 1968.

demonstrators proceeded up Duke Street on their way to the Prime Minister's office. Outside the headquarters of the Bustamante Industrial Trade Union (BITU) – the union affiliate of the JLP – they were attacked by stones and bottles thrown from both sides of the street, which led the police to intervene again to disperse the crowd. In his account of these events the Guild President, Ralph Gonsalves, has revealed that at this point several left-wing members of the University staff and some students advocated a procession through West Kingston in order to bring out the 'dispossessed' of that area. He opposed these 'adventurists', as he called them, on the grounds that the marchers were neither ideologically, organisationally nor militarily equipped to face the growing strength of the security forces which had been visibly reinforced.[33] Instead he led the march, as originally planned, to the Prime Minister's office on East Race Course. By this time it was proving harder to contain random acts of violence on people and property committed by youths who were accompanying the march. Outside the Prime Minister's office the police moved finally to break up the protest, again beating a number of students and lecturers, one of whom suffered a broken arm. By 2.30 p.m. the students were making their disorganised way back to the campus.

As the student demonstration dissipated, so thousands of unemployed youths came on to the streets of the city. They were inspired not by the issue of academic freedom but by the grievances which the banned Rodney had condemned as class and racial oppression. They attacked and looted property in the commercial quarter of Kingston throughout the evening and night of 16 October, concentrating on businesses owned by foreign investors. Among their targets were the Canadian Imperial Bank of Commerce, Barclays Bank, the Bank of Canada and Montreal, the Royal Bank of Canada, North American Life, Mexicana Airlines, Pan-American Airways, Woolworths, Bata Shoes and the offices of Esso and Shell. Businesses owned by local ethnic minorities also did not escape. Damaged property in this category included Uncle's Inn, China Radio and TV, Marzoucas Stores, C.D. Alexander and Co., Fancy Commodity Service, Jamaica Mutual, Lions' Supermarket, Bryden and Evelyn, and the offices of the Jamaica Chamber of Commerce. In addition, more than fifty buses belonging to the foreign-owned Jamaica Omnibus Service were burnt or otherwise damaged, often by being driven against shop fronts and shutters in an attempt to smash them down. The attack on the buses reflected a

33. Gonsalves, op. cit., p. 7.

separate source of popular discontent – with the bus service itself, exacerbated by a recent increase in fares. There was also at one point a clash between members of the police and the fire brigade when the police, in hot pursuit of some demonstrators, set upon and tear-gassed several firemen in the York Park fire station, with the result that the brigade at this station went on strike despite the many fires burning throughout the city. In all, the damage to property caused in the riots that night amounted to approximately £1 million. Given the level of disorder, there is surprisingly little evidence of serious personal violence. A statement from the Ministry of Home Affairs, which was not subsequently challenged, indicated that two people were killed by being shot, one was electrocuted while trying to escape after looting premises, and only twelve people were seriously injured, eleven of them policemen.

The response of the security forces was nevertheless extensive, both on Wednesday 16 October and over the following few days. Heavily-armed police riot squads and units of the Jamaica Defence Force were deployed by a joint military-police control centre set up on the Old Hope Road. Members of the Jamaica National Reserve were called up and a meeting of all justices of the peace and members of service and gun-clubs was convened to discuss the security situation. On the morning of Thursday 17 October, the day after the demonstration, the army sealed off the entrances to the University campus, which it kept under seige for more than a week. By this time the rioting was largely over. On the Thursday groups of youths intermittently threw stones at the security forces, but the only serious incident was the burning down of Uncle's Inn, a well-known Chinese-owned restaurant at Cross Roads, which had already been damaged the previous day. On Friday 18 October, despite the occasional arrest of looters, a limited bus service was restored.

Attention turned to the political reaction to the riots and, in particular, to the emergency debate in the House of Representatives held on Thursday 17 October and broadcast live throughout Jamaica on radio and television. Shearer's opening speech indicated that he intended to divert discussion away from the actions of the poor and unemployed in the city by mobilising public opinion against the students and the University as a whole. Shearer was a trade unionist by background, suspicious of higher education, and had come to the leadership of the JLP and the country in part because he was the favoured cousin of Bustamante, the party's legendary founder. Although a quiet and pleasant man, he was certainly no liberal. In his speech he began by concentrating upon Rodney who, he said, first came to the notice of the authorities in 1962, when as a student at Mona he visited Leningrad as a delegate to a congress of the International Union of Students; this body was described by the Prime Minister as 'a well-known notorious communist-front organisation'. At no time, he went on, did Rodney make any secret of 'his communist views', visiting Cuba on two occasions, while in 1968 when he returned to Jamaica, he allegedly 'lost little time in engaging in subversive activities' and organising revolutionary groups for 'the struggle ahead'. The order denying his right of re-entry into the country was signed when it became known that Rodney had 'stepped up the pace of his activities' and was widely advocating the use of force in the cause of revolution. To illustrate his point, Shearer quoted from a speech he claimed Rodney had made at the University: 'Revolution must come. We must be prepared to see it through. We must stop talking and indulging in academic exercises and act. Who will be the first to come with me down-town and take up a machine-gun?'

Shearer followed this with a deliberately divisive attack on the rest of the University. He attributed the demonstrations and violence to the actions of teachers and students who, he said, were mainly West Indians from other islands who over the previous few months had turned the campus at Mona into 'a hot-bed of anti-Jamaican organisation'. He reported that of the top five officers of a basically non-financial institution like the Guild of Undergraduates, only the treasurer was a Jamaican, and he argued that these foreign agitators had conspired to involve criminal and subversive elements in Kingston in the student demonstration. In his view, the events of the previous day showed 'real evidence of careful planning beyond the capacity of the hoodlums or the usual subversive groups with which the Government has had to deal in the past'.[34] The speech ended with the statement that the police and military forces had been given firm instructions to prevent any further breaches of law and order.

Shearer's performance effectively laid down the propaganda framework within which the government sought to anaesthetise the political impact of the riots. It fed on long-standing anti-communist feeling in the country; stimulated the latent anti-intellectualism of local society; fuelled traditional Jamaican hostility towards the rest of the Commonwealth Caribbean; and appealed to national unity in the face of what was characterised as a subversive threat to the security of the state. The opposition PNP had no answer to this emotional appeal. In his first reaction to the ban on Rodney, the

34. All quotations from Shearer in *Proceedings of House of Representatives*, 1, 1, 1968–9, pp. 392–3.

party leader, Norman Manley, had called it 'an arbitrary use of power', a 'plain denial of the rule of law' and 'a monstrous breach of human rights'.[35] Yet in the debate he did not challenge the evidence presented against Rodney or the decision to ban him, questioning only the delay with which the government had acted since it had known him to be a security risk for some months, and the inhumane method of expulsion ultimately used. The *Daily Gleaner* also backed the government's action which, in a sense, was to be expected, since the *Gleaner* was owned by the Ashenheims, one of Jamaica's leading business families, a member of which was actually a minister of state in the Shearer government. In its editorials and the columns of its influential 'Political Reporter', it joined the attack on the intellectual credentials of the University and added to the anti-communist hysteria which was building up against Rodney and other figures there. For example, in an article published on the first Sunday after the riots, the 'Political Reporter' accused the student body of being 'a pack of children playing with dangerous toys which they don't even begin to understand', and expressed his surprise that 'so many persons at the University and outside of it were deluded into believing that Rodney was fighting for black man's rights and not advocating a communist take-over of the Jamaican state'.[36]

Surrounded by the army and police, the University was in no position to defend itself against such powerful propaganda. In any case, according to Girvan, it was in 'a state of almost complete paralysis'.[37] All classes were suspended, and students, staff and administrators mostly sat and talked among themselves. Some wrote letters to the *Gleaner*, others merely fretted at their impotence. Eventually, the joint policy committee of the University produced several issues of a news-sheet called *Comment* designed to air its side of the arguments. It demonstrated that Jamaicans were numerically predominant in the student body at Mona, showed that the Guild of Undergraduates was not normally dominated by non-Jamaicans,[38] and generally sought to explain, in the words of one article, 'what a university is about'.[39] There is no reason to believe that many minds were swayed by this since the circulation of *Comment* was very limited. There was also much debate in the University about when to return to classes, and conflicts developed between the students and the Vice-Chancellor and his senior staff before agreement was

35. *Daily Gleaner*, 17 Oct. 1968.
36. Ibid., 20 Oct. 1968.
37. Girvan, 'After Rodney', p. 62.
38. *Comment*, 7 Nov. 1968.
39. Ibid., 29 Nov. 1968.

reached.[40] However, the truth of the matter was that happenings at Mona were no longer of any importance except for the University's own future, which had clearly been placed in some doubt by the crisis and the Jamaican government's reaction to it. In the city of Kingston the police were in control, and in the country generally the government's position was secure. In the short term the Jamaican political system had survived the Rodney riots.

Significance

Yet in their impact on the development of Jamaican politics and history, the significance of the events of October 1968 was considerable, although not necessarily in the sense suggested by much contemporary comment and analysis. In particular, two misconceptions of the time need to be cleared away. First, the riots were not, as Shearer implied and many feared, an attempt at insurrection or revolution. The violence was primarily directed against property rather than political figures or even members of the security forces. There were casualties among the latter and among the protesters, but remarkably few considering the scale of the disturbances and West Kingston's record of political violence in the preceding two years. As a member of the British police training team in Jamaica at the time subsequently told an academic interviewer, 'the mob used *molotovs* in 1968 but only against property, not against the security forces . . . The mob were interested in some looting and some burning, not in fighting.'[41] Nor is there any reason to think that the riots were organised. Rodney had certainly talked of the need to transform 'the black intelligentsia into the servants of the black masses',[42] and had worked during the short time he was in Jamaica to bring together radical intellectuals on the University campus, politically aware Rastafarians and the youth gangs of the Kingston ghettoes. But to believe that he could have organised an insurrectionary or revolutionary movement from these inherently dissimilar groups of people within such a limited period is unrealistic.

Nor can the students themselves be charged with planning the riots. According to Gonsalves, the main issue of concern to them at the beginning of October was student representation on the University's relevant governing bodies.[43] For the vast majority, their

40. For a fuller discussion, see Gonsalves, op. cit., pp. 16–20.
41. Lacey, op. cit., p. 98.
42. Rodney, op. cit., p. 32.
43. Gonsalves, op. cit., p. 3.

response to Rodney's banning was exactly what it seemed: anger that such a respected and popular lecturer should be so treated. Their aim was a peaceful demonstration, and its degeneration into violence must be blamed on the police. In relation to the riots that followed, the students simply played the role of catalyst. The obstacles facing radical intellectuals seeking to make connections with the unemployed of the *lumpenproletariat* were well illustrated in the brief history of the *Abeng* movement established after the riots to exploit the situation they had brought about. Named after the horn sounded by black slaves in past uprisings against the British, it published a newspaper which sold well for a while and undoubtedly raised the political consciousness of the mass urban public. Yet within two years the uneasy *Abeng* coalition had disintegrated as a result of weak organisation, factionalism, police harassment and, above all, sharp internal disagreements over ideology.[44] Thus the evidence suggests that the Rodney riots were an example of demonstrative rather than revolutionary violence. They were emotionally charged rather than coolly planned, short-lived rather than the prelude to continuing disorder – in sum, a kind of cathartic outburst by the dispossessed. By the time it was over, its force had spent itself.

Secondly, the riots were not fundamentally about race at all, despite the rhetoric of black power surrounding them. As noted earlier, the interaction between class and race in Jamaica is close and complex, but there is every reason to believe that material rather than cultural goals are the prime determinants of social conflict, especially in urban settings. The evidence for this view is found in the results of a sample survey of the population of Kingston undertaken by Carl Stone early in 1971, some two and a half years after the riots. He concluded that, despite a significant increase in black racial pride and growing sensitivity to the development of a positive black identity promoted by Rodney and the black power movement, 'the degree of hostility to whites is minimal, except within the most materially dispossessed lower class.'[45] He further argued that 'racial attitudes are largely a reflection of the relative economic discontent and material dispossession of the respective occupational strata, and that the root causes of recent changes in racial orientations in urban Jamaica are to be found mainly in the intensification of material dispossession within the manual strata.'[46] In other words, ownership of economic assets in the Jamaica of 1968 was predominantly in the

44. For a discussion, see T. Munroe, *The Politics of Constitutional Decolonization: Jamaica 1944–62* (Kingston, 1972), p. 207.
45. Stone, op. cit., p. 117.
46. Ibid., p. 116.

hands of either foreigners or local ethnic minorities, and economic frustration flowed easily into an apparent racial hostility – which in fact was more akin to class antagonism than to genuine racial prejudice. Following on this argument, the Rodney riots should thus be seen primarily as expressing the growing social and economic deprivation of the poor areas of West Kingston. The inspiration may have been the black power advocacy of Rodney and the target the property of a non-black economic élite, but the cause was poverty, unemployment, low education, poor housing and the general material and social dispossession which characterised large parts of the population of urban Jamaica.

Here lay the real political significance of the Rodney riots. They showed that there existed in Jamaican society a reservoir of antagonism to the *status quo* sufficiently strong to seize the opportunity provided by the student demonstration to come out on to the streets of Kingston and virtually take over the city centre for an afternoon and an evening. The mode of economic development of the country had generated the discontent, and the conventional party political system had failed to contain it. And although the speed with which the riots were dissipated suggested that the Jamaican social and political system was not in danger of collapsing, the riots had been a chilling warning, to those with eyes to see, of what might occur if steps were not taken to address the social failings of the Jamaican political economy and draw the poor, the unemployed and the *lumpenproletariat* back into the mainstream of national political life. This, in the event, is what occurred, and hence the long-term impact of the Rodney riots must be seen as integrationist and essentially conservative. The JLP could not respond other than by increasingly emphasising coercion, but the PNP quickly made up for its tame acquiescence in Shearer's propaganda at the time of the crisis by moving to espouse the cause of reform.

The way forward was pointed by Norman Manley in November 1968, right at the end of his political career, when he told his party that, whereas the mission of his generation had been to achieve the goal of political independence, the task of the next was to proceed to social and economic renewal.[47] The mantle was taken up by his son Michael when he assumed the party leadership the following year. Under his guidance the PNP established itself as the vehicle for the legitimate aspirations of the poor black people of Jamaica. It voiced the discontent arising from the joblessness, victimisation, coercion and corruption which grew more quickly during the JLP's last years

47. See R. Nettleford, *Mirror Mirror: Identity, Race and Protest in Jamaica* (London, 1970), p. 167.

of office and cleverly associated itself with the symbols of racial protest by sympathetically embracing the culture of Rastafarianism and the protest implicit in *reggae* music. Michael Manley himself was projected to the electorate as a populist leader in the image of the biblical figure of Joshua, successfully building up around his personality a massive expectation of change which brought the PNP a sweeping victory in the general elections of 1972.[48] By the very manner of his accession to power, Manley succeeded, at least temporarily, in achieving one of his party's new goals, namely, the legitimisation and consequent appeasement of the mass disaffection expressed in the Rodney riots. Whether or not he would be able to remove the root causes of this discontent remained an open question which only the experience of government could answer.

In themselves, however, the events of October 1968 undoubtedly marked a key phase in the development of Jamaica and indeed of the Commonwealth Caribbean as a whole. This, in a nutshell, was the moment when nationalism in the region was forced to turn from politics to economics. For Rodney himself the consequences of this change were tragic. Returning to his native country in 1974 to take up a post as professor of history in the University of Guyana, he was refused a work permit by the government in Georgetown. He devoted his energies instead to the activities of a small radical party in Guyana called the Working People's Alliance, perceived to be a threat to the government of Forbes Burnham. In June 1980 he was assassinated by a car bomb in circumstances which many have seen as implicating the Guyanese government itself beyond reasonable doubt. He died with the knowledge that in the twelve years since his name came to the fore Jamaica at least had begun to challenge the economic dependence which was the legacy of its long history of colonialism.

48. See O. Senior, *The Message is Change* (Kingston, 1972).

2

FROM MICHAEL WITH LOVE

In September 1974 the PNP government, which had already been in office for more than two years, startled the people of Jamaica by announcing that it had been converted to socialism and that henceforth Jamaica was to be considered one of the socialist countries of the world. This declaration, and the programme unveiled shortly afterwards, stimulated an intense debate in Jamaican society reaching to the roots of the problem of development and change in a profoundly ex-colonial society. The purpose of this chapter is to describe and analyse the PNP's apparent leftward move and make a preliminary assessment of the nature of the socialism which Michael Manley, as the leader of the government, was planning to introduce to Jamaica.

The first indication that something was afoot came with the disclosure in mid-August 1974 that for some time the PNP had been engaging within the party in an intensive, well-organised political education programme geared to an understanding of socialism.[1] Delegates at the fourth in a series of Sunday conferences were given copies of a statement issued by N.W. Manley on 20 August 1940, which was interesting in that it revealed that early in its history the PNP had declared itself a socialist party.[2] Norman Manley had in mind the example of the British Labour Party, but failed to prevent the emergence of a neo-Marxist faction in the forefront of party organisation and political education. In 1952, to check the growing influence of this left-wing group, four of its members – Ken and Frank Hill, Richard Hart and Arthur Henry – were expelled from the party, accused of the dissemination of communist doctrines.[3] Despite this move, the PNP never formally disavowed the socialist label, although it certainly allowed it to be laid aside in the intervening years. Nevertheless, in 1974, discussion of socialism was undoubtedly infused with the revivalist flavour of a party returning to its roots.

The new stance was publicly revealed for the first time by Michael

1. *Jamaica Daily News*, 15 Aug. 1974.
2. For a useful historical account of the party's development, see T. Munroe, *The Politics of Constitutional Decolonization: Jamaica 1944–62* (Kingston, 1972), pp. 179–92.
3. For a personal interpretation, see 'Richard Hart talks about his experiences in Jamaican politics', *Jamaica Daily News*, 8 June 1975.

Manley in his speech to the 36th Annual PNP Conference which was given, not insignificantly, in the presence of President Nyerere of Tanzania, then on a state visit to Jamaica. Manley was known to be his admirer,[4] and the visit prompted much hysterical talk of a one-party state, the elimination of the middle classes and, in fact, a JLP boycott of all official proceedings.[5] The stage was set for the PNP leader's official restatement of belief in a socialism that was flexible and undoctrinaire, standing for the 'equality of man' and holding that 'human beings are moral and capable of acting together to achieve common purposes'.[6]

These were just the barest of clues, and another month of doubt and questioning was to pass before the country was offered some more pieces to the puzzle. One of Manley's closest acolytes, Senator Dudley Thompson, made it clear that, of the many types of socialism, the one chosen for Jamaica was 'the one that suits us best, and is not a 100 per cent carbon copy of socialism in any of the other known socialist countries'. However, it was to be democratic parliamentary socialism, rejecting the idea of a police state and believing in the existence of opposition parties.[7]

For the moment Manley was content to indulge in delightful simplifications. Socialism was 'Christianity in action', he declared, as he inaugurated a housing project;[8] to a constituency conference he stated that socialism 'says no man shall be allowed to exploit his brother';[9] and then in a huge 'seminar' (not a public meeting) in the old centre of Kingston, which ended with the singing of 'Onward Christian Socialists', the obvious was revealed – 'Socialism is Love',[10] a slogan that gained immediate currency more in sarcastic jest than sincerity. This approach seemed designed to test public reaction, for by the time the details were filled in – in Manley's speech to the House of Representatives on 20 November on the

4. M. Manley, *The Politics of Change: A Jamaican Testament* (London, 1974), pp. 25–6.
5. In his Independence Day message the JLP leader, Shearer, had seen 'evidence of moves towards establishing a one party state in Jamaica', and Lightbourne, the leader of the proudly conservative United Party, charged the PNP government with trying to eliminate the middle classes. *Jamaica Daily News*, 15 and 16 Aug. 1974. The JLP boycott of Nyerere's visit derived from the invitation offered to him by the government to address the PNP conference, albeit formally in his secondary capacity as party leader. Ibid., 3 Sept. 1974.
6. Ibid., 16 Sept. 1974.
7. Ibid., 16 Oct. 1974.
8. Ibid., 17 Oct. 1974.
9. Ibid., 18 Nov. 1974.
10. Ibid., 22 Nov. 1974.

nature of the mixed economy, and then, most significantly, in a supplement to both morning papers and the one evening paper early in December – some of the earlier, wilder talk about 'burying capitalism' had subsided. Clearly, sinister warnings of demagoguery in the columns of the conservative *Gleaner*[11] and anxious expressions of concern by Chamber of Commerce spokesmen had taken their toll, since the twelve-page supplement bore the pretentious yet conciliatory title, 'Democratic Socialism – the Jamaican Model'.

As a manifesto, it was a sophisticated and skillful piece of special pleading. Readers were informed that 'many Governments throughout the world are attempting to devise methods of organising the citizens of their nations so that everyone has equal opportunities. This search has led people finally to Socialism . . . the only system of social and economic organisation that is designed to make opportunities equal and open to all.'[12] This was so because:

> Socialism is first an ideal, a goal and an attitude of mind that requires people to care for each other's welfare. Socialism is a way of life. A Socialist society cannot simply come into existence. It has to be built by people who believe in and practise its principles.
>
> Socialism is the Christian way of life in action. It is the philosophy that best gives expression to the Christian ideal of the equality of all God's children. It has as its foundations the Christian belief that all men and women must love their neighbours as themselves.

There was not considered to be a 'single road which a nation must follow to create a socialist society. Each nation must work out its methods of solving its own problems and meeting the basic needs of its people.' In an attempt to stifle scare-mongering on the lines of 'going communist',[13] the supplement declared that the PNP had 'no intention of blindly copying any foreign formula for achieving a Socialist society in Jamaica', but was 'constructing our own model of Socialism which must grow out of the application of basic prin-

11. See Colin Gregory (columnist), 'Demagogues?', *Daily Gleaner*, 21 Nov. 1974.
12. This and the other quotations immediately following are taken from the manifesto entitled *Democratic Socialism: The Jamaican Model*, published by the Political Education Committee of the People's National Party in December 1974.
13. Even in an era of international *détente*, the instinctive reaction of most Jamaicans to talk of communism was one of horror. The old, reactionary propaganda of the 1940s equating communism with, for example, the slaughter and equal division among all of the small man's cow, had laid tenacious roots. Moreover, it was not so long since the visit of two Russian ships to Kingston harbour in 1962 had been used to provoke a grass-roots scare, warning of imminent communist invasion.

ciples to the special nature of Jamaican society'.

In an important section the manifesto then listed and elaborated upon four 'fundamental aspects': the democratic political process, the Christian principles of brotherhood and equality, the ideas of equal opportunity and equal rights, and a determination to prevent the exploitation of the people. For the rest, it consisted of a personal foreword by Manley, reviewing the origins of the new socialist approach, a statement of uncontroversial basic beliefs, a list of forty 'milestones on the road to socialism', and a glossary of political terms. The only other area of serious content set out a commitment to the concept of a mixed economy, calling on the government 'to ensure that all development takes place in accordance with the needs and goals of the society', granting the private sector a 'full, integral' role, and welcoming foreign private capital provided it operated on the basis of good corporate citizenship.

In short, the document was in no way a programme of action, specifying targets and procedures for policy implementation, but a statement of progressive moral and philosophical goals, couched in the very broadest terms – persuasively argued, certainly, but marred by excessive simplifications. To imply, as Manley's introduction did, that more than 300 years of capitalism in Jamaica had ended with the departure from office of the JLP government in 1972 was fantasy, especially when many of the 'forty milestones' achieved on the road to socialism marked programmes initiated, or not opposed, by the JLP. Capitalism everywhere, not least in Jamaica, has proved resistant to more than fervent denial. It was over-dramatic too to allege that the capitalism of Jamaica had been wholly *laissez-faire* when it had always involved state regulation, and defining socialism as 'an attitude of mind' and 'a way of life' was simply avoiding the question. Nor could proponents of 'real' decolonisation have been encouraged by the attempt to gain respectability for socialism by offering, without discussion, examples of nations with democratic socialist governments that included such former colonial powers as Britain, the Netherlands and West Germany.

It was, for all that, a live party political manifesto not a philosophical treatise, and it clearly got across its major message: the PNP proposed to reform capitalism in order to make it work more to the advantage of the majority of ordinary people. There was nothing original in this aspiration, nor anything particularly radical about it. For example, the manifesto gave no detailed guidance as to the precise 'mix' of the mixed economy that was envisaged, leaving open the possibility that in practice only the mildest of bows would be made in the direction of state control. In such circumstances, crude political distinctions contrasting capitalism and socialism as totally and ideologically separate philosophies, were untenable in reality.[14] The PNP admitted that private business could 'exist either in a capitalist or in a socialist society', thereby pinpointing one of the critical tests of the quality and degree of 'democratic socialism', namely the role allowed to private business within the overall economic and political structure of society.

If at the level of ideas there were some uncertainties about the precise nature of PNP socialism, what can one say about the actual transfer of the philosophy into governmental practice during the first years of Manley's term of office, beginning when he himself argued that a strategy of change should begin? He had written in a book *The Politics of Change*, published in 1974: 'The first task that a post-colonial society must tackle is the development of a strategy designed to replace the psychology of dependence with the spirit of individual and collective self-reliance. Until that exercise is successfully embarked upon every other plan will fail.'[15] In this sphere he could unquestionably claim intensive activity in his first two or three years in power. Shortly after assuming office, the new government dramatically restored a number of civil liberties, abolished entry bans on many left-wing publications, and issued passports to people long denied them. In the field of external affairs, trade and diplomatic relations were immediately established with Cuba and other socialist countries, and Jamaica fully identified with Third World political interests; Manley even travelled with Castro to the Non-Aligned Conference in 1973 in Algiers, where he made very radical noises. On many occasions he talked about the country's need to face up to its African heritage, welcomed Black Muslims from the United States, and often used a Rastafari musical group, the Mystic Revelations, to represent Jamaica abroad. And in a symbolic move, which received much attention, he ceased to use the traditional European jacket and tie for formal occasions and encouraged members of his government to wear more suitable open-necked '*karebas*'. This kind of ritual clearing away of the accoutrements of the colonial and neo-colonial eras is easy to disparage and is by no means the beginning or the end of the problem, but it can play an important role in re-setting the psychological tone of a society.

14. The confusion of terminology and concept was wryly illustrated by the columnist, Thomas Wright. 'One gathers that the private enterprise of which the government disapproves is called Capitalism (now abolished)', he wrote, 'and the Capitalism of which the government approves is now known as "private business" ', 'Candidly Yours', *Daily Gleaner*, 28 Nov. 1974.
15. Manley, op. cit., p. 23.

Whether it does so is likely to depend on the resolution of more fundamental questions like the distribution of economic power - something which Manley also seemed fully to understand. 'It is impossible', he wrote in his book, 'to modify the distribution of wealth without considering the ownership of resources. Where the means of production are concentrated in a few hands, it is inevitable that wealth will tend to accumulate in those hands at the expense of the rest of the population.'[16] The system of ownership of the Jamaican economy must therefore 'be consistent with national objectives, and its resources must be controlled to ensure that they are used to the full and in a manner consistent with social justice.'[17] He noted that the 'commanding heights' of the economy (a turn of phrase which he commended) were almost exclusively in foreign hands, and argued from this 'that political independence and foreign economic domination of strategic sectors of the economy are mutually exclusive concepts.'[18] Turning to possible courses of action, he endorsed the by then commonplace criticisms of the strategy embodied in the so-called Puerto Rican model of 'industrialisation by invitation'[19] pursued in Jamaica in the 1960s and pointed out major weaknesses in the Jamaicanisation programme undertaken by the previous JLP government - especially its failure to modify the 'oligarchic pattern of ownership of local resources' since 'the tendency has been for the same wealthy minority to buy into the newly offered equity.'[20]

In the light of such an analysis, the policy of Manley's government was initially very mild. Rather than a wide-ranging programme of nationalisation, the dominant theme was that of partnership with existing ownership. Even in his book, Manley had retreated from his earlier theoretical analysis to argue that, 'as a matter of common sense and reality',[21] public ownership would have to work together with foreign and local private capital, at least for the foreseeable future, in such areas as bauxite, sugar, tourism and the banking system. Even in the crucial bauxite industry this was the pattern

16. Ibid., p. 77.
17. Ibid., p. 78.
18. Ibid., p. 104.
19. See N. Girvan and O. Jefferson (eds), *Readings in the Political Economy of the Caribbean* (Kingston, 1971).
20. In addition, Manley pointed to two other weaknesses of the policy. 'First, the local companies are still largely subject to the decision-making processes of the parent company operating out of its metropolitan home base. Second, the acquisition of equity under this programme leads to substantial pressures on our balance of payments and foreign reserves.' Manley, op. cit., pp. 88–9.
21. Ibid., p. 118.

adhered to, notwithstanding the furore generated in Washington and Ottawa by the heavy additional production levy, imposed in mid-1974 as an emergency response to impending national bankruptcy following the vast rise in oil prices the previous year. It is natural to be suspicious of triumphant announcements, like the government take-over of 51 per cent of the assets of Kaiser Bauxite mining operations in Jamaica, when at the press conference heralding the event Edgar J. Kaiser sat next to the Prime Minister, smiling and clutching a long-term management contract. However, in the public utilities, 'complete public ownership'[22] was envisaged, although it was not immediately achieved, and where it did occur, as in the case of the Jamaica Omnibus Service, it has to be said that no marked differences were apparent. On this particular issue the Minister of Transport, Eric Bell, was quoted as saying: 'The acquisition of the shares of the Jamaica Omnibus Service Ltd. by the Government will only result in a change of ownership of the company shares, and the company under a new Board of Directors will continue in existence as before with no change in its contractual relationships.'[23] Finally, outside 'the commanding heights', and despite his condemnation of the 'trader mentality' and the resulting 'paralysis of attitude' thus induced among Jamaican entrepreneurs, Manley proceeded to declare that 'the ordinary manufacturing sector belongs naturally in private hands.'[24]

Enough has been said to indicate the sort of economic profile Manley had in mind for Jamaica. In other areas, the government promoted discussion of schemes of worker participation, released some land to farmers under the Land-Lease project, injected some purchasing power into the slums by the provision of jobs under the Impact Programme (glorified street-cleaning), and undertook a number of valuable new welfare commitments, most notably the announcement of free secondary education for all. Yet the seminal issue of a neo-colonial economy, that of ownership of resources and the consequent distribution of power and wealth in the society, was evaded. The role played by private business in the Jamaican economy has always been vast, and was not seriously weakened by the implementation of Manley's various notions of partnership. Indeed, it could be said that by removing possible sources of tension, it strengthened the foundations of private business, both local and foreign. On this count, the first phase of Jamaican 'democratic socialism' appears a tepid brew, in no sense interrupting the conver-

22. Ibid., p. 119.
23. Quoted in D. Forsythe, 'The Piecrust Principle', *Tapia* (Trinidad), 1 June 1975.
24. Manley, op. cit., p. 120.

ging pragmatism of past PNP and JLP governments.

To explain this no more than moderate response to the radical nature of Jamaica's problems, which was well understood by Manley, more needs to be said of the power structure within Jamaican society and its effect on the political system. The fundamental point is that Jamaican politics represent an historical compromise between a capitalist power structure and the exigencies of mass politics. Popular participation has been carried as far as the vote, but mass influence on policy is severely limited by the role of organised vested interests, acting as pressure groups. The highly competitive political system in Jamaica and the heavy emphasis placed on party patronage require considerable financial support. This can only be provided by wealthy businessmen, who have thus entrenched themselves in influential positions in both the party coalitions, and who then exert disproportionate pressure on the formulation of government policy. It has been aptly said that 'the theory of competing and fragmented centres of influence that compete in the open pluralist market of ideas and value preferences merely masks the reality of concentrated oligopolistic corporate and business power over public policy.'[25] In a system of multiple-class alliances, explicitly denying overt class appeals, and where the major trade unions are not run primarily in the interests of workers, there was at this time no competing source of popular pressure on governments capable of countering the influence of this economic grouping.

The turbulent development of mass political consciousness in Jamaica in the 1930s (as throughout the West Indies) severely shook the control over society which the old plantation and commercial oligarchy had hitherto taken for granted. Faced with the growth of two large institutional parties and the ignominious failure of their own electoral challenge in the shape of a Jamaica Democratic Party,[26]

25. Carl Stone, *Electoral Behaviour and Public Opinion in Jamaica* (Kingston, 1974), p. 86.

26. All nine candidates of the Jamaican Democratic Party lost their deposits in the 1944 General Election. The character of the party has been well summarised by Munroe. It was 'in its leadership, candidates and ideology the instrument of the propertied groups. It brought together in common cause both the older landed families and the newer business groups in Kingston whose merchant houses were expanding with increasing urbanisation. Its candidates and spokesmen – such as Abe Issa and Herbert de Lisser – argued that policies of free enterprise, undoubtedly in their own interest, would advance Jamaica's welfare and development. In its ideology and organization the JDP represented one way in which the holders of economic power tried to secure a place in the new constitutional order . . . [its failure] . . . marked the beginning of the gradual shift of the economic élite from the street-corner meeting to the caucus room. Munroe, *Politics of Constitutional Decolonization*, pp. 38, 43 .

their response was to infiltrate and as far as possible steer the two popular parties. This was smoothly accomplished with the JLP, less so with the PNP where, as we have seen, resistance from a genuinely socialist left wing was not broken till 1952. As a result, the business élite has always been closer to the JLP leadership whose period in office in 1962–72 in fact marked the most successful phase of this new, more subtle technique of oligarchic domination. However, towards the end of the JLP regime, inter-élite tensions had developed between the JLP and the local capitalist class, partly as a consequence of the partisan favours bestowed on certain business figures in the way of various state concessions and contracts, and partly through a growing realisation that widespread disaffection with the inept leadership, poor welfare performance and open corruption associated with the JLP government prejudiced the stability of their own hold on the course of Jamaica's development. Manley's willingness to promise all things to all people in the 1972 election campaign, well illustrated by the vagueness of the party slogan 'Better Must Come', and his obviously immense popularity throughout Jamaica, persuaded the more liberal members of the oligarchy to switch allegiance (and financial support) to the PNP, and at least encouraged others not to oppose a PNP victory.

In this way the PNP government had the backing not only of the educated and professional middle class, which had always found its home in the PNP,[27] but, at least conditionally, of many members of the capitalist class of Jamaica. Its most ardent supporters in this group tended to be those with industrial and manufacturing interests, who had grown in strength and numbers as a result of the 'incentive industrialisation' programme and who, as subordinate partners in a network of international investment, might have been expected to gain from more resolute measures against foreign-owned industries. Historically, the JLP leadership had closer links with older elements in the business sector – those more involved in real estate speculation, usury, commerce and land ownership. Manley was concerned in the beginning not to lose the backing of PNP-minded capitalists, and they in their turn recognised their dependence on state patronage in the form of incentives, tax holidays, subsidies and import protection. In fact, he seized on this

27. The traditional strongholds of PNP support were within 'the more upwardly mobile, more respectable, more educated and less impoverished sectors in the middle, lower and upper lower sections of the hierarchy of social strata'. Stone, op. cit., p. 40. See also tables 3, 12, 13 and 14. This pattern derived from the image of middle-class respectability bestowed on the party by its founder leader, Norman Manley – in marked contrast to the coarser braggadocio of Bustamante.

inter-relationship and actively sought to promote a process of integration between the PNP élite in office and those outside the government who had control of the economy. His Marxist critics within Jamaica understood this thinking and drew attention to the consequences for the masses of this tendency for the political, bureaucratic and educated classes to merge socially with the less aloof members of the local bourgeoisie. The cabinet's intention, they argued, was that 'of inducing the oligarchy to share power with the middle classes, a sharing that will make it possible for the oligarchy to enter the mainstream of national life still retaining its hegemony over society'.[28]

This political background illuminates the government's basic economic strategy: it was to bring about the adaptation of the old, thoroughly neo-colonial, foreign-dominated economy of Jamaica into a modernised, thrusting mixed economy, with a degree of independence in its own right, which by a judicious blend of 'trickle-down' benefits and sophisticated manipulation of the symbols of change would provide sufficient welfare and psychological appeasement to contain mass disaffection, and at the same time allow PNP businessmen to forge ahead with the creation of national wealth. International capitalism was seen in a utilitarian sense as a cow to be milked to the mutual advantage of both the business and governing élites. Accordingly, Manley's initial efforts to secure state participation and partnership in the commanding heights of the economy met with the full approval of local capitalists. It was often PNP men – the Matalons, the Hendricksons, the Grahams – who sat on the new state boards,[29] and even when they did not, the slowly expanding state sector posed no threat to their interests.[30] Typically, it was Meyer Matalon, a senior member of one of the country's five leading entrepreneurial families, rather than the radical university economist Norman Girvan, a bauxite specialist, who was chosen to head the National Bauxite Commission, established in 1972 to

28. T. Munroe, 'The New Political Situation', *Socialism!* (a Marxist-Leninist journal), 1, 6 (1974), p. 10.
29. To take a single example, K. Hendrickson, chairman and largest shareholder in the National Continental Conglomerate and Caribbean Communications, was until September 1975 chairman of the island's electricity utility, Jamaica Public Service, majority owned by the state.
30. The leader column of the *Daily Gleaner* reassured its readers of this very early on: 'There is no reason why the private sector of the nation should not thrive as well or even better within the guidelines of Socialism as under *laissez-faire* Capitalism. Certainly, businessmen will be allowed fair profits and an adequate return on capital investment. There does not seem anything frightening about the kind of Socialism the government is implementing.' *Daily Gleaner*, 24 Nov. 1974.

negotiate a more favourable deal for Jamaica from the international bauxite companies. The production levy that was the fruit of this operation received widespread support from local capitalists[31] – and not surprisingly, since it had tided the whole economy, in which they all had so large a stake, over a severe financial crisis.

This, however, marked the limit of the PNP government's acceptability to the capitalist class as a whole. Despite its policies having been carefully designed not to threaten the position of those at the top of the social and economic hierarchy, tensions emerged between the government and some members of the élite alliance, and increased when the government responded to steep rises in the cost of living with budget proposals for the 1973–74 financial year that had more of a populist ring about them – including the commitment to free education, the National Youth Service programme, increases in land taxes and a freeze on rents. Many businessmen, who had tacitly supported the PNP since 1972, felt that Manley had gone beyond the terms of their 'pact', and that in consequence they had lost the initiative to Manley himself and what they saw as some of the younger zealots in his ranks. Their reaction was, first, to look again to a revitalised JLP under new leadership (realised in November 1974 when Edward Seaga was elected to replace Shearer), and, secondly, to bring greater pressure to bear on the PNP political hierarchy. This pressure undoubtedly had some short-term effect and was revealed in a darker side to PNP policies – in the Labour Relations and Industrial Disputes Act[32] and in the extraordinary Gun Court Law, passed virtually overnight in March 1974 after the shooting of a number of prominent Jamaicans. It established a new court, literally resembling a concentration camp, where all persons using firearms for criminal purposes were tried within seven days, without option of bail, and if found guilty sentenced to indefinite detention without right of appeal. This was Manley's reaction to the hysteria aroused by the growth of violent crime against the property and persons of middle- and upper-class Jamaicans and was conspicuous for the lack of any admission that the crime figures reflected the awful poverty of Kingston's urban slums.

Nevertheless, suspicions of the PNP among capitalists were not eliminated and, in fact, were given renewed credence by the announcement of the PNP political education programme and then

31. See 'Bauxite: How the PNP Liberals Satisfy The Local Capitalists and Betray the Masses', *Socialism*! 1, 1 (1974), pp. 5–14.
32. For a discussion of the LRIDA see Richard Hart, 'Anti-Working Class Industrial Legislation in Jamaica', *Socialism*! 1, 4 (1974), pp. 14–18. The bill was modelled very closely on the Industrial Relations Act passed by the Conservative government led by Edward Heath in Britain.

by the party's reaffirmation of socialism itself. They had been content to let Manley deal in the rhetoric of the masses, and indeed indulge in any symbolic manipulation that might have served to placate the evolving consciousness of the oppressed in Jamaica, a danger underlined by the 'Rodney riots' in 1968. As such, the election campaign in 1972, the PNP slogan 'Power to the People', and all the dramatic symbolism of 'the Rod' - purported to have been given to Manley by Haile Selassie, the God-figure of the Rastafarian movement - was no cause for worry. They knew, or thought they knew, what Manley was about. Similarly, the kind of psychological adjustments to the society, described earlier, were only seen as further evidence of the subtle way the government was adopting and incorporating the culture and causes of the masses. Blatant politicking - such as the way Manley was often photographed in conversation with the popular Jamaican cricketer Lawrence Rowe ('Lawrence of Jamaica') - was all part of the same game. But socialism! That appeared to break the rules. The re-adoption of socialism was seen by businessmen, even those sympathetic to the PNP, as the introduction of ideology into the neutered life of Jamaican politics, likely to arouse expectations among the mass population who would prove dangerously volatile if those expectations were to remain unfulfilled.

This was largely a misapprehension. Certainly, the espousal of socialism might have been expected to fuel the awakening consciousness of the poor and dispossessed, but such were the risks involved in any strategy of absorption and appeasement. What Manley's programme did not presage was a revolutionary departure in Jamaican political life introducing a kind of politics that articulated, rather than masked, class interests. The general policy directions of the PNP government continued the previous line of JLP policies in many ways: commitment to the use of foreign capital, non-interference with the private sector, the encouragement of tourism, the control of public utilities and an unwillingness to nationalise the bauxite industry. The world is constantly changing and the government of a small country like Jamaica, with such an 'open' economy, always has to respond to change, usually in an atmosphere of crisis. Had the JLP still been in office after 1972, it is probable that they too would have been forced by events to extend Jamaica's mixed economy and similarly divert attention from the bare bones of their commitment to capitalism by populist gestures in welfare areas. Or, to put the point in reverse, their only real alternative would have been policies of increased repression in the face of escalating mass discontent.

This, of course, is not to say that the JLP would have chosen the same set of principles to legitimise similar nationalist policies. There have always been differences of style between the parties.[33] But it is in this vein that we should interpret PNP socialism. It has been explained as follows, in Marxist phraseology: 'In order to harness and channel the rising revolutionary consciousness of the masses, to restrain them from taking a left, democratic course, Manley and his colleagues were forced to shake the dust off the old slogans of bourgeois socialism, to re-institute them and actively promote them.'[34] The tone is wrong, but the substance of the point is valid. Manley was less cynical and less opportunistic in his politics than is suggested here. The programme of political education within the PNP and the attendant re-examination of the party's ideology were set in motion as soon as victory was won in the 1972 election. The two processes converged in the re-affirmation of socialism, which therefore represented more than a short-term gambit to appease demands for change emanating from the masses. Having said that, however, there is no doubt that, following the fervour and adulation aroused by his successful election campaign and the marked fall in his popularity due to spiralling living costs and persistently high unemployment, Manley wanted to revive, around his personality, that same sense of hope and commitment among the masses seen in 1972. The PNP's historical association with socialism and the growing respectability of the socialist label within the Third World provided the obvious framework within which to bring this about. In this sense, the appeal to socialism was more in keeping with the 'Power to the People' appeal of 1972 than with the genuine socialist tendencies within the party which had been purged from it twenty years before in 1952.

The argument, in short, is that Manley's strategy, for all its dramatic co-option of such left-wing concepts as 'socialism', 'egalitarianism' and 'brotherhood', was, at heart, that of an old-school politician, manipulating the traditional Jamaican political system with enormous skill. There were present within his political career all the characteristic features of politics in Jamaica since the introduction of universal adult suffrage in 1944 – manipulation of party patronage, a search for multiple-class support, the deliberate fragmentation of class interests, and above all personalism and exploi-

33. Under their new leader the JLP immediately set up their stall, attacking socialism and advocating instead 'moderation and change without chaos'. If this can largely be explained as part of the opposition's need to oppose, it does at least demonstrate that the PNP under Manley was the more populist in terms of the force and sensitivity with which it articulated demands for social justice. Even if pursuing identical policies to Manley's government, it is unthinkable that the JLP would have striven to legitimise them by appeals to socialism!
34. Munroe, *Socialism!*, p. 8.

tation of the messianic side of Jamaican political culture. The development of collective political action in Jamaica has long been dependent on the tradition of attachment to a strong leader, and Manley's whole political style in the early 1970s was carefully designed to respond to this widespread tendency to seek psychological relief from despair and hopelessness through hero-worship. During the 1972 election campaign, PNP support was mobilised around his shrewdly-cultivated 'Joshua' image. By the use of this title, his Old Testament rhetoric and the anger and sincerity with which he denounced the suffering of the masses, he was able to appear as the heaven-sent deliverer traditionally looked to in times of need, an appeal nicely calculated to play on both the populist and religious orientations of his mass audience. By comparison with Shearer's restrained, suavely-suited business image, Manley's dramatic political personality drew an enormous and frenetic response, which has been shown to have had a tremendous impact on the voting choice of the electorate.[35]

Such an interpretation of the main dynamics of Jamaican politics in this period is reinforced by the prominence given within the socialist initiative to what might be called 'the politics of Michael'. Jamaica's saviour was no longer Joshua but Michael, and it was this message above all that was hammered home during the country-wide political education campaign that announced the party's re-conversion to socialism. At a huge meeting held in front of Norman Manley's statue in North Parade in Kingston on 21 November 1974, Manley appended to each of his announcements his personal blessing, 'This comes to you from Michael with love'. Two weeks later, the citizens of Mandeville were invited by huge press advertisements to 'Celebrate with Michael his fiftieth birthday' at a public meeting.[36] Manley, of course, is a formidable orator, managing to fuse the angry populist, almost charismatic aura of Bustamante with the image of innate accomplishment and educational superiority of his father.[37] This enables him to be just as effective addressing an hysterical mass meeting, where he slips easily and frequently into Jamaican dialect, as conversing with a more sceptical university audience on the Mona campus, where he can bandy complex philosophical arguments with the best. It is thus no exaggeration to conclude that socialism in Jamaica was made the servant of that typically Jamaican personalistic style of politics which Manley so effectively embodied.

35. *Stone,* op. cit., p. 30, esp. Table 3:7.
36. *Jamaica Daily News*, 10 Dec. 1974.
37. He has indeed been called 'Bustamanley' in the press.

Could it have been otherwise? Was there scope within Manley's own philosophy for a more radical form of socialism? There is no single answer. Within his thinking there was flexibility over exactly where the public and private sectors began and ended, and over the role assumed by the business class, and it is reasonable to assume from the tenor of Manley's writings and speeches in the early 1970s that he himself was firmly of the opinion that the balance of authority between the political and economic élites in Jamaica was too heavily weighted in favour of the latter. There was also a trend, well represented within the PNP as a party but only on the fringes of the post-1972 government, that urged a greater share of economic power for the state and harboured a vision of a sharply reduced role for the local bourgeoisie. It perceived that the commitment to socialism in itself could as well be reformist as transformative. Stone, too, has shown that in certain specific areas, such as the expropriation and redistribution of land and the nationalisation of the bauxite industry, there was significant mass support, especially among PNP voters, for radical policy changes historically excluded from discussion by the party élites who were supposedly in competition with each other, but were both generally conservative.[38]

One might thus feel that the opportunity was there for the PNP to grasp, and that Manley was perhaps always tempted by it. The fact is, however, that it was a luxury which neither he nor Jamaica could afford. The political situation in the country required him to continue his balancing act, trying to straddle simultaneously the diverging interests of the PNP business class, the political élites in his own party and government, and the mass of poorer Jamaicans, for whose plight he expressed concern regularly and with feeling. It was the kind of policy which by its very nature could not be articulated for fear of being upset. The major constraint acting on Manley was not the more usually identified features of small size or even imperialist domination but the nature of the Jamaican political system itself, and particularly the multiple-class character of the dominant political parties. Once he set himself, as he did, to work within the confines of that setting, he had to take cognisance at all times of the fact that the PNP was a coalition, incorporating the poor, the starving and the homeless but also wielding a disproportionate amount of influence at the top of the social strata, a sector of the capitalist class on whose financial backing it depended to get itself elected. In short, the social question – how power was distributed within Jamaican society – was subordinated to an attempt to revit-

38. Stone, op. cit., pp. 72–7.

alise the national question around a strategy of securing for Jamaica a greater 'piece of the action' from the dominant forces of the international economy. This was not of itself a mistake. Although Gordon Lewis has argued that such a 'subordination, perhaps necessary in the pre-Independence era, becomes a tactic of evasion in the post-Independence era',[39] that judgement is too harsh. The problem was that Manley espoused an ideal of an egalitarian society which could not be achieved within the conventional boundaries of Jamaican politics. Without directly broaching the question of the internal distribution of class power, all the other initiatives that one might otherwise have lauded from a reformist perspective come perilously close to being window-dressing, and the PNP's 'democratic socialism' merely a convenient piece of ideological labelling. On the record of his first three years in office, Manley is actually well described in his own (highly critical) definition of the pragmatist – a politician prepared to tinker but not to transform, who 'is conscious of points of pressure, seeming to require change, that arise from discontent, and seeks, in response to that pressure, marginal adjustments in the organisation of society for the purpose of relieving the discontent and removing the points of pressure'.[40]

39. G.K. Lewis, *The Growth of the Modern West Indies* (New York, 1968), p. 399.
40. Manley, op. cit., pp. 15–16.

3
THE DESTABILISATION QUESTION

The charge

The concept of destabilisation first entered the vocabulary of Jamaican politics early in 1976 when senior members of the PNP government, including the Prime Minister, began to allege that a systematic campaign was being waged by local *and* foreign forces against their very right to govern. According to Michael Manley, 'destabilisation describes a situation where some source either inside or outside a country – or perhaps two sources working in concert, one outside and one inside – set out to create a situation of instability and panic *by* design.'[1] The word had entered the lexicon of political analysis two or three years earlier because of events in Chile. As a result of a series of US Senate investigations conducted in the cathartic atmosphere of Watergate, it had been clearly demonstrated that American multinational corporations had worked hand-in-hand with US governmental agencies such as the Central Intelligence Agency (CIA) and with the Chilean military and other local reactionary elements first to destabilise, as the phrase had it, and then ultimately to overthrow the constitutionally elected socialist government of Salvador Allende. At the time when the Chilean coup occurred in September 1973, US officials – from the Secretary of State Henry Kissinger downwards – denied complicity, little realising how soon their involvement would be revealed by Congressional investigation.

In that respect, at least, it was the same in Jamaica. In June 1976 Kissinger himself was quoted as telling PNP Foreign Affairs minister Dudley Thompson that he was 'not aware of any action by the US government designed to weaken the government of Prime Minister Manley'; in the same month Deputy Assistant Secretary of State William Luers categorically denied before a House of Representatives committee that 'the US Government is doing anything to undermine or destabilise the legitimate government of Jamaica'; and the US ambassador to Jamaica, Sumner Gerard, pointedly told a group of Kingston businessmen that 'allegations of US destabilisation are scurrilous and false'.[2] Such denials were predictable and

1. Michael Manley, *Jamaica: Struggle in the Periphery* (London, 1982), p. 138. Manley's emphasis.
2. Quoted in ibid., p. 223.

were given publicity by the Jamaican government, which wanted to avoid, if possible, getting into the position of having to accuse the US administration directly. Yet it manifestly was not convinced. Its real view was expressed in an overseas interview given by the Minister of National Security, Keble Munn, in defence of the declaration of a state of emergency which was the government's response to the alleged destabilisation campaign. 'We've got all kinds of assurances from the United States government that they are not involved in destabilisation', he said, 'and we would like to be in a position to take them at face value.' But, he went on, 'everyone knows what happened in Chile, although no one could prove who was behind it until afterwards, when Watergate came along.'[3]

After the PNP won the general election of December 1976 other concerns, notably the International Monetary Fund (IMF), came to the forefront of political debate in Jamaica, and less was heard openly of destabilisation. Yet the question did not go away, and was forcefully resurrected by Manley himself in a subsequent account of his period in office in which he argued 'that Jamaica was destabilised, as we have defined the word'.[4] Although claiming that the campaign was pursued consistently between 1976 and 1980, his focus was on 1976 as the critical year. Indeed, in an appendix, a 'destabilisation diary' for 1976 was provided, itemising the events which in his view formed part of the campaign. A summary of the entries for just the one month of January gives the flavour and some of the detail of Manley's case.

January 2: The election year began ominously when the *Daily Gleaner* published an editorial replete with lies, half-truths and malicious speculation, titled 'If he fails . . .' The editor of the paper was Mr Hector Wynter, a former chairman of and candidate for the JLP.

January 4: The US Secretary of State, Henry Kissinger, left Jamaica, unsuccessful in his mission to dissuade Manley from supporting the presence of Cuban troops in Angola. Despite this failure, he assured Manley that there was no CIA interference in Jamaica, but did not add that the CIA station in Kingston had just been strengthened by the arrival of a new chief, Norman Descoteaux, a man with recent field experience in Argentina and Ecuador where it was thought other destabilisation campaigns had previously taken place.

January 5: As officials of the IMF and World Bank held preparatory meetings for a conference subsequently to be held in Kingston,

3. *The Guardian*, 18 July 1976.
4. Manley, op. cit., p. 213.

violence erupted in the ghettoes of the western sector of the city, thus providing material for a number of sensational articles filed by the large corps of foreign journalists reporting the IMF meeting.

January 6: The Minister of National Security announced the apprehension of 19 members of a group of gunmen being trained for operations against the government.

January 7: Two policemen were killed and three others injured in attacks by gunmen, provoking a stoppage of work at the police barracks until the men were personally persuaded to return to duty by Manley.

January 8: Deputy Prime Minister, David Coore, held a press conference for foreign journalists to try to counteract the exaggerated reporting of the violence which had already caused extensive tourist cancellations.

January 9: As the violence continued, Manley announced new legislation to revitalise the Gun Court: mandatory life imprisonment for illegal possession of a firearm.

January 11: Against this background Manley announced his party's proposal to establish community self-defence groups to act as an unarmed warning service and was met with a barrage of criticism alleging, *inter alia*, that he planned to introduce the 'Ton Ton Macoutes' to Jamaica.

January 12: An article in the *Wall Street Journal* claimed that the PNP government was 'the most inept of all the Western governments that fancies itself democratic'.

January 14: Revere Copper and Brass Inc. announced that its Jamaican subsidiary, Revere Ja. Ltd., was suing the Manley government over its bauxite production levy.

January 15: The traditionally dormant, middle-class, Soroptimist Club of Kingston passed a resolution calling on women to withdraw their services from their employers and communities as well as their husbands and families to protest against political violence.

January 16: Allan Isaacs, Minister of Mining and Natural Resources, was dismissed from the Cabinet for alleged leaking of government documents to the opposition and subsequently resigned from the PNP, alleging that the government was intent upon establishing Cuban style communism.

January 24: 13 people died in the eastern parish of St Thomas after eating flour subsequently found to have been contaminated with the poison parathion.[5]

5. Summarised from ibid., pp. 225–9.

And so the diary went on, charting the unfolding of events during the rest of 1976 in similar vein. As can be seen, it tells a grim story of disruption and violence. Does it amount to destabilisation? Is the charge laid by Manley susceptible to proof? To answer these questions we need to assess the available evidence as carefully and coolly as possible.

The evidence

The main problem with what one might call the case for the prosecution, as outlined above, is that it ranges loosely over a variety of types of evidence and in so doing cannot but identify several different agents of destabilisation. Admittedly, part of the case is that a number of agencies work in collusion in such campaigns – each hand, as it were, not necessarily knowing in detail what the other is up to. Nevertheless, from an analytical point of view it makes sense to consider the activities of the alleged perpetrators of destabilisation agency by agency.

The bauxite companies. There is no doubt that the multinational bauxite companies operating in Jamaica were disturbed by the implications of the production levy imposed by the PNP government in 1974. By tying the level of local taxation to the actual market price of aluminium rather than the arbitrary price at which the companies 'transferred' Jamaican bauxite to their processing plants in North America, the agreement interfered with the traditional vertical integration of the industry under constant corporate control. Although they could survive such a policy, the companies chose to fight back, initially by threatening to withdraw completely from their Jamaican mining operations (although this was never a likely option) and then by filing a suit with the World Bank's International Centre for the Settlement of Investment Disputes contesting the legality of the government levy. More seriously from Jamaica's point of view, they also moved to cut back their production of both bauxite and alumina in the island, thereby undermining the government's revenue expectations and adding to local unemployment. While some of the reductions in production were caused by the recession in the international economy, it cannot be denied that Jamaica suffered disproportionately. According to one analysis, while US companies doubled their bauxite imports from African sources in Guinea in 1975, they cut their Jamaican imports by 30 per cent.[6] In addition,

6. Sherry Keith and Robert Girling, 'Caribbean Conflict: Jamaica and the US', *NACLA Report on the Americas*, XII (1978), p. 21.

the number of strikes in the industry in Jamaica doubled between 1974 and 1975, and doubled again in the year to 1976 – an escalation of industrial action attributed by a number of local observers to deliberately provocative behaviour by a management bent on further disruption of the local economy.[7] The effect was certainly damaging: the Jamaican Bauxite Institute estimated that an 81-day strike at Alcoa, a 43-day shut-down at Alpart and a 35-day strike at Alcan during the first six months of 1976 cost the industry over 400,000 tonnes of bauxite production.[8] The companies also conducted a US press campaign blaming Jamaica for the rising cost of aluminium, e.g. claiming that higher car prices were the result of the action of the Manley government. As Sherry Keith and Robert Girling pointed out, however, the truth was that price increases in the US market bore little, if any, relation to the Jamaican levy and served mainly to boost corporate profits at a time of lower production worldwide.[9]

The US government. The US government also played a part in exerting economic pressure on Jamaica as a response to the bauxite levy. The Treasury Department, in particular, wanted to stop new official lending to the country, arguing that it would give the wrong signal to provide aid to a regime which was in dispute with several US corporations.[10] A small USAID rural development loan was cancelled, and agreement was reached within the administration that no new capital assistance should be provided while the legality of the levy was still being tested. The State Department acquiesced in these moves, although apparently with some reluctance.[11] Manley has reported that he had an affable meeting with Kissinger in 1974 at which he believed that he had forestalled any US hostility to the levy.[12] He may indeed have been right, for it is not difficult to imagine that the US government's reaction could have been considerably more vigorous than it actually was. Time was to demonstrate this, especially once the Jamaican government had begun to establish closer diplomatic links with Cuba. For example, Manley has also described a very different meeting with Kissinger during a short vacation the Secretary of State spent in Jamaica towards the end of 1975. 'Suddenly he raised the question of Angola and said he would appreciate it if Jamaica would at least remain neutral on the subject of the Cuban army presence in Angola. I told him that I could make

7. Interviews with Jamaican Bauxite Institute (JBI) personnel, July 1985.
8. *JBI Digest*, 1, 3 (1976), p. 2.
9. Keith and Girling, op. cit., p. 29.
10. J. Daniel O'Flaherty, 'Finding Jamaica's Way', *Foreign Policy*, XXXI (1978), p. 154.
11. Ibid.
12. Manley, op. cit., pp. 100–1.

no promises but would pay the utmost attention to his request.'[13] Kissinger then apparently brought up the separate matter of a Jamaican request for a US$100 million trade credit. 'He said they were looking at it, and let the comment hang in the room for a moment. I had the feeling he was sending me a message.'[14] In Manley's mind the linkage was clear, but nevertheless five days later he publicly announced Jamaica's support for Cuban involvement in Angola. The result was that US economic aid to Jamaica was embargoed till the end of the Ford administration. This had increasingly serious effects on the level of activity within the Jamaican economy during the course of 1976, although it should immediately be added that the advent of the Carter administration at the beginning of 1977 quickly brought a new, albeit temporary, warmth to US-Jamaican relations and the resumption of aid flows.

The CIA. Although obviously an agency of the US government, the CIA needs to be considered separately because of the presumption that its activities will remain clandestine. It is possible for a US administration to adopt covertly a different policy towards a particular country from the one to which it is publicly committed. Was this the case with Jamaica in 1976? Several observers have claimed that this was precisely the situation, the most significant of them being Philip Agee. After twelve years working as a CIA agent in Latin America, Agee resigned in 1969 and devoted himself to exposing his former employer's operations around the world. He arrived in Jamaica in September 1976 as a guest of the Jamaican Council for Human Rights, and during his two-week stay spoke at a number of packed meetings, stirring up great controversy as he proceeded. He claimed to be able to identify in Jamaica at the time all the typical CIA methods of destabilisation. These included spreading false information in the local and international press, funding opposition groupings, supplying arms to opponents of the government, and helping to organise all manner of social disruption by means of arson, murder and industrial action. Agee also specifically named eleven US embassy personnel in Kingston as working for the CIA, three of whom immediately left the country in what was widely taken to be a tacit admission of guilt. His accusations were given renewed publicity by an article in the December 1977 issue of *Penthouse* magazine[15] – an unusual medium – which reported that at the end of 1975 Kissinger had agreed to the

13. Ibid., p. 116.
14. Ibid.
15. Ernest Volkman and John Cunnings, 'Murder as Usual', *Penthouse*, Dec. 1977, pp. 112–14, 182–90.

implementation of such a campaign against the Manley regime and that early in 1976 the CIA station in the island had been reorganised, bringing in Descoteaux as the new chief with a budget of US$10 million to spend on various covert activities. Detailed description of these apparent activities subsequently appeared regularly in the pages of specialist American magazines like *Counterspy*.

The US press. One of Agee's claims was that the CIA was able to inspire articles in the US press which would have the effect of undermining and eventually destroying the reputation of a particular government in the minds of the US public. Again, a number of commentators have claimed that this is what occurred over Jamaica in 1976. For example, Manley's own account notes that, shortly after news broke that Jamaica was supporting Cuba in the Angola conflict, James Reston of the *New York Times* wrote 'a vicious and utterly inaccurate article'[16] about Jamaica, which seemed to start off a chain reaction in the US press. In the course of 1976 a series of articles appeared in such influential papers and magazines as the *Christian Science Monitor*, the *Washington Post, Time* and *Newsweek*, many of which gave the distinct impression that there had been a virtual Cuban military take-over in Jamaica. Violence was highlighted and often used in politically biased ways. One striking example was a story in the *New York Times* in 1976, printed under the headline 'Jamaican Opposition Leader is Shot at from Office of Ruling Party but Escapes Injury'. It was given great prominence, but later found to be utterly untrue; only a short correction was then published.[17] Moreover, academic analysis shows that such a distorted interpretation of events was not at all untypical. Marlene Cuthbert and Vernone Sparkes studied the coverage of Jamaica in the US press in 1976 and concluded that a preponderance of articles took an overwhelmingly negative view of Jamaica, emphasising political tensions and often employing crude Cold War language in the presentation of events.[18] The effect of this type of reporting on the tourist trade remains controversial. That the number of visitors coming to Jamaica fell dramatically in 1976 and again in 1977 is certain,[19] something which many have attributed to the generally violent image presented of Jamaica despite the fact that the killings were largely confined to the Kingston area, far from the

16. Manley, op. cit., p. 117.
17. Quoted in Michael Kaufman, *Jamaica under Manley: Dilemmas of Socialism and Democracy* (London, 1985), p. 121.
18. Marlene Cuthbert and Vernone Sparkes, 'Coverage of Jamaica in the US and Canadian Press in 1976: A Study of Press Bias and Effect', *Social and Economic Studies*, 27, 2 (1978), pp. 212–13.
19. See figures in Kaufman, op. cit., App. 9.

tourist enclaves on the north coast. Yet Cuthbert and Sparkes demonstrate that, although the coverage of Jamaica in the United States and Canada was equally negative, the Canadian public demonstrated a significantly greater willingness to continue holidaying in Jamaica. They speculate that the difference could well stem from the role of travel agents, the American ones they interviewed generally being readier to believe the press stories.[20] For those who think in conspiracy terms, the evil hand of the CIA can thus be made to appear as effectively infiltrating the US travel industry.

Jamaican opposition. Jamaican participants have also been identified by destabilisation theorists. They include local businessmen, JLP politicians and the owners and writers of the *Daily Gleaner*. It is certainly true that by 1976 Jamaican capitalists no longer had the confidence that some of them had initially placed in Manley. The declaration of socialism was more than they could tolerate, especially in circumstances of increasing economic contraction. Factories began to close and energy was put into smuggling wealth out of the island to Miami and other parts of the North American continent, all of which further damaged the economy. As soon as Seaga took over the leadership, the JLP also began to campaign vigorously throughout the island against the PNP's vision of socialism, engaging in such an extensive and costly range of meetings and propaganda activities as to arouse suspicion that it was drawing on resources beyond the means of its local backers. Its pitch was simplistically anti-communist, echoing much of the US press coverage and some US government opinion, but it was no less effective for that. It was also able to draw on the unstinting support of the *Daily Gleaner*, which of course was owned by one of Jamaica's richest capitalist families. Beginning at the end of 1975, it launched an astonishing barrage of vituperation against the PNP and Manley in particular. Its favourite themes were the familiar areas of the communist threat and the Cuban link. The *Gleaner* has always been a conservative newspaper, but it had traditionally worn an air of sober and serious respectability. Its abandonment of these values prompted the accusation that it too was playing a role on behalf of external interests. For example Fred Landis, who had been a consultant to the US Senate sub-committee which had investigated the CIA's covert action in Chile, prepared a pamphlet for the Press Association of Jamaica. This unhesitatingly compared the *Gleaner*'s role with that played in helping to overthrow the Allende regime by the Chilean newspaper *El Mercurio*, which had consistently and

20. Cuthbert and Sparkes, op. cit., pp. 216–18.

scurrilously attacked Allende and his colleagues and was shown subsequently to have received CIA finance and encouragement to do so.[21]

The verdict

What is to be made of all this evidence? In some areas, the facts appear very plain. Despite the mildness of the move, the bauxite companies did punish the Manley government for its institution of the levy; the US government under Kissinger and Ford did become increasingly unsupportive; the press was always imprecise and often hysterical in its reporting of events in Jamaica; and the PNP's opponents in the country were frequently vicious and unfair in their attacks on the government. In other areas, as one would expect, the evidence is less categoric. In particular, the involvement of the CIA has not been proved, which is to say it has not been admitted by official US government spokesmen. On the other hand, the circumstantial evidence that its agents were active in Jamaica in 1976 is strong – too strong, finally, to be ignored.

Even so, the problem remains of what all this adds up to. For the issue at stake is really a matter of definition. What does destabilisation mean? One should distinguish between a 'narrow' and a 'broad' definition. Understood in the broadest terms, as it often is, the concept too easily becomes a misleading shorthand expression for the fact that the world which radical governments take on is generally hostile to their aims. Opposition is generated by policies of change because powerful vested interests feel threatened, and they react. This should not be considered surprising or beyond the capacity of radical leaders to anticipate. For example, the bauxite companies pursued in connection with Jamaica nothing other than their corporate interests, as these are conventionally interpreted by big business. The US government, like any other government, does not have to feel well disposed towards the government of every country with which it has relations, let alone assist it with aid and credit. Much of the Western press is also sadly sensationalist in its interpretation of political events all over the world, not merely in Jamaica. As for the alleged treachery of the local opposition, the anxieties of Jamaican businessmen in the face of the Manley regime's stridently socialist rhetoric in 1976 are surely not difficult to explain. In terms of the business ethic, it made good sense to shift

21. Press Association of Jamaica, *Psychological Warfare in the Media: The Case of Jamaica* (Kingston, n.d.).

investment out of Jamaica. The JLP, for its part, certainly exceeded some of the boundaries traditionally imposed on an opposition by the Westminster system, but politics in the Third World is a rough game and Jamaica is no exception. In other words, these were all factors which the PNP should have been prepared to deal with. There is not really much to be gained by grouping them all together and claiming that they represent destabilisation. If that is so, every radical government must face destabilisation, simply because the system it is pledged to attack still exists and will fight back. At this point the argument becomes unprofitable and is best abandoned.

However, the concept of destabilisation can take on new force when it is understood in narrower terms. It would refer specifically to a deliberate and coordinated campaign instigated from outside a particular country and designed to undermine support for the government of that country. The tactics of such a campaign typically include covert support for opposition political groupings by a foreign power, the promotion of hostile propaganda in the press locally and internationally, the encouragement of violence and terrorism, the disruption of industrial relations, economic sabotage and indeed any form of action which generates turmoil and strife likely to have an adverse political effect on the government in question. Defined in this way, the charge that a destabilisation campaign was waged against the Manley government in 1976 is easier to substantiate. A 'smoking gun' was never found, but the weight of evidence makes it likely that the CIA was at work, in league with the JLP, the *Daily Gleaner*, and opposition businessmen and trade unionists, to undermine the elected government in Jamaica. More than that one cannot plausibly say. As Manley himself put it, 'there have been no Senate Committee hearings into the case of Jamaica and consequently no disclosures at that level.'[22] Yet, even as it stands, the statement is serious: the meaning of sovereignty and statehood for independent Caribbean countries has to be re-assessed. To obtain some perspective, however, it is important to note that the PNP won the elections with which the year of destabilisation culminated by a huge margin! It gained all but thirteen of the sixty seats in the Jamaican parliament. By this test destabilisation, narrowly defined, does not seem to have had much effect. In the longer run, the violence and the propaganda took their toll, but what really damaged the Manley regime beyond repair was the decline of the Jamaican economy after 1976. For this phenomenon explanations have to be sought beyond destabilisation.

22. Manley, op. cit., p. 237.

4

'DEMOCRATIC SOCIALISM' IN RETROSPECT

By virtue of its government's public commitment to the ideology of 'democratic socialism', Jamaica aroused more interest in the eyes of the world during the 1970s than any other country in the Commonwealth Caribbean. The PNP regime held office in all for some eight and a half years during which time, as Michael Manley himself put it, it was witness to 'some of the more controversial events'[1] of Jamaica's colourful history. The destabilisation controversy, important though it was, is thus only part of the broader question of the fate which ultimately befell Manley's government. It came to power on a tide of hope, buoyed up by the support of Jamaica's underprivileged classes for its wide-ranging programme of reform. Yet it was driven from office in 1980 in one of the heaviest electoral defeats ever suffered by a leading political party in modern Jamaica.

The whole Manley experiment constitutes dramatic evidence of the problems and possibilities that attach to 'democratic socialist' strategies of reform in trying to overcome dependence in the Third World. This chapter examines the Manley years in their totality, assesses the PNP government's particular achievements and failures and sets out some of the lessons that can be learnt from the attempt to bring about radical change in a context of underdevelopment and dependence. It begins by considering the main structural features of the political economy with which Manley and the PNP had to grapple.

Class, state and capital

At the beginning of the 1970s, when the Manley government came to office, the economy of Jamaica was unquestionably more complex and diverse than ever before in the island's history, but not necessarily any less dependent on external forces as a result. The development of bauxite, tourist and manufacturing sectors within the economy had all been based on foreign private investment. This came not from traditional British sources but predominantly from the United States.[2] The cumulative effect was to shift the economic

1. Michael Manley, *Jamaica: Struggle in the Periphery* (London, 1982), p. ix.
2. See N. Girvan, *Foreign Capital and Economic Underdevelopment in Jamaica* (Kingston, 1971).

orientation of Jamaica away from Europe to North America—a process so marked by 1972 that it would not be too much to suggest that within a decade of independence Jamaica had been effectively transferred from British colonial control into the less overt but still highly effective domain of US hemispheric power.

The fact of the continuing external domination of the economy had also influenced the structure of the country's class system. In particular, it generated a relatively weak domestic capitalist class. The local visibility and assertiveness of this class should not be allowed to give an exaggerated impression of its power. As we have seen earlier, it maintained its position in the local economy only by securing subordinate agency relationships with foreign firms and by generally effecting a deferential alliance with foreign capital. It then became dependent for further growth on state patronage in the form of subsidies, incentives, import protection, tax holidays and the like. Increasingly, therefore, Jamaican capitalists were forced to cultivate the local political élite which since independence had come to control the state, and to act as subordinate clients of this grouping. Stone neatly summed up the relationship, noting that 'the alliance between members or sectors of the capitalist class and ruling politicians is one that grows out of the weakness of that class rather than its strength.'[3]

The unformed character of the capitalist class at the beginning of the 1970s extended to the working class, the peasantry and the unemployed. The last of these typically lived at or around subsistence level and devoted their energies to the search for individualistic solutions to their dilemma, ranging from crime to gangsterism; it is questionable whether they possessed any sort of collective consciousness at all. The urban working class grew in size during the economic expansion of the 1960s, but remained only partly organised. Because of the small scale of many of the industrial plants established under the import-substitution programme the level of unionisation was low and labour relations were paternalistic. The unionised sector of the working class did possess a capacity for collective action but tended to limit its activities to narrowly defined issues such as industrial disputes and wage bargaining. Similarly, the various agricultural associations which developed to represent the interests of small peasants devoted their efforts mainly to extension work, the improvement of marketing facilities and the distribution of state subsidies. In short, few channels had been forged by which ordinary lower-class Jamaicans could bring their particular interests

3. Carl Stone, *Class, Race and Political Behaviour in Urban Jamaica* (Kingston, 1973), p. 50.

to bear on the shape of the country's political economy.

As in other dependent societies in the Third World, the presence of a considerable measure of external domination and the underdeveloped nature of local class relations placed heavy demands on the state. Despite its position of relative economic subordination to powerful overseas economic interests, it could nevertheless direct the domestic political system by channelling state patronage in clientelist fashion both to the depressed masses and to the local capitalist class. To this extent, the Jamaican state possessed a degree of autonomy which at one and the same time was both real and qualified. Reference to the existence of this 'relative autonomy' on the part of the state is critically important, not only because of the room for manoeuvre in the real world which it identifies but also because it addresses one of the most fundamental of recent intellectual debates about Third World politics. Some analysts have taken the view, in more or less classic Marxist terms, that the post-colonial state has no choice but to act in the interests either of the local or a metropolitan bourgeois class.[4] Others have argued that the petty bourgeois class, which generally acceded to political power at independence, has been able to use its control of the state to establish itself as a new bureaucratic bourgeoisie.[5] However, neither of these theses is supported by the facts of Jamaica's class structure at the beginning of the 1970s. The political managers of the state were far from being instruments of the country's capitalist class, nor were they completely in the power of international capital, although the latter was clearly a force to be reckoned with. Nor were they so powerful economically and politically as to constitute a new ruling class in their own right. As we have explained, they represented instead what may reasonably be called an indeterminate petty bourgeoisie, which might 'go either way' in terms of development strategy depending on the outcome of political pressures. Again several writers have adopted this line, but none has put the point more succinctly than Roger Murray: 'The essence of the matter is that the post-colonial state has simultaneously to be perceived as the *actual* instrument of mediation and negotiation with external capitalism and as the *possible* instrument of a continuing anti-imperialist and socialist

4. Colin Leys has adopted both positions at different times. See C. Leys, *Underdevelopment in Kenya: The Political Economy of Neo-Colonialism* (London, 1974) and C. Leys, 'Capital Accumulation, Class Formation and Dependency – The Significance of the Kenyan Case', *The Socialist Register, 1978* (London, 1979), pp. 241–66.
5. See, for example, C. Meillassoux, 'A Class Analysis of the Bureaucratic Process in Mali', *Journal of Development Studies*, VI (1969–70), and Issa Shivji, *Class Struggles in Tanzania* (New York, 1976).

revolution'.[6] Emphasis should be given to the contrast in Murray's formulation between actuality and possibility. It encapsulates in a few words the very essence of the struggle which Third World states inevitably engage in if and when they embark upon strategies for overcoming dependence.

Manley's strategy of change

From the moment in 1969 when he became leader of the PNP in succession to his father, Michael Manley demonstrated a clear understanding of the nature of the political economy produced in Jamaica by the post-war era of expansion. As a former trade union leader, he was aware that the social benefits of economic growth had been spread thinly and that there were pockets of alienation within the urban environment which on more than one occasion during the 1960s had exploded into violence. It was by addressing himself to this discontent, and by adopting a dynamic approach to such issues as unemployment, poverty and political participation, that Manley was able to lead the PNP to victory in the 1972 elections. The result reflected the broad range of support which Manley received from the young, the unemployed, large sections of the working class and peasantry, most of the professional and administrative middle class and intelligentsia and even some of the more liberal members of the capitalist class disaffected by the economic failures of the previous JLP government.[7] It could not be interpreted as anything other than a most decisive mandate for change.

By the time he assumed office, Manley had also developed a coherent vision of the programme of change he wished to introduce. In the domestic sphere this consisted of three basic commitments. The first was to create an economy that would be more independent of foreign control and more responsive to the needs of the majority of the people. This required a wide range of initiatives including land reform, the creation of co-operative farms, the promotion of worker participation and measures to achieve a more equitable distribution of wealth, but it revolved at heart around the extension of state control into the 'commanding heights' of the economy. In the various public utilities Manley envisaged the swift implementation of complete government ownership, but admitted that 'public ownership will have to work together with foreign and private

6. Roger Murray, 'Second Thoughts on Ghana', *New Left Review*, 42 (1967), p. 31 (my emphasis).
7. See Carl Stone, *Electoral Behaviour and Public Opinion in Jamaica* (Kingston, 1974).

capital'[8] in such areas as bauxite, sugar, tourism and banking. He rejected expropriation, and asserted that 'the question is not whether to use foreign capital in development planning' but how to bring it into 'harmony with national aspirations'.[9] He also accepted the permanent existence of a mixed economy. In his own words, 'once certain priorities have been overtaken in the field of human resources, infrastructure and certain strategic areas of the economy, private enterprise is the method best suited to the production of all the other goods and services which are necessary to the functioning of an economy.'[10]

The second feature of the strategy was the development of a more egalitarian society, not only in terms of opportunity but also in the deeper sense of mutual respect and access to benefits. To this end Manley sought to use the state to ensure that certain basic rights were enjoyed by all Jamaicans. Education, previously narrow and élitist, was to be expanded and opened to all classes; resources in the health service were to be concentrated on preventive medicine in the countryside rather than sophisticated hospital care in the capital; certain laws were to be amended to improve the legal position of employees and of women, especially mothers; and significantly the government was to accept responsibility for organising massive work programmes of unemployment relief as a positive social duty. A common theme in all these proposals was a commitment to the use of public expenditure to reduce social inequality.

The third aspect of the programme was political. Manley was critical of the remoteness of traditional multi-party democracy in Jamaica, particularly its tendency to confine itself to the act of choosing a party to form a government every five years. To this he posed the alternative, not of the single-party state but what he described as 'the politics of participation'. This called for basic political engineering to 'create the institutions through which people feel continuously involved in the decision-making processes',[11] even as governments faced the need to compromise or take unpopular decisions. Accordingly Manley proposed the revitalisation of Jamaican local government, the establishment of community councils, the involvement of the public in economic planning, the deployment of the political party as an instrument of mass political education and communication and a host of other measures

8. Michael Manley, *The Politics of Change: A Jamaican Testament* (London, 1974), p. 118.
9. Ibid., p. 106.
10. Ibid., p. 215.
11. Ibid., p. 68.

designed to intensify popular mobilisation.

The various elements of this strategy of change were conceived by Manley as 'a third path'[12] for Jamaica and the rest of the Caribbean, in which both the Puerto Rican and the Cuban models of development were rejected. In his view the Puerto Rican model was in effect the policy pursued in Jamaica in the 1950s and 1960s, emphasising economic growth and foreign investment but neglecting social welfare. In contrast, the Cuban model was one of revolution with impressive social achievements but based on the Marxist-Leninist view of democracy which allowed no political rights outside the concept of the dictatorship of the proletariat. For Manley both models also stood condemned by their respective dependence on each of the two superpowers. It was, as he put it, 'self-evident to us that we want to be pawns neither of East nor West, economically or politically'.[13] Only the third path offered Jamaica and the Caribbean the possibility of choosing real independence.

This last point is important because it highlights a clearly articulated international dimension to Manley's programme of change. Manley understood from the outset that domestic reform could be secured only if his government was able to negotiate better terms for Jamaica in all its dealings with the international economy. To some extent this was met by the proposal to bring such industries as bauxite and sugar partly into public ownership, but it was also deemed to require a radical revision of the direction of post-independence foreign policy. Manley worked from the perception that Jamaica was a part of the Third World: he attached considerable weight to the development of a globál Third World economic strategy designed to increase collective self-reliance, and favoured the creation of an organisation of bauxite-exporting countries on the lines of OPEC. More generally, he proposed the adoption of an open foreign policy envisaging relations with a variety of countries beyond the circle of Jamaica's traditional partners, including those whose ideologies and political systems were communist. Notice was also given of Jamaica's readiness to support wars of liberation in Africa. In short, Manley sought to 'establish the fact that the entire world is the stage upon which a country, however small, pursues this perception of self-interest'.[14]

Thus Manley's thinking contained a number of diverse elements which make it difficult to categorise. In this the ideological label he himself adopted, that of 'democratic socialism', does not necessarily

12. Manley, *Jamaica: Struggle in the Periphery*, p. 38.
13. Ibid., p. 221.
14. Manley, *Politics of Change*, p. 130.

help. Manley has recorded that in 1974, when the PNP came to choose a name around which to mobilise support for its programme of change, it considered three possibilities:

> Christian socialist was rejected on the grounds that it might sound like a political ploy. We decided not to use the word socialist alone because it seemed to invite too much speculation. Quite apart from communism, there were a number of African socialist states organised on a one-party basis. Then again, the local communists were at that time in semi-hiding under the term 'scientific socialist'. Since we were neither communist nor seeking to establish a one-party state, it seemed to invite unnecessary risk to use the term socialist without qualification. In the end, we settled on democratic socialist. The democratic was to be given equal emphasis with the socialist, because we were committed to the maintenance of Jamaica's traditional and constitutional plural democracy; and more importantly, because we intended to do everything in our power to deepen and broaden the democratic process of our party and in the society at large.[15]

One notes the care with which Manley and his party tried to establish the particular nature of the ideas that were to guide their attempt to reshape the political economy, and one can appreciate the reasons for their choice. Respect for democracy was genuine; furthermore, it was indispensable for securing popular support in Jamaica, where the concept is well embedded in the political culture, while there was an obvious attraction to the idea of reaffirming the PNP's original socialist appeal which had been dormant since the party had expelled its small Marxist faction in 1952. From the analytical point of view, however, 'democratic socialism' is hardly the most precise term in the political vocabulary, since it begs all sorts of questions as to the content of the socialism and the reality of the democracy, quite apart from the mode of their attainment.

It is more accurate to view Manley's approach to politics as a complex, but not inconsistent, combination of several strands of thought. First, he is a nationalist, committed to the service of Jamaica, the assertion of its place in the world and the achievement of a greater degree of economic independence for it within the international capitalist system. Secondly, he is an egalitarian, determined to bring the benefits of reform to all sectors of society. 'Social organisation', he has written, 'exists to serve everybody or it has no moral foundation . . . The fact that society cannot function effectively without differentials in rewards together with the fact that men are manifestly not equal in talent must not be allowed to obscure the central purpose of social organisation. That is, and must always be,

15. Manley, *Jamaica: Struggle in the Periphery*, p. 123.

the promotion of the welfare of every member of the human race.'[16] Thirdly, he is anti-Marxist, and disavows, either explicitly or by implication, all notions of class struggle and proletarian dictatorship as methods of political and social change. As he put it, the promotion of class conflict is 'unacceptable morally, divisive socially, obstructionist economically and a source of tension'.[17] Fourthly, he is a believer in the reformist capacity of the state, in the areas of economic management and social policy as well as over the matter of national self-assertion. In short, Michael Manley is best described as a populist.

For those familiar with the way this term has conventionally been used in the analysis of Latin American and Caribbean politics, such a statement may not immediately clarify the issue, for populism has been notoriously difficult to define with precision. Yet there is a firm basis for recognition of the phenomenon in the work of Torcuato di Telli, who has constructed a typology from the study of a number of varying political situations.[18] He characterises populism as a political movement enjoying genuine and extensive mass support (typically drawn from rural migrants recently arrived in the cities in combination with the previously organised working class), but *not* organised along narrow class lines. In other words, it is a weapon which successfully synchronises divergent class interests, achieving this by means of a fertile mix of charismatic leadership, nationalist rhetoric and redistributive neo-socialist ideas on economic and social issues. Such a profile adds up to a distinctive type of radical politics. It categorises more accurately than any other available label the strategy of change which Manley brought to bear on Jamaican society in the turbulent eight years that followed his election victory in 1972.

Reform and re-election: March 1972–December 1976

The first two years of the PNP government brought a number of significant social reforms but no decisive break with the previous direction of economic policy. The reforms included the release of some land to farmers under the Land-Lease project, the inauguration of crash programmes of job creation to relieve unemployment, and the introduction of a number of new welfare commitments, including the announcement of free secondary education for all. Foreign-owned electricity, telephone and omnibus

16. Manley, *Politics of Change*, p. 18.
17. Ibid., p. 41.
18. T. di Telli, 'Populism and Reform in Latin America' in Claudio Veliz (ed.), *Obstacles to Change in Latin America* (London, 1965).

companies were nationalised, but with compensation, and there was a reorganisation of the various statutory corporations in the state sector – which served to ensconce some of the PNP's supporters among the capitalist class in important management positions. Overall, it was an even-handed start, entirely in keeping with the government's multi-class electoral base.

A turning-point for the Manley administration occurred in 1974. The fact of dependence made Jamaica more than usually vulnerable to the economic crisis which came to a head all over the world. Its economy simply could not withstand the effects of the sudden rise in the oil price and the generalised economic recession that followed. In one year, 1973/4, the island's oil import bill rose from J$65 million to J$177 million.[19] Other import prices rose in consequence, especially food and manufactured goods, putting further pressure on the cost of living and the balance of payments. Foreign capital inflows declined, as did income from tourism, and although the price of sugar reached high levels towards the end of 1974 it plummeted in 1975. In addition, the government's own measures of welfare reform had considerably increased state expenditure, and this, in an economy lacking the resources to sustain such a sudden expansion, meant that the public sector debt also increased dangerously. Between 1972 and 1974 it rose by 56.7 per cent from J$332.6 million to J$520.8 million; more significantly, the foreign component of the debt rose even more steeply, from J$117.3 million to J$206.3 million, an increase of 75.6 per cent.[20] It was the cumulative impact of this severe economic situation rather than political commitment in itself which persuaded the Manley government to press ahead quickly with the more radical of its proposed reforms.

The first sign of this change of gear came in January 1974 when the government announced its intention to renegotiate the tax agreements signed with the US- and Canadian-owned bauxite and alumina companies. These agreements had not been altered since the early 1950s, when the industry was first set up in Jamaica, and produced only a token tax yield for the government. After four months of inconclusive talks, Manley abrogated the agreements and imposed a novel method of raising revenue. This was a production 'levy' on all bauxite mined or processed in Jamaica, set at 7½ per cent of the selling price of the aluminium ingot instead of a tax

19. National Planning Agency, *Economic and Social Survey: Jamaica 1979* (Kingston, 1980).
20. Claremont Kirton, 'A Preliminary Analysis of Imperialist Penetration and Control via the Foreign Debt: A Study of Jamaica' in Carl Stone and Aggrey Brown (eds), *Essays on Power and Change in Jamaica* (Kingston, 1977), pp. 80–1.

assessed according to an artificial profit level negotiated between the companies and the government. It was an extremely effective mechanism from the Jamaican point of view, raising the revenue from the industry from a meagre J$22.71 million in 1972 to no less than J$170.34 million two years later.[21] Interestingly, the new policy received support and a good deal of impetus from the Jamaican capitalist class, whose economic wellbeing depended on substantial imports of goods not only for personal consumption but as inputs for their 'final touch' manufacturing industries, and was being threatened by a shortage of foreign exchange. Their role was recognised by the appointment of two leading members of the class, Meyer Matalon and Patrick Rousseau, as chairman and vice-chairman respectively of the National Bauxite Commission, which presided over the negotiations with the companies. Many of the benefits of the increased revenue also went to these industrialists. To handle the additional money, the government created a Capital Development Fund, whose official purpose was to bolster the productive capacity of the economy. Management was again placed in the hands of Meyer Matalon, and the bulk of its budget was directed into the construction industry. This worked to the particular advantage of companies owned by Jamaican capitalists.[22]

For the government, the institution of the levy marked only the beginning of a 'bauxite offensive'. It initiated talks with the companies aimed at the purchase of majority control in their local operations, set up the Jamaican Bauxite Institute to provide it with independent data on the technical side of the industry, and played the leading part in the formation of the International Bauxite Association (IBA), a producers' cartel inspired by OPEC. At first, the response of the aluminium corporations to these moves was aggressive: they filed a suit with the World Bank's International Centre for the Settlement of Investment Disputes contesting the legality of the levy, pressed the United States government to intervene on their behalf with the Jamaican government, and began to transfer bauxite and alumina production from Jamaica to other parts of the world. The Jamaican share of the world bauxite market fell from 19 per cent to less than 14 per cent between 1973 and 1976, while that of countries like Australia and Guinea showed a marked increase.[23] Yet the companies ultimately reached an accommodation with the Manley government;[24] they realised that new tactics were needed to

21. National Planning Agency, *Economic and Social Survey: Jamaica 1976* (Kingston, 1977).
22. See Sherry Keith and Robert Girling, 'Caribbean Conflict: Jamaica and the US', *NACLA Report on the Americas*, XII (1978), p. 21.
23. Ibid., p. 24, Table 7.
24. Ibid., pp. 23–4.

guarantee continued access to the Jamaican ore for which many of their alumina plants were specifically geared, and resolved to accept the production levy and the government's joint venture proposals. Under these the government purchased all the land the companies owned in Jamaica and 51 per cent of their mining operations. The companies kept their refining plants and retained management control for at least the next ten years; in the unspoken part of the agreements they also maintained their superiority in technology, control of the market and access to capital. In these circumstances the government's challenge to the position of the bauxite companies appears rather more muted.

Perhaps the longer-term significance of the new bauxite policy was that it brought the Manley government to the attention of the US administration. Bauxite is a mineral of strategic importance, and in the mid-1970s the United States drew approximately half its supplies from Jamaica.[25] It seems that at first the US government was prepared to tolerate Jamaica's action, and in the course of a lengthy meeting in 1974 Manley personally sought to explain the idea of the levy to Kissinger. The part of the government's bauxite strategy most likely to arouse Kissinger's opposition was in fact the formation of the IBA; potentially, at least, this touched a raw American nerve in that it purported to promote a wider Third World resistance to Western economic interests. Such a commitment was, of course, an integral part of Manley's programme of change, and was to contribute to the hostility which he quickly came to arouse within the US government.

The main cause was Cuba. Not long after assuming office, Manley had incurred the displeasure of the US ambassador, who considered him largely responsible for the decision of the independent Commonwealth Caribbean countries to announce their full diplomatic recognition of Cuba. In September 1973 he came under further suspicion for flying to the Non-Aligned summit meeting in Algiers aboard Fidel Castro's private plane. Manley's attendance at the conference was indicative of the prominent role he and his government intended to play in the Third World movement and, in particular, in the diplomacy surrounding the call for a 'New International Economic Order'.[26] It also marked the beginning of a friendly relationship between the PNP government and the Cuban regime, which agreed to provide Jamaica with technical assistance in school construction and fishing. In the middle of 1975 Manley paid a

25. Ibid., p. 19, Table 5.
26. See Chapter 9.

state visit to Cuba to express his thanks, and with Castro at his side, made an impassioned anti-imperialist speech before cheering crowds. These moves raised real if unfounded doubts in Washington about the extent of Jamaica's commitment to the West. In American eyes the doubts were more than confirmed by Manley's public declaration of support for Cuba's decision to send forces to assist the Marxist regime in Angola, despite a clear warning from Kissinger only days earlier that to do so would incur US displeasure. The announcement was made out of the sense of morality that typified Manley's approach to international relations, but nevertheless ensured that US economic aid to Jamaica was halted until the matter was reopened by a new president.

Although these geopolitical considerations were the primary cause of the worsening of US–Jamaican relations, the situation cannot have been helped by the other important initiative of the Manley government in the aftermath of the economic crisis in 1973–4, namely the PNP's reaffirmation in September 1974 of its commitment to 'democratic socialism'. The launch was widely and deliberately publicised although, as we have seen, the manifesto contained little that was new, and defined 'democratic socialism' as a commitment to four principles already fundamental to Manley's approach to politics: the democratic political process, the Christian principles of brotherhood and equality, the ideals of equal opportunity and equal rights, and a determination to prevent the exploitation of the people. Certainly the direction of the government's policy was not noticeably changed by the declaration of support for socialism. The intention was rather to mobilise the people more actively behind the PNP's strategy of change. Following a fall in popularity in the face of rising inflation and persistently high unemployment since he had come to power, Manley felt it necessary to revive the populist fervour of his 1972 election campaign. In this sense the reaffirmation of socialism was conceived as a means to greater mass mobilisation and not as a shift of course.

The campaign did nevertheless have one important unintended consequence. It marked the limit of the PNP's acceptability to members of the local capitalist class. Until this point they had gone along with Manley's rhetoric, sometimes uneasily but generally reassured that this type of politics was necessary to maintain social order in Jamaica. And although they were less than happy about the government's developing friendship with Cuba, they were not inclined to see too many dangers in it for themselves. But the public espousal of socialism struck them on the raw. In the first place, it fed a long-standing suspicion of ideas within Jamaican political culture, which the business sector fully shared; and secondly it threatened to arouse among the masses too great a sense of their latent power, which the capitalist class feared that Manley would ultimately be unable to assuage. In short, socialism seemed to open all sorts of doors behind which the spectre of revolution had hitherto been conveniently locked.

From this point onwards, domestic and international opposition to Manley's programme of change came together and worked in tandem. Politically, local capitalists turned their energies towards a resuscitation of the JLP; economically, they contracted their investments in Jamaica, exported foreign currency illegally, and migrated in large numbers to North America. Those who stayed created such a mood of panic in the private sector that the corporate economy was gradually drained of activity. From outside Jamaica there appeared to emanate all the signs of 'destabilisation' we have previously discussed: inaccurate foreign press reports calculated to undermine the tourist industry, unexplained violence and arson in the ghettoes of Kingston, vicious attacks on the Manley government in the columns of the *Daily Gleaner*, and allegations of a strong CIA presence among United States embassy personnel in Jamaica. Most damaging of all was the credit squeeze to which the country was subjected: the US Agency for International Development (USAID) turned down a request for a food grant, the US Export-Import Bank dropped Jamaica's credit rating from the top to the bottom category, and commercial banks ceased all lending to the island. In combination with the decline in the production of bauxite immediately after the imposition of the levy, these measures brought about a catastrophic deterioration in the foreign exchange position.

In response Manley allowed the process of socialist mobilisation to take off more intensively than the terms of his original strategy dictated. While the economy was temporarily shored up by means of bilateral loans from friendly governments, such as those of Trinidad and Canada, the attack on the country by 'imperialist' forces was made the theme of the PNP's 1976 election campaign. Until then Manley had endeavoured to preserve a balance between the left and the right in the party, but now he gave his support to the left and allowed the party secretariat to organise a heavily ideological campaign. The communist Workers' Liberation League (WLL), which had been formed in December 1974 under the leadership of Dr Trevor Munroe, a lecturer in politics at the University of the West Indies, adopted a position of 'critical support' and itself played an important role in putting leftward pressure on the government. In a sense the campaign was hugely successful because, despite the desperate condition of the economy, the PNP was re-elected in December 1976 with a massive majority, winning forty-seven out of the sixty seats. However, although nobody realised it at the time, the victory meant that Manley's initial conception of the politics of change had failed. The PNP no longer represented the majority of people of all classes. Its support among the capitalists and the middle class had disappeared and been displaced by gains among the working class and the unemployed.[27] The overall effect was to polarise class voting patterns and rob Manley of his chance of leading a genuinely populist movement of reform.

The IMF and retreat: January 1977–October 1980

In the heady atmosphere that followed the election, the extent to which the nature of Manley's victory had undermined his original strategy was not realised. Instead the result was interpreted by many in the PNP as an endorsement of the socialist mobilisation of the preceding year. Before the election, the government had thought that Jamaica's dire economic situation necessitated an appeal for assistance from the IMF. A provisional set of measures had been worked out, and the foreign exchange markets closed as a prelude to their implementation. After the election, however, this policy was cast aside in the face of intense opposition from the PNP left wing, supported by the WLL. They were doubtful of the efficacy of the monetarist approach of the IMF when applied to Third World economies, and argued that in the short run Jamaica could survive the foreign exchange crisis by careful rationing of earnings, supplemented by loans and other kinds of material support from socialist bloc and progressive OPEC countries. Manley's personal position is not known, but he powerfully articulated the government's defiance of the IMF in a speech to the nation on 5 January 1977:

> the International Monetary Fund, which is the central lending agency for the international capitalist system, has a history of laying down conditions for countries seeking loans . . . This government, on behalf of our people, will not accept anybody anywhere in the world telling us what to do in our country. We are the masters in our house and in our house there shall be no other master but ourselves. Above all, we are not for sale.[28]

27. See Carl Stone, 'The 1976 Parliamentary Election in Jamaica', *Journal of Commonwealth and Comparative Politics*, XV (1977), pp. 250–65.
28. Michael Manley, Speech to the Nation, 5 Jan. 1977, mimeo (Kingston, 1977).

Accordingly, the government announced a very different programme of economic measures to the deflationary package implicit in the proposed IMF agreement. To be sure, certain moves were perhaps intended to keep that latter option open, such as the imposition of a pay moratorium and a higher tax on petrol, but they could not disguise the dominant influence of the left on the government's post-election thinking. There was to be no devaluation, which was the main demand of the IMF. Several left-wing economists from the University of the West Indies, led by Norman Girvan, were brought in to strengthen the national planning apparatus. Radio Jamaica was to be purchased as part of a political education programme led by the newly-formed Ministry of National Mobilisation, whose first head was Dr D.K. Duncan, the PNP's left-wing General Secretary. Negotiations were also announced for the take-over of three foreign banks, including Barclays, and the island's only cement factory, owned by the Ashenheim family. Finally, the preparation of a Production Plan, to be based on suggestions made by the ordinary people, was set in motion. The strategy as a whole envisaged the mobilisation of Jamaica's exploited classes against local and foreign capitalist control.

It turned out to be only a brief interlude in the political economy of the Manley years. As Fitzroy Ambursley has observed, these initiatives brought the PNP to 'the Rubicon of retreat or social revolution'.[29] At this point Manley could have embarked fully upon the committed socialism of class confrontation, a road along which he had tentatively set out – albeit under pressure of external events – during the mobilisation of 1976 and in the immediate aftermath of the election. The goal of a populist programme of change supported by all social classes would have had to be abandoned, and a different sort of politics erected in its place. There can be no doubt that this was the aim of the left, both inside and outside the PNP. However, there were still those in the party who shied away from this prospect and would, as Manley put it, 'have looked askance at all these young Turks of the left, often sporting beards, tams and jeans, playing so prominent a part in affairs'.[30] The left themselves argue that in the final analysis Manley himself was to be found in this category, betrayed by 'his lack of confidence in the capacity of the masses of black Jamaican people to assert their productive creativity' – a view that 'derives from a brown Jamaican petit-bourgeois

29. Fitzroy Ambursley, 'Jamaica: the Demise of "Democratic Socialism" ', *New Left Review*, 128 (1981), p. 82.
30. Manley, *Jamaica: Struggle in the Periphery*, p. 155.

perspective'.[31] Certainly nothing in the evolution of Manley's thought would have predisposed him to accept the ideology of class politics being urged upon him. As noted earlier, his mind worked along entirely different lines. At any rate, he retreated. The announcement that negotiations would resume with the IMF was made in April 1977, and from that moment the story of the Manley government became, in essence, the story of its relationship with the Fund.

Manley has subsequently claimed that he had 'no choice at that time'[32] but to do as he did, and within the limits of his own politics, that may well be true. At home, the call for 'people's planning' produced a massive response, but of half-baked, unrelated and often trivial ideas, and it foundered on the harsh reality of the lack of technical and economic knowledge at the mass level. Also, there was never very wide support for the anti-imperialist implications of the left's strategy. A national poll conducted by Carl Stone in May 1977 showed, by contrast, that 76 per cent of the population favoured the receipt of US aid[33] – hardly the ideal political base from which to challenge the hegemony of international capitalism. Abroad, the constraints were even tighter and, from the left's point of view, not short of irony: as part of the post-election plan, tentative efforts were made to seek financial aid from the socialist world, and an (unpublicised) approach was made to the Soviet Union. They proved unsuccessful:[34] Jamaica had not prepared the ground in any way for forging this connection, and was not otherwise of sufficient political or military significance to attract large-scale Soviet support. At the same time as this rejection was becoming manifest, signals were emanating from Washington that the new administration of President Jimmy Carter, which had replaced the Ford-Kissinger team at the beginning of 1977, was looking for a more friendly relationship with the Caribbean, beginning with Jamaica. Prompted by Carter's ambassador to the United Nations, Andrew Young, an old friend of Manley, the aim of US policy seemed to be to coax Jamaica back into

31. George Beckford and Michael Witter, *Small Garden . . . Bitter Weed: The Political Economy of Struggle and Change in Jamaica* (Morant Bay, 1980), p. 93.
32. Manley, *Jamaica: Struggle in the Periphery*, p. 155.
33. Carl Stone, *Democracy and Clientelism in Jamaica* (New Brunswick, 1980), p. 176.
34. According to one account, 'the Soviets were so unenthusiastic about acquiring another ward in the Caribbean that they laid down prerequisites for aid that bore a striking resemblance to the standard IMF regimen for a country in Jamaica's position' J. Daniel O'Flaherty, 'Finding Jamaica's way', *Foreign Policy*, XXXI (1978), p. 148.

the Western camp. The opening was seized upon by the moderates in the Manley government, who included the Foreign Minister, P.J. Patterson, to argue for a return to the traditional focus of foreign relations. The conjuncture of these two pieces of diplomacy was critical and, in so far as the United States made it known that the resumption of aid would be easier if Jamaica repaired its relations with the IMF, it paved the way for the decision to resume talks.

Initially Jamaica was able to exercise a good deal of bargaining power in its negotiations with officials of the Fund.[35] In the early rounds the main sticking point was the scale of the devaluation required. The government proposed a dual exchange rate: a 37.5 per cent devalued 'special rate' applicable to traditional exports and inessential imports, but a 'basic rate' at the old level for government transactions, essential imports of foods and medicines and, most important, bauxite exports, the value of which would thereby be maintained. The Fund opposed this and the government's slight easing of its wage guidelines, but Manley was able to use his personal friendship with James Callaghan and Pierre Trudeau, Prime Ministers of Britain and Canada respectively, as leverage to bring some influence to bear on the IMF Board. In the end, however, it was probably the readiness of the Carter administration to 'lean' on the IMF on Jamaica's behalf that forced the Fund to settle largely on Jamaica's terms. The amount to be provided was US$74.6 million over the two years to June 1979, subject to the economy meeting the well known IMF performance tests. In the circumstances the agreement was relatively satisfactory from Manley's point of view. Additional foreign exchange would become available, the basic imported goods on which the island's poor depended would be spared a huge increase in price, and the government's general programme of extending public ownership could be slowly advanced. In 1977 the National Sugar Company took over several more of the island's sugar estates, and a State Trading Corporation was established with a view to eventually handling all imports.

However, the embrace of the IMF was not to prove so warm for long. In a development utterly unexpected by Manley, the economy failed the first performance test in December 1977. On the day in question the net domestic assets of the Bank of Jamaica exceeded the required ceiling of J$355 million by a mere J$9 million, or 2.6 per

35. The subsequent discussion of Jamaica's relationship with the IMF relies heavily on Norman Girvan, Richard Bernal and Wesley Hughes, 'The IMF and the Third World: the Case of Jamaica, 1974–80', *Development Dialogue*, 11 (1980), pp. 113–55.

cent. The Fund seized on this as evidence of irresponsible domestic economic management, suspended the next tranche of the loan, and returned for further talks to be conducted in an altogether harsher manner. There is no need to follow every aspect of the negotiations, for there was little that the government could do but agree to a virtually total overturn of its previous economic policies. A new agreement was finally concluded in May 1978, providing US$240 million over three years, but depending upon the introduction of, in Manley's words, 'one of the most savage packages ever imposed on any client government by the IMF'.[36] It contained as its centrepiece the reunification of the exchange rate, along with a further immediate general devaluation of 15 per cent, to be followed by a 'crawling peg' arrangement under which there would be further mini-devaluations every two months (which amounted to 15 per cent over the first year of the programme). There were also to be drastic cuts in the size of the public sector, a cutback in the operations of the State Trading Corporation, sharp tax increases, price liberalisation to guarantee a 20 per cent rate of return on capital invested by the private sector, and finally a mandatory limit on wage settlements of 15 per cent a year, in comparison with the predicted increase in the cost of living of some 40 per cent.

By this stage, what else could the government do? In terms of domestic politics, the PNP left was a defeated force in the struggle within the party, its decline symbolised by Duncan's resignation as Minister of National Mobilisation in September 1977, while the moderates and conservatives who dominated the Cabinet could neither prevail on the IMF to soften its position nor think of any alternative source of foreign exchange. As the tone of his speeches and public appearances at the beginning of 1978 indicated, Manley himself was subdued. Internationally, the Jamaican government had lost even the qualified support of the Carter administration, partly as a result of internal changes within that government, notably the declining influence and eventual resignation of Young, but also because Manley insisted throughout Jamaica's economic traumas on maintaining a radical and pro-Cuban foreign policy. He entertained Castro on a state visit to Jamaica in October 1977, and repeatedly praised the social and economic achievements of the Cuban revolution. He also continued to assert aggressively Jamaica's commitment to a New International Economic Order. In the light of his experience of the IMF, one can appreciate his reasons for doing so, but in the short term – and by 1978 that was the only

36. Manley, *Jamaica: Struggle in the Periphery*, p. 160.

consideration relevant to the Jamaican economy – it was not the most effective way of improving his country's bargaining position with Fund officials.

For Manley the tragedy was that the IMF recipe could not work for a structurally dependent economy, so lacking in productive capacity, as Jamaica's was. It is now a commonplace of political economy analysis to say this,[37] very much as a result of Jamaica's experience. The fact is that, although the Manley government proceeded to carry out every single aspect of the new agreement in both letter and spirit, the economy never recovered. The harsh economic medicine did not generate additional inflows of foreign capital or halt the outflow of Jamaican capital, with the result that the economy became locked into a vicious deflationary spiral, with predictable consequences for employment and living standards. Even the bauxite levy was lowered slightly in an attempt to induce the companies to increase production and expand their investment in the industry. Yet in December 1979 the economy once more failed a performance test, and again this was largely because of factors outside governmental control, in particular further increases in the oil price. The Fund demanded huge public expenditure cuts as the price of continuing the assistance programme, only to find that opinion had hardened in the country in the course of the long and difficult relationship with the IMF. In a clear sign of the changing mood, the WLL, which had been transmuted into the Workers' Party of Jamaica (WPJ) in August 1978, announced that it was prepared to extend its policy of 'critical support' for the PNP into an actual alliance. Within the PNP itself, Dr Duncan was re-elected to the post of General Secretary in September 1979 and set in train a detailed discussion of the government's economic policies. The impact was catalytic: a special delegates' conference in January 1980 gave enthusiastic support to proposals that the government should find a 'non-IMF' path, and urged it to resist the full extent of the budget cuts being demanded. Eventually, in March 1980, the national executive committee of the party voted by a two-to-one majority to break with the IMF and start implementing an alternative programme. The Cabinet accepted this, and Manley announced that elections would be held before the end of the year to enable the people to decide on the economic strategy the country should follow.

This was to be the final lurch in what has been referred to as 'the

37. A good summary of this argument is provided in Nick Butler, *The IMF: Time for Reform*, Young Fabian pamphlet (London, 1982).

zig-zag politics'[38] of the Manley regime. A new left-wing Finance Minister was appointed, and some attempt was made to renegotiate the country's commercial debts, but little emerged by way of concrete policy.[39] Once his original strategy had been upset – paradoxically – by the great electoral success of 1976, Manley was never again able to develop a coherent approach to the management of the political economy. Instead the pattern was one of endless vacillation in which he danced alternately with the domestic left and the international right. As he did so, the economy deteriorated and whatever chance he and his party had of being re-elected was destroyed. Elections were finally held on 31 October 1980, and the PNP was massively defeated by the JLP, winning only nine out of sixty seats in parliament, the party's lowest-ever representation.[40] In the view of Norman Girvan, the UWI economist and head of the National Planning Agency under Manley, the IMF had at last 'succeeded in manipulating the Jamaican political process to re-establish the political conditions in which the previous model of dependent, unequal capitalist development may function.'[41]

Conclusion

The heavy electoral defeat suffered by the PNP was hardly surprising in view of the government's overall record over the preceding eight and a half years. It had promised so much and in the end achieved so little. The economic statistics alone are revealing: between 1974 and 1980 there was a cumulative fall of 16 per cent in gross domestic product, while unemployment rose from 24 to 31 per cent and the cost of living by an enormous 320 per cent. The exchange rate against the US dollar moved from approximately J$0.88 to J$1.76, and as we have seen, foreign exchange reserves and foreign capital inflows fell dramatically over the period.[42] One could continue the catalogue of figures, and it would not brighten the picture. For ordinary Jamaicans, the reforms of the Manley government had produced a severe decline in living standards, worse

38. Beckford and Witter, op. cit., p. 99.
39. See the interview with Hugh Small, the new Minister of Finance, published in the *Guardian Third World Review*, 1 Oct. 1980.
40. For a fuller discussion see Carl Stone, 'Jamaica's 1980 elections', *Caribbean Review*, X, 2 (1981), pp. 4–7, 40–3.
41. Girvan *et al.*, op. cit., p. 155.
42. For these and other statistics see National Planning Agency, *Economic and Social Survey: Jamaica 1979* (Kingston, 1980).

unemployment, acute shortages of basic goods in the shops, and a mood of depression that pervaded the whole economy and society. Against this dismal background the government's few achievements in the social field and in foreign affairs cannot be said to count for much.

What went wrong? Manley's own analysis has emphasised external considerations – the US government, the CIA, the IMF and so on. He concluded his account of his government with the observation that 'when the news of the PNP's defeat in the elections of 1980 reached Washington, champagne corks popped. The hawks were celebrating.'[43] This is part of the explanation, of course, but not all of it. International factors bore heavily, and at times oppressively, on Manley's regime, but their impact can be properly understood only in relation to the type of politics he was trying to pursue. To go back to the beginning, Manley's initial strategy of change was intelligently conceived. Its implementation was unlikely to be easy, but there was no reason to think it impossible either. The post-colonial state enjoyed a significant degree of autonomy, and if led with sufficient political skill and sense of *realpolitik*, it ought to have been able to restructure the political economy along the lines Manley proposed without arousing the implacable opposition of either the indigenous capitalist class or international capitalist interests as a whole. The former had a good deal to expect from such a strategy, both economically as businessmen and politically as leading citizens; the latter had not too much to lose from schemes of joint ownership in terms of real economic control, and something of distinct value to gain if social tensions were thereby reduced and the country's politics stabilised accordingly. In short, an accommodation was possible. The international economic crisis which came to a head in 1973–4 made the task of achieving it more difficult, because it forced Manley to increase the pace of change, but again it is doubtful whether this made it inherently unattainable. After all, the bauxite levy was supported by the local capitalist class, and was eventually accepted with more or less good grace by the US government and the corporations themselves, leaving Manley still balanced on his tightrope.

However, two other initiatives, both avoidable, finally upset his balance. The first mistake concerned the direction of foreign policy, particularly the developing friendship with Cuba and the ostentatiously offered support for its involvement in the Angolan civil war. Manley has defended these policies as non-negotiable matters

43. Manley, *Jamaica: Struggle in the Periphery*, p. 237.

of principle. However, with his romantic view of the world, he underestimated the reality of Jamaica's strategic location in the US sphere of interest. In the last analysis the relationship with Cuba, which produced only minor technical assistance, did not justify in material terms the opposition it engendered from the United States. It was not integral to the government's domestic reforms or even to the wider pursuit of changes in the international economic order, and, in the context of US paranoia over the role of Cuba in the Caribbean, would have been better avoided. The second mistake concerned the PNP's readoption of 'democratic socialism' as the ideological framework for reviving populist support for its policies. The choice of label proved counterproductive: it alarmed even those local capitalists who till then had supported Manley, further perturbed the US government and effectively gave official approval to the activities of the relatively small left-wing element in Jamaican politics both inside the PNP and outside it in the WPJ. Other ways of mobilising the Jamaican people existed which need not have incurred such heavy costs.

These two mistakes were critical. Both served to over-politicise what Manley was trying to do and make his policies appear more radical and threatening to established interests than they actually were. They aroused unnecessary opposition at home and abroad, which not only badly damaged the country's economy but undermined Manley's intended strategy of change. He was unable to rebuild the class alliance on which he had come to power, and although for a time he seemed to toy with the idea of embarking on a complete disengagement from the capitalist world economy, sustained domestically by the adoption of the politics of class confrontation and internationally by Soviet support, his government was largely without a strategy from the moment it became embroiled with the IMF. Manley thus got caught in that no-man's-land between rhetoric and reality in which so many populist politicians all over the world have found themselves. His failure teaches the need for consistency of purpose in the politics of development. If the strategy is to be fully socialist, it must be followed all the way – and this of course means that the state must be capable of maintaining the productive level of the economy, sufficient outside support must be available, the party must be committed and tightly organised, and a certain level of class mobilisation must be present to sustain the regime through the transition period. Manley never intended to lead Jamaica down this path, knowing how unrealistic an option it was in the circumstances in which he had to work, but some of his language and policies nevertheless suggested that this was his goal, thereby bringing upon his government a predictable wave of opposition. Equally, if the strategy is to be populist in character, as it was in Manley's case, it must be so not only in implementation but in style and presentation. Manley had no need to lose the support of either his local capitalists or the US government, yet he sacrificed both and found that without the former he could not run the economy and without the latter he could not manage the external environment in the way his programme of domestic change required. Faced by the antagonism of these two powerful interests, the Jamaican state was left with minimal space for manoeuvre.

In summary, Manley's 'democratic socialist' experiment offers important lessons to proponents of change in the Third World. The task of overcoming, or even adjusting, dependence will never be easily accomplished, least of all in difficult economic circumstances such as those which prevailed in the mid- and late 1970s. Yet success will never be approached unless policy is implemented and articulated as consistently as it is conceived. Manley failed in the end largely because he got himself into a muddle.

5

SEAGA'S FIRST YEAR

On 31 October 1980, following the stunning victory of the JLP over the PNP in the general election, a new government was formed in Jamaica. Under its leader, Edward Seaga, the JLP had consistently portrayed the PNP as a communist-influenced party incapable of managing the island's economy properly and intent upon creating a one-party state. It attacked the Manley government's establishment of close ties with neighbouring Cuba, its rhetoric of anti-imperialism, its links with the WPJ, and, above all its decision in December 1979 to sever its connection with the International Monetary Fund in favour of an 'alternative' non-IMF path of economic development. The JLP argued that this move would fatally damage Jamaica's reputation in the West and that only a return to traditional free enterprise policies under its management could save the island from bankruptcy. With the economy steadily deteriorating, this analysis of Jamaica's ills won increasing support from the electorate and ultimately produced a massive victory for the JLP in the 1980 election.

This result was a personal triumph for Seaga. Born of Syrian stock and by training a sociologist, he had been Minister of Development and later of Finance and Planning in the 1962–72 JLP government and had earned respect as one of the leading 'modernisers' of that administration. Towards the end of 1974 he took over the leadership of a rather demoralised party from Shearer, but initially found it difficult to establish himself in the public's esteem. At the time of the 1976 election, public opinion polls had shown Manley to be three times more popular with the Jamaican people than his rival. Manley's charismatic personality symbolised the struggle for equality and justice which was the foundation of the PNP's 'democratic socialist' appeal, whereas Seaga's image was that of the technocrat committed to more efficient operation of the *status quo*. Gradually his elaborate and statistically detailed attacks on the PNP's performance in office began to catch the public mood, and by 1980 he had acquired a reputation as something of a financial wizard, a man who in contrast to Manley's denunciations actually understood the workings of the international economic system in which Jamaica had to survive. His Harvard education, his smart suits and his experience as a former Minister of Finance all served to project an air of competence and stability.

In his new government Seaga appointed himself Minister of Finance, and although the former party leader and Prime Minister Hugh Shearer was made Foreign Minister, Seaga also took charge of shaping the main features of Jamaica's revised foreign policy. In just a year he transformed the character of Jamaican government.

The IMF loan

The first priority of the JLP government on assuming office was to raise sufficient financial assistance from the local banking system and from abroad to prevent the Jamaican economy from going bankrupt. Since the Manley government's abandonment of IMF support, the economy had been sustained from month to month by short-term loans, and by the end of the election campaign was in a desperate position. In his first address to the nation, Seaga declared dramatically that there was only enough foreign exchange to last for four more days! Loan agreements were quickly signed with the Venezuelan government to tide the economy over the immediate crisis and a commitment given to initiate talks with the IMF as soon as possible. This statement of intent was the critical step, and was the announcement which Western governments and bankers had been awaiting. It gave due notice that the mainstay of Seaga's economic policy was to consist of close alliance with the Western economic system.

The government's extensive talks with the IMF resulted in the announcement in April 1981 that the Fund was to lend Jamaica US$698 million over three years. Most of this amount was provided under the IMF's extended fund facility, but some US$48 million constituted compensatory financing designed to offset shortfalls in export earnings. The agreement was also (in the language of the IMF) 'front-loaded', which meant that 40 per cent of the loan could be drawn in the first year of the agreement's term. To ensure payment of subsequent tranches of the loan, the government had to meet certain targets. Limits were set on the net amount of domestic bank credit distributed to the public sector and on the extent of the domestic and international reserves held by the Jamaican Central Bank. The government further agreed not to introduce multiple currency practices (as the Manley regime had done) and not to place new restrictions on payments and transfers for current international transactions. Finally, a ceiling was placed on new external borrowing by the government.[1]

1. *Caribbean Contact*, 9, 1 (May 1981), p. 2.

What was interesting were the conditions which the IMF did *not* see fit to impose on the Seaga government compared to the way it had treated the PNP government's requests for support. Crucially, there was no demand for a devaluation of the Jamaican currency and no insistence on the erection of wage and price controls – both of which the IMF forced on the Manley regime as the price of its assistance. Nor were the restrictions on domestic public sector borrowing made to apply to the private sector, while the ceiling on government borrowing abroad excluded loans to re-finance existing debts and loans from foreign governments and their agencies or multilateral lending organisations. In short, Seaga was able to negotiate much more favourable terms with the IMF than his predecessor. He cleverly deployed his anti-communist, pro-Western credentials for all to see, and they won him his due financial reward.

The whole episode offered a textbook illustration of how a loan from the IMF could put the stamp of financial respectability on a country which had been effectively frozen out of the international money markets. The signing of the loan agreement with the IMF opened the way to further inflows of financial support for Jamaica's beleaguered economy. These included loans from the World Bank, Western commercial banks and a variety of donors operating through the Caribbean Group for Co-operation in Economic Development. Some estimates placed the value of this extra support as high as US$350 million.

Local and foreign capital

Consistent with Seaga's readiness to work with the IMF was his commitment to free enterprise at home. He had long believed that private individuals could run businesses more efficiently than government officials, and accordingly established a disinvestment committee to try to rid the public sector of a number of enterprises set up during the Manley era. He also phased out nearly all the various restrictions and licences with which the previous administration had entangled the private sector in its effort to control the consumption of scarce foreign exchange. The new government thus sought to minimise its own role in the functioning of the economy and looked to local private capital to play a big part in restoring the Jamaican economy to growth. As Seaga himself told the Jamaica Manufacturers' Association just after his election, in December 1980, 'I can promise you no more than that we will offer you the climate for this turnaround; but I will be fully conscious of the fact that as a government we can only set the tone, set the climate and provide the policies.'[2]

Seaga, through his personal connections with the Jamaican business class, must have known that it has traditionally lacked independence; it has always relied heavily on the protection and patronage of the local state, and been dependent even then on association with foreign capitalists for whom it has generally functioned as a kind of junior partner. In the previous few years, it had also been further weakened by migration and the ideological attacks made on it by the PNP left, and thus was hardly likely to provide the JLP government with the dynamism it needed to revive the economy. Seaga appeared to realise this and made it clear that the government would not protect local businesses from foreign competition. In his first budget address, he told parliament that the country's long-standing policy of industrial protection was to be discontinued, the idea being that if imports of cheaper products were allowed, the cost of living would be reduced and the consumer would benefit. Faced with the incursion of cheaper products, he said, local producers would be compelled to switch to the production of items for which they had viable markets.

The unavoidable consequence of this stance was that foreign capital would come to play an even larger role in the Jamaican economy than in the past. Far from being worried about this outcome, Seaga went out of his way to encourage foreign businessmen to invest in Jamaica. He spoke of his intention to pursue an export-oriented model of economic development, involving the attraction of foreign-owned 'enclave' industries importing almost all their inputs, except labour, and producing almost exclusively for export. To this end he won President Reagan's support for the creation of a joint Jamaican/American 'Committee on Foreign Investment and Employment', designed to channel new investors to Jamaica. The Committee met under Seaga's chairmanship and was led by prestigious figures: on the American side, the former chairman of the Chase Manhattan Bank, David Rockefeller, and on the Jamaican side, Carlton Alexander, chief executive of the Grace Kennedy Group, one of Jamaica's largest private companies. It split into various sub-committees, and at first concentrated its attention on areas such as garment manufacturing, electronics assembly, woodwork, printing, horticulture and tourism.

Indeed, the emphasis again placed on tourism was illustrative of the whole Seaga approach to economic recovery. When he took

2. Ibid., 8, 10 (Feb. 1981), p. 7.

office, tourist arrivals on the island were running some 40 per cent below those for 1979, whereas the figures for July 1981 indicated a 10 per cent increase over arrivals in the same month the previous year. The tourist industry, relying predominantly on American demand, obviously benefited from the favourable reports about Jamaica which started to appear in the Western media, but it was also directly encouraged by the government which considerably increased the tourist development budget and sponsored a new weekly air link between London and Montego Bay, which was expected to be operated by Air Florida.[3] In another typical move, the government instructed the state-owned National Hotels and Properties Company, set up by the Manley government to manage a number of hotels it had taken over as the only means of keeping them operational, to offer several of its properties for lease and possible sale. At least two American hotel groups quickly expressed interest.

The American connection

In the wider geopolitical sense, all Seaga's actions in his first year of office were built upon the American connection. It underpinned the IMF negotiations, the provision of financial support generally, the openings offered to foreign capital and the planned revitalisation of the tourist industry. Indeed, it is not too much to say that in the year following his election Jamaica emerged as probably the most committed 'client-state' of the United States government in the Caribbean area, a status neatly symbolised by Seaga being the first foreign head of state to be invited to the White House by President Reagan after the latter took office at the beginning of 1981.

Seaga made a speech in Washington calling on the United States and its allies to put together a rescue programme for the Caribbean Basin region along the lines of the Marshall Plan prepared for Europe after 1945. After his visit, the concept of a 'Mini-Marshall Plan' gathered support and was discussed again during a conference held at Nassau in the Bahamas in July 1981, when the US Secretary of State and the Foreign Ministers of Canada, Mexico and Venezuela agreed to adopt a co-ordinated approach to the provision of development aid in the Caribbean.[4] On the surface, such a proposal appeared to support the Reagan administration's contention that it was sincere and benign in its attitude to the Third World and not

3. *The Guardian*, 27 Aug. 1981.
4. See Mo Garcia, 'The Caribbean Aid Plan', United States International Communication Agency, 14 July 1981.

obsessed, as its critics alleged, with the military and security dimensions of underdevelopment. But neither in scale nor focus did the plan, later enacted as the Caribbean Basin Initiative (CBI), merit comparison with the huge American effort to provide for the recovery of Europe after the Second World War. The emphasis was not on aid in the conventional sense, but rather on the elaboration of means to stimulate the working of free enterprise in the region. Furthermore, it is apparent that the aid plan, as conceived in the mind of the Reagan government, was intended to discriminate politically between the territories of the region, rewarding friendly states like Jamaica under the JLP and punishing by exclusion states that were deemed to be too close to the Castro regime in Cuba.

The Seaga government was not in the least embarrassed by this aspect of the aid plan. Indeed, it fully shared US suspicions of Cuba's role in the region. In its election manifesto, the JLP proclaimed its intention to 'halt the expansionist movement of Communist imperialism' in the Caribbean,[5] and immediately on assuming office Seaga asked the Cuban government to withdraw its ambassador to Kingston, Ulises Estrada, a man whom Seaga had previously accused of interfering in Jamaica's domestic affairs. Diplomatic ties with Cuba were maintained, but the Manley government's policy of vigorous support for the New International Economic Order and Third World issues in general was quietly set aside. During the election campaign Seaga had observed somewhat disparagingly that, if Manley had spent a quarter of the time he devoted to 'struggling' around the world in the cause of the NIEO to fighting for a better US quota for Jamaican rum and lower tariffs in general for Jamaican products entering the American market, the country would have been noticeably more prosperous. In this respect, Seaga followed his own counsel. Alignment with the West and a corresponding hostility to Soviet and Cuban influence became the touchstones of Jamaican foreign policy.

Prospects and problems

What were the prospects for Seaga's Jamaica after its first year, and what problems might it have been expected to encounter? The various dimensions of Seaga's policy undoubtedly added up to a coherent and integrated approach to Jamaica's problems. They collectively represented the unabashed pursuit of a policy of peri-

5. Jamaica Labour Party, 'Change without Chaos', Kingston, Oct. 1980.

pheral capitalist development, unconcerned by, and indeed committed to, the proliferation and intensification of ties of dependence on the dominant centres of the international economy. As such, Jamaica saw in twelve months the complete reversal of the Manley government's efforts to win for the territory a greater degree of independence in its relationship with the world economic system.

For a while, it seemed that the Jamaican people liked what their government was doing. A public opinion poll carried out by Stone in January 1981, just three months after the election, found that the close ties that were developing between Seaga and President Reagan were supported by as much as 85 per cent of the Jamaican electorate; only 10 per cent condemned this relationship as a willing subordination to imperialism. Moreover, fully 70 per cent of those polled endorsed the new JLP government's overall performance in running the country over the October–January period.[6] These trends were confirmed in March by the results of local government elections, which produced JLP victories in all parishes for the first time in the country's history of two-party politics.

Nevertheless, the JLP had cause to be wary of some features of its electoral performance. Its support, though considerable in 1981, was inevitably fragile because it contained so many PNP defectors (30 per cent of the party's 1976 vote) who could easily switch back to their former allegiance. Nor was the JLP's victory in October 1980 quite as sweeping in terms of votes cast as its dominance of the seats in the new parliament suggested: it won 59 per cent of the votes to the PNP's 41 per cent, scarcely a negligible share for a defeated party. Seaga also had to come to grips with the fact that he had unavoidably inherited the political legacy of Manley. The intense politicisation of the Manley period had created a more aware public opinion in Jamaica, and popular aspirations for social justice, inspired by the PNP's socialism, were not extinguished but were re-directed at the JLP. As Stone's survey work illustrated, the shift in the political mood of Jamaica towards a desire for a more business-like leadership 'was clearly predicated on the assumption that greater administrative competence could ease the burdens on the poor'.[7] Like Manley, Seaga was bound to find that a favourable image would serve him well for a while, but that ultimately the Jamaican people would judge him and his government according to the material benefits generated by their policies.

This raises the question of the performance of the Jamaican economy and the prospects of success for Seaga's programme of

6. Carl Stone, 'Jamaica's 1980 elections', *Caribbean Review*, X, 2 (1981), pp. 42–3.
7. Ibid., p. 40.

revitalisation. According to the original government figures, the economy was expected to grow by 12 per cent during the three years of IMF support – 3 per cent in the first year, 4 per cent in the second and 5 per cent in the third. Such a swift recovery proved easier to predict than to carry into effect. The Bank of Jamaica's publication of its review of the economy for the year ending April 1981 indicated a continuing depression. It stated that the major economic sectors of bauxite, sugar and bananas had performed below expectation, and revealed that although there was an increase in the dollar value of exports, the current account recorded a deficit of US$13.5 million at the end of April, compared with a surplus of US$44.1 million at the end of April 1980. This was no doubt explained by the ending of restrictions on imports. Yet the general tenor of the Bank's report contradicted the impression of confidence that the government had been trying to create to such an extent that Seaga felt it necessary to recall parliament after it had gone into summer recess to reassert his claim that the economy was definitely showing signs of recovery. In this statement he gave a significantly lower projection than before of the economy's anticipated growth rate in that financial year, and suggested that the worst possibility was zero growth and the best just 2 per cent.[8]

Of course, it should not have been surprising that the Jamaican economy would need some shaking out of the debilitating effects of seven consecutive years of declining Gross National Product. There was little doubt that the considerable inflows of foreign capital which Seaga set himself to attract to Jamaica would in time refloat the economy back to a path of economic growth. The deeper question concerned the extent to which renewed growth would solve the more intractable features of the Jamaican political economy – high unemployment and underemployment, unequal distribution of income and inadequate welfare for many poorer Jamaicans. Jobs were the most vital requirement and the biggest problem. Most of the industries attracted by programmes of 'industrialisation by invitation' tend to be highly capital-intensive and unsuited to the special needs of labour surplus economies like Jamaica. For example, an academic analysis of the incentive legislation programme operated by the previous JLP government showed that as many as 146 industries had to be set up to create a mere 9,000 jobs;[9] whereas at the end of 1981 some 263,000 people

8. *Jamaica Daily News*, 6 Aug. 1981.
9. O. Jefferson, 'Some Aspects of the Post-War Economic Development of Jamaica' in N. Girvan and O. Jefferson (eds), *Readings in the Political Economy of the Caribbean* (Kingston, 1981), p. 112.

were officially out of work and in reality many more. Under the JLP government of the 1960s, in which Seaga was Minister of Finance, the fruits of growth went mainly to the upper and middle echelons of Jamaican society, and only a small amount was able to 'trickle down' to the poorer sections. In so far as it remained JLP policy to allow market forces to determine the distribution of benefits, then the level of social and political tension was bound to rise, and the JLP would have difficulty in securing the second term in office which has become almost an established feature of the Jamaican electoral cycle.

6

THE 1983 ELECTION

Elections in Jamaica have always been highly charged. Vivid, turbulent, often violent, they have provided since 1944 natural points of climax to the country's political life. However, the 1983 election was different. It was no less vibrant than usual, although it was happily less violent than that of 1980, and it was certainly far from being uncontroversial. The election was exceptional in that it was called by the JLP government after it had only been in power for little more than three years, and was boycotted by the PNP which resolved not to put up candidates in any seats. The result was, in effect, a 'non-election': the JLP 'won' all the sixty seats in the parliament, thereby giving rise to the taunt that it had established a 'one-party state' in Jamaica. However true that charge may be, it was clear that something strange was happening and that the tradition of two-party democracy in the island had been seriously threatened. What had brought about this situation?

Background factors

The economy. By the time it approached the third anniversary of its election to office, the honeymoon which the Seaga government had briefly enjoyed with the Jamaican electorate had ended. The cause was the state of the country's economy. So far from presaging recovery, or 'deliverance' as the JLP had expressed it in 1980, the intervening period had witnessed an escalation of economic problems. The combination of a post-victory import boom, the poor performance of traditional commodity exports and the inability of the manufacturing sector to move quickly to open up new export markets generated increased pressure on the balance of payments. The consequent foreign exchange problem was exacerbated by the considerable leakage overseas of earnings from the tourist industry, the one bright spot within the economic picture. By January 1983 the situation had become so critical that Seaga had to establish a two-tier exchange rate which, despite official denials, effectively devalued the Jamaican dollar. The effect was a significant increase in the price of imported goods and a boost to inflation.

At the end of March 1983 the illusion of Seaga's special skill in managing the country's finances was shattered when it was announced that Jamaica had again, as in the Manley era, failed an IMF performance test. Disbursements under the extended fund facility initially agreed in April 1981 were suspended, pending talks.[1] By introducing a package of austerity measures (including new taxes and reduced foreign exchange allowances for imports) in anticipation of IMF demands, Seaga was able to negotiate a waiver on the supply of funds, only to find that in September the economy once again failed its quarterly IMF test. As a result, discussions about a new stand-by credit agreement were initiated.

The September failure and the initiation of new talks with the IMF were at first kept secret. Even so, the political consequences of the worsening economic situation can be imagined, especially since increased unemployment and the renewal of 'hard times' for the poor were in stark contrast to the conspicuous consumption enjoyed, at least for a couple of years, by business people in particular and the wealthy middle classes in general. The resulting decline in popular support for the JLP government was charted in Stone's regular opinion polls. A commanding 28 per cent lead in May 1981 fell to 7 per cent a year later. Then, for the first time, in October 1982, the PNP pulled ahead of the JLP - by 43 to 38 per cent - and proceeded to maintain that measure of ascendancy into 1983.[2] It was not so much that the PNP had been able to arouse a renewed faith in its capacity to govern, but rather that its association with the poor, with public expenditure and the expansion of welfare policies regained its appeal as the issue of the economy again took precedence in the public mind over anti-communism and similar issues. Thus, by the autumn of 1983, the prospect of being the first Jamaican government since independence to lose office after just one term loomed ominously before the JLP.

Grenada. Grenada had been a salient issue in Jamaican politics ever since March 1979 when a coup in the tiny Eastern Caribbean island first brought the People's Revolutionary Government (PRG) to power. As Grenada's new prime minister, Maurice Bishop, was to reveal later, Jamaica under Manley's leadership had been the first state to respond to the revolution's call for assistance and solidarity, and had offered help even before Cuba.[3] Close ties were

1. *Latin America Regional Report: Caribbean*, RC-83-04, 13 May 1983.
2. Carl Stone, *The Political Opinions of the Jamaican People* (Kingston, 1982).
3. Maurice Bishop, *Forward Ever! Three Years of the Grenadian Revolution* (Sydney, 1982), pp. 111, 129.

subsequently developed between the PNP regime and the revolutionary government in Grenada – so much so that when the PNP lost office in 1980 a number of the more left-wing cadres in the party were recruited by the Grenadians to serve in technical, administrative and educational roles. Bishop was also very much a leader in the charismatic mould of Manley. In short, the Grenadian regime was widely seen in Jamaica as a kindred spirit of the PNP.

By contrast, the incoming JLP government endorsed United States concern over Grenada's potential as a revolutionary bridgehead within the Commonwealth Caribbean. In addition, it strongly and repeatedly criticised the PRG for its failure to hold elections, its suppression of the main newspaper in Grenada, and its generally illiberal stance on human rights. All were issues capable of striking a chord with the Jamaican electorate, although it should be said that there is no evidence that in 1981 and 1982 they had yet made any impact on local opinion. Nevertheless, within the forum of the Caribbean Community, Seaga continued his efforts to weaken support for the Grenadian regime. In the weeks preceding a CARICOM Heads of Government Conference held at Ocho Rios in Jamaica in November 1982, he joined with the then prime minister of Barbados, Tom Adams, in proposing an amendment to the CARICOM treaty which, by committing member-states to the maintenance of parliamentary democracy, would have had the effect of excluding Grenada from the organisation. Seaga himself was quoted as saying, in reference to Grenada, that there had appeared in the Commonwealth Caribbean 'something called people's democracy, and this was the Cuban model which we reject'.[4] At the summit Bishop retorted that fundamental human rights should also be deemed to include the right to life, a job, education, good roads, electricity and piped water, and in a speech to a public rally on his return to Grenada, he went on to accuse Seaga and others of deference to US imperialism. 'Every morning at breakfast', he told the crowd, 'one of them had to go over to the Americans to take the morning instructions, every lunch-time one has to go down and report how the morning went, and at night another set had to go across and tell them how the rest of the afternoon went and plan strokes for the next morning.'[5] At the conference, the proposed amendment did not in the end win general support, but relations

4. *Latin America Regional Report: Caribbean*, RC-82-07, 20 Aug. 1982.
5. Maurice Bishop, 'Address by Comrade Maurice Bishop to Bloody Sunday Rally, Seamoon, St Andrew's, 21 November 1982' in M. Bishop, *One Caribbean*, Britain/Grenada Friendship Society (London, 1983).

between Bishop and Seaga worsened and subsequently became very sour. Indeed, after November 1982 the relationship was in some ways not far short of a vendetta.

Electoral reform. The PNP and the JLP had been arguing intermittently about electoral reform since at least the beginning of the 1970s. In the 1972 election, despite having won, the PNP felt aggrieved because the Shearer government had refused to update the 1969 electoral lists. No-one who had reached the voting age of twenty-one after 21 October 1969 was allowed to vote in the general election, with the result that some 200,000 Jamaicans were effectively disenfranchised. After the 1976 election it was the JLP's turn to express dissent. Although the distribution of the popular vote had changed in favour of the PNP by only 1 per cent, the party had increased its majority of seats from one of 36:17 to one of 47:13. The JLP attributed this to the government's manipulation of constituency boundary changes and to illegal registration procedures adopted by the PNP – charges which received some support from subsequent psephological analysis.[6] By contrast, other JLP allegations, such as the claim that the State of Emergency imposed by the Manley government to contain violence impaired its campaigning efforts, had little if any substance.

Nevertheless, Seaga seized the opportunity to begin a campaign both inside and outside the country in favour of electoral reform. This was a part of what one can only describe as the JLP's general attempt to destroy the legitimacy of the Manley government by promoting the idea that the PNP was prepared, if necessary, to subvert the democratic rules of the game in order to stay in power and complete the transition to communism in Jamaica. To its credit, the PNP responded as positively as it could, and in November 1978 reached preliminary agreement with the opposition to set up an electoral advisory committee.[7] It was to consist of seven members, two appointed by Manley as prime minister, two by Seaga as leader of the opposition, and three including the chairman by the Governor-General on the recommendation of the first four members. The committee was in turn to recommend to the Governor-General the appointment of a director of elections, and

6. Carl Stone, *Democracy and Clientelism in Jamaica* (New Brunswick, 1980), p. 168.
7. For background, see G.E. Mills, 'Electoral Reform in Jamaica', *The Parliamentarian*, 62, 2 (1981), pp. 97–104.

would then preside over a reform of the electoral system designed to eliminate flaws in the registration and voting procedures.

The committee was only just established in December 1979 when it had to begin preparations for the election announced by Manley after his government had decided to break with the IMF. Because of pressure of time, the committee's plan to introduce a voter identification card with a photograph had to be postponed, but a most careful enumeration of voters was undertaken, and new checks to prevent impersonation were built into the procedures at polling stations.[8] For all the violence which disfigured the 1980 campaign, there was general agreement among participants and observers that the new measures ensured less abuse of the electoral system than had been known in any previous election. The achievement was largely due to the dedication and hard work of the committee members and their reputation for integrity, especially perhaps that of the chairman, Professor G.E. Mills, a former senior civil servant and professor of government at the Mona campus of the University of the West Indies.

It therefore seemed as if the basis had been laid for non-partisan management of the Jamaican electoral system. The committee was subsequently upgraded to an electoral commission, and once the dust from the election had settled, it set about preparing a new enumeration of voters, this time with full identification cards. The issue only became controversial again during the budget debate in 1982, when Manley questioned the JLP government's good faith in the matter of proceeding with the reforms. He warned that 'we will not regard ourselves bound to any of the normal rules of cooperation or participation unless the solemn pledge given in 1980 is kept and adhered to in its strictest form'.[9] Seaga responded with an unequivocal declaration that the government intended to ensure that 'the full programme of electoral reform on which we agitated as an opposition is completed by us as a government . . . inclusive of the photo identification card . . . for the next election.'[10] His reply appeared to resolve the matter satisfactorily, and was widely regarded as a commitment by the government that a general election could not, and would not, be held until the reform process and the new enumeration were completed. According to the schedule to which the electoral commission was working, this would not have been before the spring of 1984, the time when the parish council elections would be due.

8. See ibid.
9. *Daily Gleaner*, 30 April 1982.
10. Ibid., 1 May 1982.

Precipitating events

Dramatic events were to intervene. In a period of no more than ten days in October 1983 the deep political tensions hitherto contained within the revolutionary government in Grenada came to a head. Maurice Bishop was overthrown, arrested and subsequently murdered, along with a number of other ministers opposed to the dominant clique within the regime. The latter then proceeded to seize power in what was essentially a military coup. Throughout the region the reaction of ordinary people and politicians to the news was one of shock and outrage. Whatever views may have been taken of the politics of Bishop and his comrades, the killings offended the strong cultural commitment to peaceful political change which pervades the entire Commonwealth Caribbean, unquestionably including Jamaica. The only exceptional feature of the Jamaican situation was that more precise evidence of the feelings of horror emerged in the course of the regular national opinion poll conducted by Stone. This showed that interest in Grenada among Jamaicans was unprecedentedly high. Only 15 per cent of the sample had no opinion on Bishop's death, while the vast majority - some 70 per cent - condemned it as cruel and wicked.[11] A particularly interesting feature of the poll was the apparent feeling of many Jamaican citizens that the scenario of events in Grenada could plausibly have occurred in Jamaica if the PNP had won the 1980 elections. The basis of this fear was that Manley could have been outmanoeuvred by left-wing elements in the party, aided and abetted by domestic and foreign communist support, just as it seemed Bishop had been. This was underlined by the fact that significant sections of public opinion (43 and 35 per cent respectively) assumed that Cuba and the Soviet Union were responsible for Bishop's fall,[12] despite a lack of evidence supporting this view. In fact, the *Gleaner* chose not to report Fidel Castro's forthright speech condemning Bishop's killers.

The main message of the poll was not difficult to discern. The bloody events in Grenada had revived the powerful anti-communist and anti-Cuban sentiment which had so dominated the 1980 election campaign but which had since been noticeably assuaged. The impact of this on the fortunes of the main parties, as revealed in the poll, was immediate. PNP support fell from 41 to 38 per cent, while that of the JLP rose from 38 to 43 per cent - a substantial swing. A mood was thus generated which broadly welcomed the subsequent US invasion

11. Carl Stone, 'The Jamaican Reaction: Grenada and the Political Stalemate', *Caribbean Review*, XII, 4 (Fall 1983), p. 60.
12. Ibid.

of Grenada and certainly supported the decision of the JLP government to involve Jamaican forces in the operation, albeit in a minor supporting role. The government was unapologetic in defence of its involvement, presenting it as a way of teaching the communists a lesson. The PNP was left with the difficult task of explaining its abhorrence of the acts of violence against Bishop and the other ministers and at the same time its disagreement on principle with the invasion on the grounds that the conflict in Grenada was an internal matter that should have been resolved by economic and diplomatic pressure. It was a stand which in the climate of the time could easily be ridiculed as weak and indecisive. According to a later poll, a large minority of PNP supporters themselves broke ranks and supported the JLP's position on the invasion.[13]

However, the Stone poll did more than simply reveal where the Jamaican electorate stood on Grenada: it actually altered the course of events by redefining the agenda of public debate in Jamaica. Confronted with these various findings and embroiled in difficult negotiations with the IMF over a new agreement to respond to a worsening economic situation, Seaga took swift action 'to deepen the "Jamaicanisation" of the Grenada issue'.[14] He accused the Soviet embassy in Kingston of being involved in espionage and dismissed a junior civil servant in the Jamaican foreign ministry for allegedly meeting a KGB agent. Some two dozen people associated with the PNP and the WPJ were also named as having recently visited Cuba, Grenada and the Soviet Union, the implication being that while so doing they might have been involved in 'anti-Jamaican' activities. Seaga himself visited Grenada in triumph after the American invasion put an end to the coup which had overthrown Bishop, and used his access to Grenadian government documents captured by the Americans during the invasion to show that the PNP had taken part in an allegedly subversive meeting in Nicaragua with other Socialist International parties in the region. The tactics deployed were those of the classic 'red scare': they reached the height of implausibility in mid-November when the government expelled four Soviet diplomats and a Cuban journalist ostensibly for plotting to kill a senior officer in the protocol division of the Ministry of Foreign Affairs.

The effectiveness of propaganda does not, of course, depend on its truthfulness. The reality was that the self-destruction of the Grenadian revolution had given the JLP an electoral oppor-

13. Ibid., p. 61.
14. Anthony Payne, Paul Sutton and Tony Thorndike, *Grenada: Revolution and Invasion* (London, 1984), p. 211.

tunity that it could not have imagined a few weeks earlier. Even so, it would not necessarily have been seized if the country's economic prospects had looked brighter. The reality in this sphere was that a major devaluation of the currency was emerging as the price of a new IMF agreement. This would be bound to have a severe impact on the cost of living to add to the 18 per cent inflation already experienced in 1983. In the circumstances, the temptation to call a snap election before the effects of the devaluation worked through the economy, before the Grenada issue was forgotten and before the new voters' list (with all its new members) was ready, was plainly compelling. There is a view that it was Seaga's wish to announce the devaluation and the dissolution of parliament at the same time but that he could not secure the agreement of the Cabinet, several of whose members took the JLP's commitment to complete the process of electoral reform seriously. In the event, it hardly mattered.

On 23 November Seaga announced the details of a new economic package which included the devaluation. The PNP leaders who would have been most likely to respond to the government's announcement - Manley and the party chairman Patterson - were both out of the island. In their absence, the general secretary, Paul Robertson, who had replaced D.K. Duncan earlier in the year, issued a statement condemning 'in the strongest terms the deception enacted on the Jamaican people by the Prime Minister'[15] and calling for his resignation as Minister of Finance. The attack on his personal integrity provided Seaga with the chance for which he had been hungering and which his Cabinet had possibly denied him earlier. Calculating that he needed more than the two remaining years of his first term of office for his economic policies to bear fruit, he called an election on 25 November, scheduling nomination day for 29 November, just two working days later, and election day itself for 15 December.

The PNP was put firmly on the spot. The national executive committee hastily convened to debate the question of contesting the election. Some members felt that the party had a good chance of increasing its representation in parliament, even on the old lists, and were ready to take up the challenge, but the vast majority, including Manley, were opposed to participating. Their argument was both principled and pragmatic. On the first count, the calling of the election abrogated the inter-party agreement on electoral reform, and the party had stated clearly on several occasions that it would not take part in the election on such terms. On the second count, the

15. *Daily Gleaner*, 24 Nov. 1983.

PNP knew that it had been disadvantaged by Seaga's ploy. Candidates were not yet selected, policy had not been fully worked out, and funds were short. In addition, Stone's polls showed the PNP to have a commanding lead among 18–20 year olds, precisely the group which would be disenfranchised if the 1980 voter lists were used. In short, the party feared being drawn into an election it could not win and preferred the retreat of an official boycott. Nomination day thus closed with JLP candidates unopposed in fifty-four constituencies and challenged only by independents in the other six.

The campaign

Despite this, both major parties waged intense campaigns up to election day, realising that the prize was just as much in the field of public opinion as in parliamentary seats. At a series of mass meetings around the island, the PNP reiterated its claim that the government had breached a solemn pledge. At a rally at Halfway Tree in Kingston, for example, Manley demanded that 'the minute the new system is ready . . . this country must have elections the very next day. As long as 100,000 dead men in and 180,000 live men out, no elections.'[16] He also announced that the party planned to start the so-called People's Forum as an arena for the expression of opposition opinion. The PNP was sensitive to the charge that it too had not played fair by the democratic process by boycotting the election, and wanted to be seen to be discharging its responsibilities to its supporters as assiduously as it could. To this end sixty 'constituency representatives' were named in place of actual MPs. The 'bogus' election was undoubtedly its overriding campaign theme, but it also attacked the government on its management of the economy. A full-page advertisement in the *Gleaner* – the first to be taken out by the party for several years – was entitled 'The Fairy Tale of Deliverance', and cited statistics on what had gone up (prices, the trade deficit and external debt) and what had gone down (production, employment and exports) in Seaga's time.[17]

In response, the JLP tried to make the most of its affinity with the Reagan administration and its role in the Grenada 'rescue mission'. On the economy, it claimed that the basis of recovery had been laid, but that 'five more years' were needed to complete the task. More and more, however, the party was forced by the sheer vigour of the

16. Ibid., 2 Dec. 1983.
17. Ibid., 18 Dec. 1983.

PNP's campaign to address the issue of the holding of the election itself. JLP spokesmen and supporters argued variously that no binding pledge had ever been given; that a prime minister in the Westminster system had the legal right to call an election at any time; that Seaga had simply outwitted Manley; and that the PNP was scared of a fight. Yet they never fully succeeded in allaying the worries of many voters about the election of a 'single party' parliament. As the campaign closed, the consensus of neutral observers was that the PNP had easily won the argument on the election issue. It had been able not only to portray itself in shining armour as the defender of democracy but also to demean the JLP with the image of the cheat.

The result

The result was a foregone conclusion in that the JLP won all sixty seats. Very few people actually voted. Even in the six constituencies where there was a contest, only some 25,000 people turned out, compared to three times that number in 1980. However, another result of a sort was 'declared' by the inestimable Carl Stone who conducted one of his polls during the course of the campaign. His figures show that on the old voters' list the JLP had a slight lead - 50.6 to 49.4 per cent; but that within the electorate as a whole the PNP was ahead by a full 10 per cent - 55 to 45.[18] Although opinion on the calling of the election and the boycott largely reflected partisan attachments, he also found that a large majority of the Jamaican public had been persuaded by the PNP's argument that new elections should be called immediately the new register was ready. Even 25 per cent of JLP supporters took this view.

On the basis of the two 'results', both parties were able to draw some comfort. The JLP was returned to office and thus postponed having to go to the country again till late 1988. Seaga therefore achieved his major objective of winning more time to see the fruits of his economic policies. Despite PNP protestations, it was never realistic to suppose that he was going to respond to the demand for renewed elections on the new register. For its part, the PNP was revitalised by the election. It had been a sluggish opposition party until galvanised by Seaga's deceitfulness, but entered 1984 with substantially more vigour, and indeed in an angry mood. The main loser in the contest was perhaps the Jamaican electoral process itself. The situation produced was one where a minority party held all the seats

18. Stone, *Caribbean Review*, p. 62.

in parliament at a time of great economic difficulty. It was not a healthy political development for the long term, and was not appreciated by Jamaicans. The irony underlying its emergence was well expressed by the Anglican Bishop of Kingston, Neville DeSouza, shortly after the election was over. 'We went to Grenada', he said, 'to help them preserve the democratic way of life, and found that within a month we could well have presided over the demise of ours.'[19]

19. Quoted in Anita M. Waters, *Race, Class and Political Symbols: Rastafari and Reggae in Jamaican Politics* (New Brunswick, 1985), p. 289.

7

VIOLENCE AND PROTEST IN 1985

The pressure that had been building up within the Jamaican political system as a consequence of the harsh programme of economic readjustment pursued by the Seaga government finally burst into the open in January 1985. As was widely reported in the international media, there occurred two days of demonstrations in which roads were blocked with piles of debris and cars and property burned amidst several confrontations between protesters and the security forces. In total, seven people were killed and some fifteen wounded.

The spark which ignited the protests was the announcement during the evening of 14 January that from midnight the price of a gallon of premium gasoline would be increased from J$8.99 to J$10.90. Other similar sharp increases were made in the prices of diesel fuel, kerosene and cooking gas. The official *Jampress* news release tried to explain that the increases were virtually inevitable given the collapse of the country's currency over the previous year from a rate of J$3.40/US$1, when the price of petroleum products had last been fixed, to approximately J$5/US$1 at the time of the announcement.

This did not stem the anger of those who heard the news. Many PNP supporters telephoned the party's headquarters on Hope Road in Kingston, where the PNP executive happened to be holding its weekly meeting, and demanded a response. Wary of its public image, the party took care that it should not be seen to issue any specific instructions to its members and activists, but it nevertheless gave approval for the organisation of 'spontaneous' demonstrations. The executive realised that it could no longer hold back the hostility to the Seaga government felt by so many of its followers. Many elements in the party had been wanting to launch some such action ever since the gas price protests which the JLP affiliate, the National Patriotic Movement, had so successfully mounted against the Manley government in January 1979. The increase in price then had brought the cost of a gallon of gasoline to a mere J$3.20 - a sign of just how far the external trading position of the Jamaican economy had deteriorated in the intervening years.

Once it became apparent on the morning of 15 January that a protest was under way - and late-night listeners to Radio Jamaica reported hearing at about 2 a.m. that some streets were already blocked - large numbers of ordinary Jamaicans with no particular

PNP connections, and especially unemployed young people from the poorer parts of Kingston, rallied to the road blocks, which they assembled with whatever material came to hand – garbage, old tree trunks, car tyres and pieces of masonry. The effect of the action was to bring the country virtually to a standstill for the day. Public transport was disrupted and children who had gone to school early and employees whose work places were unable to open were faced with no alternative but to make their way home on foot. As the day progressed, a number of clashes took place between the people manning the barricades and representatives of the police and security forces, leading to deaths and injuries. By nightfall there had also occurred some outbreaks of looting and burning of shops, supermarkets and other business premises.

Yet there is no doubt that what transpired was an overwhelmingly popular protest expressing anger and hurt at the squeeze which the Seaga government had been imposing on the economy for the previous two or three years. Some commentators tried to deny the validity of this interpretation by suggesting that 'a lot of those road blocks went up so that the people who man them could extort money from motorists'[1] before letting them through. Others, such as Wenty Bowen, writing in the influential regional newspaper *Caribbean Contact*, claimed that members of the Marxist Workers' Party tried to take over a number of the protests for their own purposes.[2] This suggestion was firmly challenged in a letter published in the next issue of *Contact*. In it, UWI lecturer Brian Weeks reported that he had walked the streets of Kingston on both days of the demonstration, and commented:

> . . . nowhere could one find a WPJ, PNP or any other 'party' barricade. What was immediately obvious was that in many communities WPJ members and supporters were engaged in the blocking of roads, but *alongside* and not apart from representatives of the PNP. . . What is unfortunate about Bowen's article is that it leaves the impression of a sharply divided opposition, with a small, opportunistic WPJ hanging on to the coat-tails of the PNP. This is totally opposite to the spirit of the roadblocks which was one of camaraderie and which lacked sectarianism. There was little if any talk of party differences as all the participants engaged in the main task of registering their first sharp protests against the painful direction of the Seaga government.[3]

Indeed, the signs were that the WPJ was itself taken by surprise by

1. Carl Wint, 'A futile gesture', *Daily Gleaner*, 21 Jan. 1985.
2. Wenty Bowen, 'Jamaica smoulders,' *Caribbean Contact*, 12, 9 Feb. (1985), pp. i, ii.
3. *Caribbean Contact*, 12, 10 March (1985), p. 3.

the intensity of the movement of protest and was nearly outmanoeuvred as a result. The WPJ General Secretary, Dr Munroe, had to issue a statement officially declaring that his party supported the demonstrations – which he too characterised as 'spontaneous' – and had been active within them.

In reality, the debate over spontaneity versus organisation in movements of popular protest misses the main point. Research into the sociology of political violence nearly always reveals the two forces working in combination. Where sustained protest against unpopular governments occurs, it is usually party activists who launch the movement, but widespread popular support and independent action which keep it alive and give it its strength and political importance. The evidence available strongly suggests that this was the pattern of events in Jamaica at the beginning of 1985.

For its part, the JLP government's initial reaction was rather subdued. In an emergency statement to a virtually empty House of Representatives, Seaga reported what had taken place and urged the country to remember 'the future which we are all struggling to rebuild'. There had recently been a time, he said, when Jamaica had no future; 'now there is a future emerging, but with political pain.' The economy, he claimed, was already beginning to show signs of stabilisation, although it would admittedly be a while before the benefits became evident in daily life. He thus concluded that the demonstrations 'without a doubt have been political in origin',[4] something which as the leader of a government with a deep commitment to democracy he accepted would take place from time to time.

As Seaga recovered from the shock of the violence his manner became more assertive. Responding two days later to a call from the PNP for an immediate freeze of all prices, he said there was no possibility of reducing the price of gasoline until the country produced a sufficient level of foreign exchange to improve the value of the currency. Moreover, he was not the sort of leader who considered 'demands' from the opposition. Much was also made by the government subsequently of the fact that on the second and third days of the protest several cane fields had been set on fire and electricity supplies had been tampered with in rural areas. In a speech to a party meeting in Mandeville at the end of January, Seaga went on to the attack: 'Evidence of sabotage and damage to the economy as a result of the recent demonstrations has now reached such proportions that the country must now be told of the extremes to which the organisers went to try to jeopardise the economy of Jamaica.'[5] It was

4. *Daily Gleaner*, 16 Jan. 1985.
5. Ibid., 28 Jan. 1985.

all highly reminiscent, he went on, of the strategies set out in a 'communist' handbook in his possession called *How to Sabotage an Economy*.

Given Seaga's political style, this was a predictable party political response. However, it sheds doubt on the extent to which, initially at least, he grasped that the protests were a warning signal to his government that the people of Jamaica could not take much more deflation of the economy. Whatever Seaga's thinking, this point was clearly appreciated by some of his allies. For example, the Private Sector Organisation of Jamaica, while condemning any illegalities contained in the protests, nevertheless called for urgent tax reforms 'as a first step towards bringing some measure of relief to the burdens of the people'. More generally, it urged the government to respect 'the severe hardships which Jamaican families have had to ensure as we go through this necessary but difficult and painful period of economic adjustment'.[6]

In contrast to this note of responsibility and concern, Seaga seems to have been more immediately preoccupied with the potential damage to the country's tourist industry, not least because of the sensational reporting of the protests in North America.[7] According to government sources, there were some 15,000 room/night cancellations in the two weeks following the demonstrations, mainly from American bookings. As a consequence, the major holiday and villa chains laid off some of the temporary workers already employed in north coast hotels in anticipation of a successful winter season. To try to prevent any worsening of the situation Seaga quickly departed to the United States for a series of meetings with journalists and editors of major US publications such as *Newsweek*, the *Wall Street Journal* and the *Washington Post*. This visit was presented as a vital step towards restoring Jamaica's image abroad as an attractive holiday destination and investment location, but it was regarded by opposition politicians in Jamaica as displaying Seaga's perverse political priorities.

The protests also revealed much about the attitudes of the PNP in opposition. Although responsible for the initial decision to launch the public protest, the PNP thereafter adopted a low profile: none of its major figures appeared at any of the demonstrations. In his initial statement Manley defended the right of Jamaican citizens to make peaceful, legitimate protests against their government and ritually called for Seaga 'to go', but at the same time he required 'the people

6. Ibid., 18 Jan. 1985.
7. For illustration and discussion, see Tony Best, 'Jamaica's Problems - US media views', *Caribbean Contact*, 12, 10 March (1985), p. 4.

of Jamaica to ensure that any demonstration of its anger is conducted in accordance with the laws and that there is due respect for the lives and property of all citizens'.[8] On the second day he called for the ending of the demonstrations, arguing that the point had already 'resolutely' been made and that several national institutions, particularly the health service, were almost at breaking-point because people could not get to work.

Accordingly, the PNP advanced a 'formula for national peace and stability', to be built upon four minimum conditions:

(*a*) an immediate freeze of all prices;
(*b*) the process of meaningful dialogue with consumers, trade unions, and persons engaged in commerce and industry, must begin;
(*c*) discontinue the auction of foreign exchange which has led to the weekly devaluations of the Jamaican dollar and the fact that the Seaga administration has no alternative but to increase prices on a daily basis; and
(*d*) no further layoffs – the further reduction in the public sector envisaged by the IMF must be abandoned at once.[9]

Clearly, the PNP considered that it had nothing to gain from encouraging street politics beyond the need to allow its people to let off steam. Since its defeat in 1980 the party had worked hard to divorce itself from the extra-parliamentary left in Jamaica, Manley himself insisting upon the ending of all ties, formal and informal, with the WPJ. The PNP sought to appear, above all, as a party interested in electoral opportunities. Indeed since December 1983, when it boycotted the snap election called by Seaga on the old voting lists, its main political appeal had been to call for a new election once an up-to-date register was ready. It manifestly did not want that campaign to be undermined by an apparent attachment to quasi-revolutionary politics. In the immediate aftermath of the protests, some observers even went so far as to suggest that the PNP did not want to take power *by any means* at that moment, since it had no more idea about how to generate economic recovery than the incumbent JLP government.[10]

Notwithstanding this point, the PNP unquestionably used the protests to increase the stakes in its attack on the government. At a huge rally held in Montego Bay at the beginning of February, it announced the inauguration of a 'relentless political campaign' to

8. *Daily Gleaner*, 17 Jan. 1985.
9. Ibid., 18 Jan. 1985.
10. *Latin America Regional Report: Caribbean*, RC-85-02, 22 Feb. 1985.

force the holding of elections on the new register, which was by then ready. A resolution, entitled 'The Declaration of Sam Sharpe Square' after the place where the meeting was held, was presented to the crowd. It declared that the campaign 'shall not cease until Seaga calls general elections to restore the credibility of government, to restore confidence in the words of a prime minister and government, to restore integrity in public life, and to restore true democracy in Jamaica'. A full denunciation of the government's economic policies and of the country's dependence on the IMF was also made, but the emphasis was deliberately placed on the alleged lack of political authority of the JLP government in the absence of a mandate from the electorate. Specifically, therefore, 'due notice and fair warning' was given that 'the PNP, because of the unprecedented situation which has arisen by reason of Seaga's political double-cross, does not regard as necessarily binding any economic, social or cultural arrangements promised or entered into hereafter by the Seaga administration as of the fourth day of February 1985.'[11]

The declaration sounded dramatic, as was intended, and provoked critical comment on the grounds that, by traditional conventions in two-party political systems, successor administrations honour the commitments of their predecessors in office. This, however, was a side issue: the real point was that the PNP was choosing to appeal to the country on the basis of democracy rather than socialism. The substance of the party's socialist commitment was left unspecified and was indeed never made clear. With the polls and all informed opinion suggesting that the PNP would win any election called at the time, Seaga was hardly likely to take up the democratic challenge; hence, the question of the PNP's programme did not arise. This was precisely the calculation which many felt that the PNP itself had made and which thus fuelled cynicism as to the party's real intentions.

Seaga certainly seemed to have come to this view. Claiming that his government had repeatedly laid its plans and strategies on the table for all to see, and chiding the PNP for still having theirs 'locked away in a cupboard full of skeletons',[12] he subtly changed his political tactics following the gasoline price protests. Having been further shaken by the unexpected announcement that the Alcoa alumina refinery was to cease production at the end of February, he took the decision to be more candid with the Jamaican people about the state of the country's economy. In quick succession in the middle of February there occurred a prime ministerial broadcast to the

11. *Daily Gleaner*, 5 Feb. 1985.
12. Ibid., 28 Jan. 1985.

nation live from parliament, a breakfast meeting with journalists at Jamaica House, and a long television interview with three academics from the University of the West Indies. A series of working dinners with various influential sectors of Jamaican society, starting with the trade union leadership, quickly followed.

This flurry of communication was designed to alert Jamaicans to the seriousness of the economic situation and to reassure them of the effectiveness of the government's measures. Seaga's message on each occasion was stark and simple. 'I ask you to believe', he told the nation on television, 'that there is no alternative to these strategies even though they hurt and I know they hurt. The choice is not between pain and pleasure, but between pain and greater pain.' Although he reported that the country would be able to meet the targets in the current agreement with the IMF, which expired at the end of March, and so would be able to negotiate a new deal, he did not attempt to conceal that the Alcoa closure, in particular, created serious problems. He called it 'a monstrous blow', and said that it would cost Jamaica J$125 million in direct revenues, a loss which would be quickly made manifest in the budget for the coming year starting in April. Finally, Seaga warned that 'worse was yet to come, if signals we are now receiving are correct.'[13] This was taken to be a reference to rumours that the 1 million tonne Alpart refinery might also close because of the decision of one of its owners, Atlantic Richfield, to pull out of the metal business and the apparent inability of the other partners, Kaiser and Reynolds, to take up the slack. Reynolds had in any case ended its own bauxite-mining operations in Jamaica the previous June.

For all the prime minister's efforts to put the harsh choices before the country, the *Daily Gleaner* was unimpressed. In an editorial headed 'National Crisis', it accused Seaga's speech of lacking any hint of the spirit of national rapprochement it considered necessary for the solution of the country's problems. The paper declared that the time had come for the leaders of the two major parties, JLP and PNP, to bury the hatchet and sit down together to seek a common approach. 'We support the exhortation to face the challenge', it added, 'but we do not think the nation can do it divided.'[14] This led to a series of calls for unity and consensus from media columnists and callers to phone-in programmes, extending eventually even to members of Seaga's cabinet. The Agriculture Minister, Dr Percival Broderick, caught the mood by urging the Governor-General to

13. Ibid., 21 Feb. 1985.
14. Ibid., 22 Jan. 1985.

convene a forum for discussion so that what he called an 'agenda' for government could emerge. Unsurprisingly, government and opposition were at one in rejecting such proposals. Seaga pithily dismissed 'the angelic chorus' and the 'harpists': he knew that, in practice, he still had some time before he would have to face the electorate. Equally, the PNP chairman, P.J. Patterson, said that his party would be wary of entering such a dialogue in view of the 'recent double-cross' it had suffered at the government's expense in connection with the 1983 election.[15] It preferred to picket the daily foreign exchange auctions at the Bank of Jamaica as a way of highlighting the economy's decline, while at the same time continuing to call for a timetable for new elections.

Both sides knew that, since the economic crisis would not go away, the political crisis had to be played out. Jamaica's problem was that consensus and dialogue between the politicians, even if achieved, would not in themselves provide an answer to the deep-seated difficulties faced by the economy. The country's ills derive instead from the historic structure of the Jamaican economy. The irony was that since Seaga always dismissed this argument as an alibi when it was advanced by Manley in the 1970s he could not use it himself in the 1980s.

15. Caribbean News Agency (CANA) feature, 7 March 1985.

8

ORTHODOX LIBERAL DEVELOPMENT IN THEORY AND PRACTICE

The period of JLP government which began in November 1980 merits consideration as a distinct era in the management of the Jamaican economy. Seaga's time in power has been characterised, as he promised, by a complete rejection of the 'democratic socialist' aspirations of the Manley years, but it has not lacked ideological shape in its own right. To some extent, this was unexpected. The key to Seaga's successful appeal to the Jamaican electorate in 1980 was his reputation as a manager and fixer. He was the experienced technocrat who understood the international economic system and had the necessary connections outside the country to get the economy growing again; by contrast, Manley was presented in JLP propaganda as the ideologue who unwisely allowed his personal political philosophy to dictate policy at the expense of pragmatic common sense. In this light, the surprise has been the rigidity with which the JLP government itself pursued a model of economic development derived directly from theory.

The ideological framework within which the Seaga regime sought to manage the political economy of Jamaica was that of orthodox liberal development, as refined in the 1980s by such leading international institutions as the IMF and the World Bank. Indeed, so close was the relationship established by the government with the IMF that it is not too much to claim that the Jamaican economy was under international, rather than national, management. This chapter examines the overall economic record of the Seaga period and sets out in detail the phases of policy through which the pursuit of economic revival passed. It starts by explaining the notion of structural adjustment which has lately become the centrepiece of liberal theories of economic management and which the Seaga government enthusiastically embraced.

Structural adjustment

The political economy of structural adjustment can only be understood in the context of the debate about the working of the international economy, and the role of the IMF within it, which has gone on throughout the post-war period. Between 1945 and 1973 large US balance of payments deficits financed the whole international trading system, which meant that there was no fundamental payments disequilibrium for developing countries as a group. During these years it was generally accepted that those countries which did get into balance of payments trouble and had consequently to turn to the IMF for help had done so because they had in some way mismanaged their economic affairs, rather than because there was a general lack of liquidity in the global economy. Moreover, in a world of growth the IMF remedy of a temporary deflation of demand, combined with the provision of credit, quickly restored external balance and recreated the basis for economic expansion. Relatively little controversy attached to the IMF's approach. Since 1973, however, all that has changed. Developing countries have had to cope with major oil price rises, a deterioration in their terms of trade and sharp increases in the rates of interest determining debt service repayments. Indeed, the decline in their general balance of payments position has been 'so continuous and so serious that there can be little doubt that it can only be described as "structural" or "fundamental" in its nature.'[1]

In such conditions IMF prescriptions were no longer capable of generating an automatic economic recovery, and the harshness of their terms attracted growing political opposition within the Third World. Jamaica's experience with the Fund under the Manley government, although far from unique in its time, was central to the emerging critique. The argument came to a head in 1980 at a major conference on the international monetary system jointly organised by Jamaica and Tanzania, another state whose reforming approach had been broken on the back of an IMF intervention. The conference drew up the 'Arusha Initiative', which *inter alia* condemned IMF policies as 'a form of political intervention' designed to subordinate states to 'the free play of national and international market forces' to the advantage of the 'traditional centres of power' in the world.[2] It called instead for a major shift of resources from the richer to the poorer parts of the world so as to enable deficit economies to produce their way out of balance of payments problems. The legitimacy of the Fund was damaged by such criticisms and a response was soon forthcoming – the development of the concept of structural adjustment.

The thinking underlying this new approach was well set out by

1. E.A. Brett, *The World Economy since the War: The Politics of Uneven Development* (London, 1985), p. 219.
2. 'The Arusha Initiative', *Development Dialogue*, 2 (1982), pp. 14–16.

Guitan, one of the Fund's theorists, in an IMF publication in 1982. He accepted the argument that the payments imbalances existing in the world economy in the 1980s were structural in kind and could therefore only be dealt with on the basis of longer adjustment periods than had been deployed in IMF programmes in the past. A new recognition was also given to the need for production - to be achieved, it was said, by means of 'foreign borrowing strategies that directly enlarge the amount of resources to the member', thus allowing 'higher levels of expenditure . . . as well as higher growth rates over the medium term.'[3] Having incorporated this extra emphasis on the transfer of resources to developing countries, Guitan then felt able to defend the IMF against the charge that its preoccupation with deflation served primarily to retard, rather than promote, growth. Yet, as Brett has pointed out, this concession did 'not leave orthodoxy far behind'.[4]

For, as it turned out, the domestic adjustment policies favoured by the IMF were little changed from those of the 1970s. According to Guitan, they include:

> public sector policies on prices, taxes, and subsidies that can contribute to eliminate financial imbalances and to promote efficiency in public sector activities; interest rate policies that foster the generation of domestic savings and improve inter-temporal resources allocation; exchange rate policy that helps to control absorption and the external accounts but is also a powerful tool for development; and incomes policies that keep claims on resources from out-stepping their availability.[5]

The technicality of the language cannot mask the hostility shown to all forms of state intervention in economic management or the merits that are seen to attach to low wages, the complete rejection of protection as a trade policy, or the disregard for the impact the programme would have on domestic prices. Indeed, devaluation was recommended as the best means to control imports. In short, there was little real change in the IMF's approach: its new prescriptions were more sensitive to the timing and pace of the adjustment being demanded, but were still firmly based in liberal orthodox economics.

The logic on which such liberal thinking depends is simple. If a country suffers from a balance of payments deficit it means that its currency (in effect, its commodities and products) is less in demand than the foreign currencies with which it trades. The country can

3. M. Guitan', 'Economic Management and IMF Conditionality' in T. Killick (ed.), *Adjustment and Financing in the Developing World* (Washington, DC, 1982), p. 88.
4. Brett, op. cit., p. 223.
5. Guitan in Killick, op. cit., p. 88.

correct its payments deficit by allowing its currency to 'float' until it finds its correct level or by devaluing sufficiently to eliminate the distortion. This would discourage imports and promote exports. It is also presumed that the country would attract enough extra foreign investment to generate more production in the medium-to-long term to offset short-term inflation. It does not need to impose import or export controls as the market mechanism should do the job perfectly well. The market, in turn, dictates all the other required fiscal measures such as regulation of the money supply to control public expenditure, the removal of subsidies, and the privatisation of state enterprises. In this way society is returned to the environment of the free market, debts can be repaid, and the integrity of an open international trading system is preserved.

Such an ideology is as crude as it is simple, which is one of the main reasons why Seaga, who has had to operate within a competitive electoral system, has not been prepared to articulate it as clearly as the IMF technocrats. Nevertheless, it is evident that this is the nature of the structural adjustment which the JLP government sought to effect in Jamaica after 1980. Although Seaga may not have spelled out the extent to which his policies constituted a coherent programme along these lines, the fact did not escape the more alert of local commentators. Everton Pryce, for example, argued that the JLP was pursuing 'a package of elusive structural adjustments', composed of five different, but related, elements:

(i) a 'stabilization' policy, designed to adjust the imbalance in the economy between earnings and spending and effected via tight monetary policies, devaluation and increased taxation;
(ii) resource transfer from domestic to export production – even at the expense of dislocation, closures, unemployment and the possible extinction of whole areas of domestic production;
(iii) import deregulation, or the liberalisation of imports, with the aim of preparing local producers to compete in export markets;
(iv) an incomes policy intended to strengthen the capitalist sector in the hope that it would invest and provide the desired engine of growth; and
(v) borrowing, with whatever economic and political dependence resulted.[6]

His formulation is a fair summary of the Seaga approach. What needs to be stressed, however, apart from the coincidence with contemporary IMF thinking already identified, is its novelty in Jamaican terms. It is wrong, for example, to see it simply as a return

6. Everton Pryce, 'Jamaicans in Agony', *Iere* (June 1985), p. 4.

to the 'dependent capitalism' pursued by the JLP in the 1950s and '60s. Naturally, there were important similarities in that private capital, domestic and foreign, was to be the main motor of growth, and scant concern was registered about the perils of dependence on the international capitalist economy. Yet the differences were equally striking, notably the crucial commitment to shift the economy from import substitution to export orientation. The government's long-term goal was to achieve a growth in non-traditional exports, especially manufactures, and thus break out of the constraints of both primary commodity production, with its inherent market instability, and import substitution industrialisation, with its inherent market limitation. The new vision, in other words, was of Jamaica as the Taiwan of the Caribbean.[7]

IMF Management

Phase I: November 1980–October 1983. The Seaga administration began in an atmosphere of great confidence. Negotiations were immediately opened with the IMF and quickly brought to a successful conclusion. An Extended Fund Facility agreement was signed in April 1981 and provided for a loan of US$650 million over three years on remarkably lenient terms.[8] In addition, the government received a further US$48 million from the Compensatory Financing Facility to offset shortfalls in traditional export earnings. Having achieved the IMF seal of approval at such an early stage, the government could move ahead and mount a further massive borrowing and refinancing operation over the next two years. The sources of the loans were so diverse that they implied the existence of a coordinated international rescue of the Jamaican economy. The immediate gain was the provision of ample foreign exchange with which to rehabilitate traditional industries and stimulate new ones; the long-term price was a substantial rise in foreign debt, which increased from an estimated US$1.2 billion at the end of 1980 to US$3.1 billion by the end of 1983.[9]

On the basis of this financial support and the increased foreign investment which the government expected to attract once it had been demonstrated that the Jamaican economy was again solvent, ambitious growth and production targets were set in almost all

7. For a discussion of the East Asian element in Seaga's economic thinking, see Peter Berger, 'Can the Caribbean Learn from East Asia?', *Caribbean Review*, XIII, 2 (1984), pp. 7–9, 40–1.
8. For the details, see *Government Ministry Paper*, April 1981.
9. *Daily Gleaner*, 1 June 1981.

sectors, none more so than in the crucial bauxite and alumina industry. In June 1981 Seaga revealed plans to increase the annual production of bauxite from the 1980 figure of 12 million tonnes to no less than 26 million tonnes within three years; alumina production was to be similarly expanded from 2.4 to 8.6 million tonnes, primarily on the basis of a proposed joint investment between Alcoa, the government and several Norwegian firms to double the size of Alcoa's refinery in Jamaica.[10] But just as the government was making great play of this future expansion, the company was announcing a cut-back in production because of decreasing world demand for alumina. Despite warnings from local experts and opposition politicians, the government was unquestionably caught out by the recession in the bauxite market. The other companies operating in Jamaica followed Alcoa's lead with the result that, far from expanding hugely as anticipated, bauxite production fell disastrously to only 7.3 million tonnes in 1983. Government revenue from the industry fell accordingly from US$206 million in 1980 to US$137 million in 1982.[11]

This was a severe setback - and one against which the Seaga regime could not have protected itself other than by a more accurate prediction of market trends. It appealed for immediate assistance to its main overseas ally, the United States, which responded in December 1981 by ordering 1.6 million tonnes of Jamaican bauxite for its strategic defence stockpile. Although the purchase helped to maintain production for a while, its contribution to the balance of payments was limited by the US insistence on paying for the bauxite, in part, by the barter provision of agricultural products. The balance of payments problem caused by the fall in bauxite production was exacerbated by the poor performance of other traditional agricultural exports. Sugar production declined by 50,000 tonnes between 1980 and 1982, and banana production by 11,000 tonnes over the same period.[12] Only tourism offered some consolation, the number of visitors increasing from 1980 levels in response to a vigorous publicity drive and the favourable image which Seaga presented to North American audiences. The difficulties experienced by these long-standing foreign exchange earners inevitably placed responsibility for the generation of economic growth on non-traditional exports at a much earlier stage in the process of structural adjustment than had been anticipated.

10. Ibid.
11. National Planning Agency, *Economic and Social Survey: Jamaica 1982* (Kingston, 1983), pp. 9.3–9.5.
12. Ibid., p. 8.1.

How, then, did this sector of the economy respond to the Seaga government's entreaties? Despite the establishment of joint US-Jamaican business committees and the much-publicised involvement, at President Reagan's personal request, of David Rockefeller, the fact was that foreign investors were extremely cautious in their response to the new opportunities being offered. There were several reasons for this: apart from a general disinclination to invest in new activity at a time when international interest rates were at unprecedentedly high levels, there were Jamaica's reputation as a place of violence and extremism (a legacy of the 1970s), the continuing problem of bureaucratic inefficiency, and new concern over the adequacy of the country's basic infrastructure. To begin with, the Caribbean Basin Initiative was a source of great hopes for future investment, but its delayed implementation and the exclusion of textiles, clothing and a number of other categories of goods markedly reduced its impact on the Jamaican economy. As a result, although the government could point to the large number of investment enquiries handled by Jamaica National Investment Promotion Ltd. (JNIP) - the new agency set up in 1981 to facilitate the inflow of foreign investment - the number of projects actually initiated in the first year or so was very few. Moreover, even when foreign businessmen were persuaded to set up new operations they often borrowed on the local market rather than bring in foreign funds. As for the response of the Jamaican capitalist sector, that was accurately encapsulated in E.H. and J.D. Stephens' wry observation that it persisted in its 'traditional preference for quick and easy profits over entrepreneurial risk-taking, new investments and a search for new markets'.[13] In consequence, the figures show that non-traditional exports rose from J$197 million in 1980 to only J$235 million in 1982[14] - by no means enough to offset the poor performance of the traditional sector.

The government's development strategy was itself partly responsible for the unwillingness of Jamaican businessmen to take chances in export markets. Put simply, they could make money more easily at home in conventional import-export activities. The policies of deregulating the economy and liberalising the flow of imports fuelled an enormous consumer boom in 1981-2 as the rich and the middle class imported the luxury items forbidden to them during the foreign exchange squeeze at the end of the 1970s. This launched what a local

13. E.H. and J.D. Stephens, *Democratic Socialism in Jamaica* (London, 1986), p. 255.
14. National Planning Agency, *Economic and Social Survey: Jamaica 1982*, p. 8.1.

gibe referred to as 'the era of the three V's' - Volvos, videos and venereal disease, the last of these associated with the revival of the tourist industry. Although politically attractive (and thus to some extent necessary) as a way of pleasing the government's better-off supporters, the import boom created serious difficulties. First, it raised popular expectations about improvements in the standard of living to new and dangerous heights; secondly, it made it impossible for local manufacturers to preserve their hold on the domestic market, let alone prepare to launch themselves into the export battle; thirdly, it put out of business many small farmers who could not compete with cheap food imports once restrictions had been lifted; and lastly, and most critical of all, it worsened the already shaky prospects for Jamaica's balance of payments.

By the middle of 1982 the Jamaican dollar, which was officially valued at J$1.78 to the US dollar, was trading on the black or 'parallel' market at nearly twice that figure. In what amounted to the offer of a measure of legality to this system, the government at first tried to draw some of the parallel market dollars - many of which had been earned illegally from trading in *ganja* - into specified imports intended to help local manufacturing. It issued so-called 'no-funds licenses' which permitted businessmen to pay for certain goods without recourse to the Bank of Jamaica. By January 1983, however, it was forced to go a step further and openly institute a two-tier exchange rate. Seaga's aim was to encourage exports by making imported inputs for manufactured goods less expensive than imported goods for consumption. The former would continue to be priced at the official rate, the latter at a rate expected to level out around J$2.70.[15] This amounted to a hidden devaluation of the currency, an issue of particular political sensitivity because of the JLP's earlier attacks on the Manley government's policies in this area. The most immediate effect of the introduction of the dual exchange rate was, of course, on prices, thereby threatening the one undisputed economic achievement of the Seaga government to this point, namely the reduction in inflation which had accompanied the liberalisation of imports and the capture of the local market by cheaper foreign goods.[16]

The worsening balance of payments crisis was bound sooner or later to affect the quarterly tests to which the economy was subject as

15. For the details of the system's operation see Michael Witter, 'Exchange Rate Policy in Jamaica: A Critical Assessment', *Social and Economic Studies*, 32, 4 (1983), pp. 27–9.
16. See Derick Boyd and Everton Pryce, 'Jamaica's Devaluation Spree', *Caribbean Contact*, 12, 5 Oct. (1984), p. 6.

part of the 1981 IMF agreement. The moment of failure came in March 1983 when the deficit reached the figure of US$150 million: the Fund promptly suspended further disbursements and Seaga had no alternative but to plead for a waiver. In order to impress the IMF he introduced a series of austerity measures which included new taxes, public spending cuts, reduced foreign exchange allocations for imports and the shift of many more items to the more expensive parallel market rate. The idea was to curb the use of precious foreign exchange on non-essential imports by pricing them out of the reach of most people. As such, the move was an extension of the previous devaluation, and had the same inflationary consequences over an even wider range of goods including many basic items such as gasolene. Jamaicans felt the impact of the squeeze, but the reaction of Seaga's external backers was favourable. The IMF generously granted the waiver, the World Bank produced two more loans, and the US government offered US$25 million in emergency balance of payments assistance as well as agreeing to make a further purchase of bauxite for its strategic reserve. It was an impressive demonstration of solidarity in support of Seaga by the dominant forces of the international liberal economy.

What is striking is that it failed to remedy the situation. The level of production in the Jamaican economy had fallen so low that it could not be corrected simply by devaluation and deregulation. In October 1983 the IMF again suspended payments following a protracted dispute with the government over figures relating to the failure of the September test. It was announced that the agreement was to be terminated six months early and negotiations were started on a new package of assistance, with Seaga and his colleagues in a much weaker bargaining position than in 1980–1.

Phase II: November 1983–March 1985. The talks with the IMF took place against the background of pressure on the exchange rate. The government had miscalculated the balance of supply and demand for foreign exchange: the decision to push so many extra imports on to the parallel market caused a rapid 'bidding-up' of the price to over J$3.00 by the end of October. The Fund focused on this as a sign of the continuing uncompetitiveness of Jamaican exports and made a unification (i.e. another devaluation) of the exchange rate its main demand in return for the provision of a new stand-by credit. The original intention was that this new arrangement would run for fifteen months from the beginning of January 1984, but it soon became clear that the IMF had other demands which it wanted implemented *before* it agreed to the loan, not after it had been approved and disbursed. Its approach can be aptly described in military terms as a 'pre-emptive strike'. In this connection the key announcement came at the end of November 1983: the Jamaican dollar would henceforth be fixed at a single rate, initially set at J$3.15, but adjustable every two weeks by the Bank of Jamaica in a kind of 'managed float'. This signified a devaluation of no less than 43 per cent for any item hitherto traded at the former official rate, and was only the first of a series of harsh economic measures introduced at the behest of the IMF. The controversial snap election in December thus served to clear the political decks for the austerity that was to come.

Having achieved its goal of a substantial devaluation, the major remaining IMF demand related to the size of the government's budget deficit, which it wanted to see reduced from the existing figure of 15.6 per cent of GDP to single figures within just one year. Yet even before the task of meeting this requirement could be properly confronted its achievement was jeopardised by another damaging development within the bauxite industry. In March 1984, apparently without giving any prior warning to the government, the American company Reynolds announced that it was shutting down its bauxite operation in the island. It blamed the international recession, although some felt that an argument with the government a year or so earlier about the distribution of the US stockpile contract between the companies operating in Jamaica was at least partially responsible. Seaga expressed his bitterness that a company which had worked in Jamaica for over forty years should behave in such a way, and admitted in a state of shock that the loss to the fiscal budget being planned for 1984–5 could be as much as J$100 million and the short-fall in the foreign exchange budget some US$30 million.[17]

If, therefore, the IMF target was to be met, the level of deflation had to be even more severe than had been projected. For political reasons Seaga introduced a two-stage remedy: he raised taxes by J$138 million in a 'mini-package' in April and then extended the process by a further J$45 million in the regular budget in May. In addition, public expenditure was reduced and many civil servants and other public sector workers were sacked, adding to the already high levels of unemployment. Food subsidies were also cut, although a minimum level of support for basic commodities was maintained. Other measures designed to appease the IMF included restrictions on domestic credit, the promise of accelerated divestment of state enterprises, and a more intensive policing of the leakage of foreign

17. *Caribbean Insight*, April 1984.

exchange from the tourist sector – which was notorious for the way that it was able to siphon money to Miami. It should be noted too that while these measures were being introduced piecemeal in the first half of 1984 the Jamaican dollar continued to slide on the floating exchange, reaching the figure of J$4.15 by June. Eventually, enough was deemed to be enough. Jamaica's second major IMF loan in the Seaga era came into being five months late in June 1984: it provided US$143 million, well below the US$180 million the government had been hoping for since the end of 1983, divided between stand-by credit and compensatory finance, and was only scheduled to last until the end of March 1985. With the loan in place, debt rescheduling was again possible and shortly afterwards the Paris Club agreed to 'roll-forward' US$135 million of external debts due for repayment before March 1985.

It was hoped that the loan would give the Jamaican economy the necessary breathing space in which the prescribed free market remedy, as applied by the IMF, could at last begin to work. The Fund itself issued a statement, declaring optimistically that the measures that had been introduced would 'place fiscal and credit policies on a sounder footing in order to improve the balance of payments and restore conditions for the implementation of structural reform'.[18] One can imagine the reaction therefore both inside and outside the country when, almost immediately, the economy failed the quarterly test at the end of September. Seaga had to travel to Washington in person to seek the by now familiar waiver. On this occasion the Fund accepted his argument that the failure was more technical than real (some agreed foreign loans had not been paid on time); the only two conditions attached to the continuation of the credit were his removal of the last vestigial attempt to manage the level of the Jamaican dollar and the decision that it should float 'freely' from the beginning of December. Yet by the time the end-of-year test came round the position of the reserves was no better and two loans from the US government, which still supported the Seaga regime loyally, were hurried through to secure the pass. Despite government denials, it was now clear that another IMF agreement was coming to an ignominious end.

Seaga's problem was that not only did he have to satisfy the IMF's demands, he also had to manage the domestic political situation in Jamaica, which by the beginning of 1985 was becoming more and more tense. The economic boom of 1981 had long since disappeared, inflation stood at 30 per cent; the currency had floated downwards

18. IMF press release, June 1984.

to J$5.00; and unemployment (notwithstanding the initiation of a number of job training programmes) was estimated at 25.6 per cent of the labour force. In this last respect the unpalatable fact was that the creation of 6,705 jobs which the JNIP proudly announced as the result of four years of trying to promote new investment in manufacturing industry barely exceeded the 6,200 jobs which the government itself was prepared to cut from the public sector to secure the second IMF loan.[19] In the circumstances, the riots and protests which followed the gas price increases in January 1985 were, if anything, overdue. Even so, the government was shaken by the extent of the anger felt by ordinary working-class Jamaicans at its economic policies and was further taken aback by the announcement shortly afterwards that Alcoa was to follow in the footsteps of Reynolds and close down its alumina refinery, pending a revival of market conditions. The government's conclusion, however, was not that the adjustment programme needed to be abandoned or amended, but that the people would have to be made more aware of the stark choices facing Jamaica as a result of the economy's plight – especially as the next round of IMF talks was about to begin.

Phase III: April 1985–April 1986. The new policy of candour was inaugurated in a nationwide television address delivered by Seaga in April 1985. He spoke of the need to secure a further IMF deal, but warned that there would have to be costs in the form of more public sector job losses, higher interest rates and still heavier taxation. The sole ray of hope he could offer was the news that the Alcoa plant would open again in July under a leasing arrangement whereby production and marketing would be undertaken by a new government company, Clarendon Alumina Production Ltd., with Alcoa retaining operational responsibility. Seaga claimed that buyers had already been found for virtually all of the plant's capacity, albeit at loss-making prices. The government's willingness to intervene in this way was highly revealing: it showed how desperate it had become to preserve the basis of the bauxite industry for the future and to prevent any further redundancies in the meantime. Critics also noted that there were boundaries to its own acceptance of a policy of complete reliance on the market.

As the government promised, the next IMF agreement was soon announced. It represented a 20 month credit of US$120 million to run from August 1985 to March 1987 and was deemed to require a further reduction in the size of the government's budget deficit.

19. *Caribbean Insight*, Aug. 1984.

Apart from threatening more jobs, this permitted a wage rise of only 10 per cent for public employees at a time when inflation was more than three times that figure. The political reaction to the announcement was both swift and fierce: within two weeks the country was in the midst of the first general strike in its post-independence history. For several days towards the end of June essential services were either closed down or maintained at only minimum levels and a call from Seaga for an immediate return to work was rejected. Yet the truth was that the action stemmed from despair rather than calculated planning, and the initial solidarity of the strikers was fairly quickly undermined by the government's uncompromising insistence that if the lifeblood of IMF credit was to be kept flowing, there really was no more money available for wage increases. For all that, the strike indicated in a more tangible way than hostile opinion polls the extent to which Seaga's programme had lost the support of the bulk of the country. The fact that the JLP-affiliated Bustamante Industrial Trade Union took part was particularly damaging.

Although the strike's collapse was generally seen as a victory for Seaga, subsequent events suggest that it may have had a significant impact on his political tactics. The period following the strike brought no sign that investment and enterprise were responding to the cheap labour economy created in Jamaica by the massive devaluation of the currency over the preceding two years. Indeed, the economy continued to worsen. Alpart suspended production at its alumina refinery in August 1985, with more loss of jobs and revenue; official forecasts warned of a decline in gross domestic product of as much as 6 per cent in the year; tourism fell back in the aftermath of the gas price disturbances; and the exchange rate reached almost J$6.00 to the US dollar at the end of September. There was nothing new in this further manifestation of economic decline except for the evidence of growing political opposition, not just from the unions, but from a more active PNP which was well in the lead in opinion polls. It was this opposition which seems to have persuaded Seaga of the need to adopt a softer stance to improve his domestic political position. The IMF annual meeting in Seoul which Seaga attended in October was treated to a description of the 'huge toll in human suffering' experienced as a result of the 'over-hasty' reform programme demanded by the Fund in countries like Jamaica. It was not the substance of the programme that he challenged but its pace; seven years, rather than three, would be a more appropriate adjustment period.[20]

20. Ibid., Nov. 1985.

The political thinking which lay behind his plea was quick to emerge. The economy had failed the September quarterly test, several loans had been delayed, and once again the government required a waiver. In the face of restiveness among leading figures in his own party and a further fall in the currency to J$6.40 (at which point the Bank of Jamaica did intervene financially to arrest what had become an almost uncontrollable slide) Seaga knew that he could only mollify the Fund by in effect arguing the opposition's case: namely that the Jamaican people could not take any more deflation of the economy. Accordingly, a team from the IMF and the World Bank was invited to the island to witness the 'progress' that had already been made towards structural adjustment and to hear the arguments for an easing of future terms. As a token of its faith the government took a step towards the further reduction of its budget deficit by introducing another emergency tax package in January 1986. This included the imposition of an annual licence on the TV satellite antennae, the 'dishes', which had become the new symbols of prosperity in the far-off days of the 1981 import boom. The Fund was unimpressed. Although a waiver was granted to enable more credit to be drawn while negotiations continued, it became apparent that the visiting team was demanding the maintenance of restrictive measures. At the same time pay disputes with the teachers, police and junior doctors, as well as protests from students at the University of the West Indies about the introduction of tuition fees, kept up the political pressure on Seaga and reduced his room for concessions to IMF orthodoxy. In short, an impasse had been reached.

Phase IV: May 1986–September 1987. The first move to end the stalemate was made by Seaga in May 1986, when in an extraordinary reversal of policy he introduced an expansionary budget designed to regenerate economic growth. Its main features were a reduction in interest rates; a pledge to hold the exchange rate at J$5.50; the use of temporary controls to reduce the price of basic foods, animal feed and cement; and an increase in capital expenditure from J$1.4 billion in the previous fiscal year to J$2.1 billion in the forthcoming year. In contradiction of earlier warnings, no new taxes were imposed. The change of approach was evident, but quite what it meant was unclear. The budget had been delayed for a week following arguments about strategy with the joint mission and, on the surface at least, appeared to reflect a decisive rejection of IMF thinking. Seaga also observed enigmatically that the government had prepared, but would not disclose, 'a contingency programme in the event that there is any insistence by the institutions on returning this time to further devaluations, budget cuts, reduction of services, redundancies and no growth'[21] – for which he now disclaimed all responsibility. Conversely, conspiracy theorists in the opposition parties were inclined to argue that the budget was a ruse cooked up with the IMF and designed to generate sufficient short-term popularity to win another election, after which orthodox management could be resumed with a vengeance. Memories of the December 1983 election were clearly still fresh.

The most likely interpretation of events falls somewhere between the two scenarios. The crucial background factor was the fall in the market price of oil in early 1986 which gave the balance of payments an unexpected boost and provided the government with rather more room for manoeuvre economically than had been anticipated. It quickly took advantage of the situation by buying three years supply of oil at a price of US$10 per barrel. With regard to the IMF, the probability is that Seaga saw the oil windfall as providing the best chance to bargain for the softening of terms of which he had first spoken in Seoul, and certainly the May budget did not indicate the adoption of a non-IMF strategy of any kind, least of all that attempted by Manley in 1980. In September Seaga went to Washington for more talks, having revealed that part of his tactics involved delaying repayments to the Fund. This was a high risk policy, since the running up of arrears with the IMF unquestionably meant a moratorium on any new loans or debt rescheduling agreements. Indeed it was debt, and the threat of default, with which Seaga was trying to bargain.

According to leaks from Jamaican government sources the issue in dispute was the currency. Attempts to rescue the stalled third agreement, which had until the end of March 1987 to run, were abandoned in favour of discussion of a completely new three-year programme. As a prerequisite, the Fund wanted a further devaluation to take the rate from J$5.50 to J$6.06; the government countered with a proposal to move to J$5.91 in the fiscal year 1987–8 and then to J$6.43 a year later. It defended this position by claiming that it maintained the rate in real terms and was not therefore a means to further restructuring – this was why the Fund's officials were reluctant to accept it. As an alternative Seaga proposed a wage freeze, only to find that as soon as this came into the open all the major trade unions in the island including the BITU rejected it emphatically. There was clearly some very tough bargaining between the government and the Fund, and for a long while no accommodation could be reached. Gradually, as the discussions proceeded, the

21. Ibid., May 1986.

government's expansive talk in May of resumed growth of some 5 per cent was dropped and replaced by more sluggish forecasts. Perhaps the US administration was also signalling its disapproval of the poker game being played by Seaga when at the end of 1986 it announced both a substantial cut in aid to Jamaica and a reduction in the country's sugar import quota into the US market.

Finally, in January 1987, the JLP government's fourth major agreement with the IMF was concluded. It was for a loan of US$132.8 million over fifteen months running until 31 March 1988. Seaga presented it as 'a major breakthrough'. 'The negotiations were long and tough', he declared, 'but they were worth it. We were determined to avoid any up-front devaluation of the Jamaican dollar. We did so! But we must maintain this with a low inflation level.'[22] This last point was a reference to the main condition of the agreement, which was a government commitment to reduce the rate of inflation in 1987/8 to only 7 per cent, about half the existing level. With this need in mind, the list of price controls on basic foods imposed the previous May was retained and new controls instituted on fertilisers, animal feed, herbicides, pesticides, medicines and educational textbooks. Pay guidelines were also announced limiting increases to 10 per cent in the year, compared with the previous year's average settlement of 12.5 per cent. Import duties were further reduced, giving extra-regional goods even easier access to the Jamaican market and acting as a downward pressure on prices, albeit to the disadvantage, as before, of local manufacturing interests.

Nevertheless, Seaga's relief was justified, at least for the moment. The IMF had retreated from its demand for an immediate devaluation and had allowed him more time in which to sort the situation out. Once more, debt rescheduling within the framework of the Paris Club was made possible by the signing of the IMF deal, and various debt-swap schemes were mooted. The government was also able to point to renewed economic growth at an annual rate of 8 per cent for the first quarter of 1987, largely on the basis of an improvement in tourist earnings. Finally, increased expenditure in the budget added to the air of economic optimism being projected in official circles in the run-up to the election. Even so, the new IMF agreement posed dangers for the government. Under questioning, Seaga was forced to admit that a devaluation was likely to take place at the end of the fifteen-month period if the inflation target was not met. With the trade unions reacting angrily to the proposed pay guidelines,

22. E. Seaga, 'Statement to Parliament on the International Monetary Fund Agreement, January 13 1987' (Kingston, 1987), pp. 7–8.

problems quickly arose – nurses, doctors, teachers, civil servants and the police all rejected government pay offers. The reductions in import duties also presaged another consumer boom led by the well-off, which could worsen the trade deficit and thus put renewed pressure on the exchange rate. The Jamaica Manufacturers' Association expressed its unhappiness at this move, and added that further job losses and factory closures in the local economy were threatened. In short, Seaga's claim that 'we have now left behind us the bitter part of these programmes'[23] may prove to be premature: his dramatic plea to the IMF won a temporary easing of terms – but that is all.

Conclusion

The arguments which beset Jamaica's dealings with the IMF in 1986–7 do not alter the fact that the dominant approach taken to the management of the island's economy after October 1980 was that of orthodox liberal development theory. Admittedly it is not clear whether such a policy arose out of a genuine ideological commitment to liberal economics on the part of the Seaga government or a more calculating assessment that in the international environment of the 1980s there was no practical alternative. Perhaps it does not really matter which was the case: the model was pursued, for one reason or another, with more or less complete loyalty to its classic form. The Seaga period thus stands as a test-case of the validity of the whole liberal development tradition when applied to conditions of dependency. So what is to be said of its record of achievement in Jamaica?

The first point to make is that a high social and human price has undeniably had to be paid by very many Jamaicans. An OXFAM report published in May 1985 examined social conditions in the island and concluded that they were 'deteriorating dramatically'. It observed:

> As inflationary measures push up prices, the purchasing power of consumers declines because of rising unemployment and low pay. As cuts in public expenditure erode social service provisions, standards of health care delivery and education fall. As the Government balances its books, poverty is on the increase and people are suffering.[24]

23. Ibid., p. 11.
24. Belinda Coote, *Debt and Poverty: A Case Study of Jamaica* (Oxford, 1985), p. 20.

Since then the situation has worsened, not improved. The government was forced to admit as much, but defended itself against charges of callousness and indifference to human suffering by arguing that any set of alternative policies would cause even worse suffering. As Seaga himself said on one occasion, 'if the government did not take strict action, what is ahead would be so disastrous that the hurt we feel today would be nothing more than a pimple on the face of the country'.[25] It is reasonable to assume that at the outset the government did not grasp the extent of the social damage which its economic policies would incur; but equally important to note is that, having discovered, it was still prepared to ask Jamaicans to pay the cost.

Secondly, it is also the case that a high political price has had to be paid by all Jamaicans, not just by many. This refers not to party political considerations but to the loss of sovereignty over national affairs which the Seaga government has accepted and promoted. It is a commonplace of the analysis of Third World politics that post-colonial states find it hard to make a reality of the formal sovereignty which they possess in the international political system. It is more unusual for such states to acquiesce, apparently peacefully, in the effective subversion of that sovereignty. Yet that is what occurred in Jamaica under Seaga. The government allowed itself to become little more than a caretaker or clientelist regime which administered the country and its economy on behalf of the US government and major multilateral agencies like the IMF and the World Bank. Stone has written that 'it would not be an exaggeration to suggest that a process of economic recolonisation has occurred in Jamaica to the greater benefit of foreign capital and consultants and at the expense of local labour and capital as well as local professionals'.[26] As his regular newspaper columns indicate, Stone is neither a friend of the PNP nor a Marxist, which makes his observation all the more telling. What one might, for want of a more elegant phrase, call the 'de-nationalisation' of the state is thus another by-product of the application of liberal development thinking to Jamaica.

Even in the face of demonstrable economic success there would, therefore, be a powerful social and political critique to be made against Seaga's development strategy. It might be thought that the economic gains were greater than the social and political losses, but in the end that is a question of values, a matter of personal judge-

25. *Caribbean Insight*, Nov. 1984.
26. Carl Stone, 'Democratic State in the Caribbean: The Case of Jamaica', unpublished paper presented to the symposium on The Role of the State in the Caribbean, University of the West Indies, Jamaica, May 1985, p. 94.

ment. However, when the economic record is also poor there is little to weigh in the balance. The critical evidence is not so much the level of wages, the increase in prices, the state of the currency, or even the size of the foreign debt. It is the fact that consistent and substantial economic growth has not been achieved. The cheapening of labour, the devaluation of the currency, the liberalisation of imports, the borrowing of money – all of these policies were designed to stimulate the economy into export-led growth. This they manifestly failed to do. The government's own figures record moderate growth in 1981–3, a small contraction in 1984 and then a massive fall in 1985 of no less than 4.53 per cent. Resumed growth of 2.2 per cent in 1986 – largely on the basis of lower oil prices, the general international upturn and Seaga's own reflation in the May budget of that year – should not obscure the fact that the Jamaican gross domestic product, measured in constant prices, was barely more in 1986 than 1980.[27] Over the first six years of the Seaga regime average annual growth was a trifling 0.44 per cent – scarcely the stuff of economic miracles.

Why did this happen? Seaga's answer was to blame the international recession in general and the decline in the bauxite industry in particular. Aside from noting the irony of Seaga's use of such explanations (in Manley's time everything that went wrong with the economy was held to be the consequence of 'mismanagement'), it has to be conceded that external markets have been depressed and that this made the task of breaking out into export-led development all the more difficult. Equally, the recession in the bauxite industry was unquestionably damaging. Bauxite production in 1985 amounted to only 5.97 million tonnes, compared to 12.05 million tonnes in 1980; correspondingly, foreign exchange earnings from the industry fell over the same period from US$313.99 million to US$138.70 million.[28] It was a huge shortfall to make up and would have severely disrupted any economic strategy. The question remains as to whether it is sufficient as the sole, or even main, explanation of the failure of the Seaga programme to deliver the promised revival of economic growth.

As late as April 1984, in a speech to foreign journalists, Seaga was still arguing that, had bauxite production continued at 1980 levels, 'we would have surpassed the reduction of deficit at the target level which we had set for ourselves in our Agreement with the Inter-

27. Planning Institute of Jamaica, *Economic and Social Survey: Jamaica 1986* (Kingston, 1987), p. 1.9.
28. Ibid., pp. 8.5 and 8.7.

national Monetary Fund, that we would have surpassed the surpluses which we had targeted also . . . that we would have significantly improved our growth performance and nearly achieved our unemployment target'.[29] The claim was unconvincing at the time and has been rendered no more plausible since. By 1987 the state of the Jamaican economy was such that it was impossible to believe that, even with the maintenance of bauxite production, the exchange rate would have been much higher, or the balance of payments much improved, or the level of debt much lower, or the social costs of the reduction in the government's budget deficit much less marked. Bauxite was an inadequate scapegoat. The real culprit was a policy which had deliberately sought to deflate the economy in order to make it more competitive in world markets.

Understood in this way, considerable doubts begin to attach to the relevance of the whole approach of liberal development thinking when applied to structurally underdeveloped economies which have to make their way in a world economy characterised by the monopoly power of established countries and companies. The evidence from Seaga's Jamaica is that liberalisation undermines the position of small and medium-sized domestic producers; does not necessarily attract large influxes of foreign capital, even though wages may be low; forbids the state from playing any significant part in the production process; and leads inexorably to unemployment and de-industrialisation rather than growth and expansion. Add to that the social costs brought about by rising prices and collapsing public services and the political price paid in terms of exaggerated dependency and client status, and it is apparent that Jamaica has suffered as comprehensive a failure of development under Seaga as it did under the very different policies of Michael Manley in the 1970s.

29. Edward Seaga, *The Recession and Jamaica – Problems and Solutions*, address by the Prime Minister to the Inter-American Press Association Conference, Kingston, 1984, p. 6.

9

JAMAICA AND CUBA

Jamaica and Cuba are close neighbours, being separated at their nearest point by only 100 miles of sea. They share a climate and topography, they have both experienced a long and difficult history of imperialism, and they still struggle today to cope with the economic legacy of plantation agriculture. As one writer has noted, both countries have had to 'come to terms with the uniquely New World experience of being dependent suppliers of tropical primary products for Western European or North American markets'.[1] It is also true that Jamaica and Cuba have gone their separate ways politically – the one westwards, the other eastwards – to the point where it is difficult to discern which of them is the more firmly integrated within its chosen geopolitical system. As a consequence, Cold War barriers have frequently been placed in the way of closer bilateral relations between the two neighbours.

For all this, they have never been able to keep their roles and interests in world and regional affairs totally separate; the gravitational pull of their common Caribbean destiny has been too strong. The result has been that ever since the Cuban revolution they have danced an uneasy *pas de deux* – sometimes friends, sometimes enemies, sometimes pretending the other does not exist. Each seems to have conducted its relationship with the other, not in terms of its potential or intrinsic merits, but rather in subservience to other orientations and interests which it has wished to pursue or safeguard. As it unfolds, therefore, the story of the relationship between Jamaica and Cuba reveals in an unusually telling way the extent to which the modern development of the Caribbean has been shaped by the interplay of the many different links and associations with the outside world which the region has accumulated in the course of its history.

The Cuban perspective

Cuban foreign policy since 1959 has striven both to defend and advance the revolution at home and to promote national liberation

1. M. Cross, *Urbanization and Urban Growth in the Caribbean* (Cambridge, 1979), p. 5.

abroad. As with its domestic policy, it has been a blend of pragmatism and idealism, of nationalism and socialism, in combinations that have varied over time. Nevertheless, several specific phases of development can be delineated.

Revolutionary subversion. The first phase covers the 1960s and was marked by Cuba's endorsement of revolutionary action in other Third World countries, particularly within Latin America. In the earliest years the 'adventures' it supported were amateurish and romantic in conception, drawing directly upon and attempting to repeat, in what were considered similar circumstances, the successful formula of the Cuban revolutionary war against Batista. Panama, Haiti, Nicaragua and the Dominican Republic were chosen as the sites for such action, but in every case the enterprise proved to be an utter failure. Subsequently, a more sophisticated approach emerged in which local forces were more evident, and revolutionary change, rather than simply a change of political regime, came to be identified as the protagonists' principal goal. Venezuela was the main target of this policy, which quickly brought Cuba into direct conflict with the government in Caracas and with the Inter-American system at large as constituted by the Organisation of American States (OAS). Following a Venezuelan initiative, the OAS decided in July 1964 to impose diplomatic and economic sanctions against Cuba, effectively isolating it in Latin America (with the exception of Mexico which refused to implement the policy). Jamaica was not a member of the OAS at the time and was thus not required to participate. In fact, it is noteworthy that throughout the 1960s, even after the process of decolonisation had begun, the Commonwealth Caribbean states were excluded from Cuba's policy of revolutionary subversion. They were regarded as part of the British sphere of influence.

Cuba's immediate response to OAS sanctions was to step up support for subversive activity in Latin America, particularly in Venezuela, Colombia and Guatemala where by this time there were established guerrilla movements and the chances of success were deemed to be higher. Yet even these ventures failed, which led to changing assumptions and finally to an explicit recognition of the inability of armed struggle alone to bring about the desired changes. Cuba's developing relationship with the Soviet Union was central to this shift of policy. Much to the disappointment of the Cubans, the Soviet Union made clear that it regarded the strategy of revolutionary exhortation as both naive and dangerous. It was concerned at the response such activity might provoke from the United States and, preoccupied as it was in other parts of the world, was unwilling to sponsor Che Guevara's call for the creation of 'two or three' or even 'four or five more Vietnams' for the United States in Latin America and the Caribbean.

By 1968 Cuban-Soviet relations had reached their nadir. But thereafter, due to continued US hostility to the Castro regime, the defeat of the guerrilla strategy symbolised by the death of Guevara in Bolivia in 1967, the growing diplomatic isolation of Cuba within the western hemisphere and, not least, the economic pressure imposed by the Soviet Union through such measures as the delay of petroleum shipments, Havana was forced to draw closer to Moscow, regardless of ideological misgivings. Castro recognised the necessity of *rapprochement* in 1968 in giving qualified approval to the Brezhnev doctrine of 'limited sovereignty', as exercised in the invasion of Czechoslovakia. Mutual concessions were also subsequently made concerning revolutionary strategy, in that the Soviet Union agreed to give some support to guerrilla insurgency in Latin American and Caribbean states with extremely pro-American and anti-communist regimes, and the Cubans accepted the Soviet case for adopting peaceful diplomatic methods as the means in the first instance to challenge US hegemony in the hemisphere.

Progressive diplomacy. Cuba's abandonment of the export of revolution did not lead quickly to the formation of a new foreign policy. For three or four years after 1968 the Cuban government turned inward, preoccupied with the ultimately unsuccessful drive to produce 10 million tonnes of sugar in the 1970 harvest. Its retreat from the extensive foreign involvements of the previous decade was so striking that one writer was moved to talk of Cuba's pursuit of 'socialism in one island'.[2] By 1971, however, the second phase in the development of Cuban foreign relations can be said to have begun. It was effectively inaugurated during an extended visit paid by Castro to Chile, in the course of which he endorsed Allende's electoral road to socialism as authentic and deserving of support. This apparent new pragmatism was given some theoretical sustenance by the creation of the concept of the 'progressive' government, defined rather loosely by the Cubans as 'any government which sincerely adopts a policy of economic and social development and of liberating its country from the imperialist yoke'.[3] Relations with such governments were to be developed on the basis of solidarity, which went further for Cuba than the existence of a common under-

2. J. Petras, 'Socialism in One Island: A Decade of Cuban Revolutionary Government', *Politics and Society*, 1, 3 (1971), pp. 203–24.
3. Cited in R. Espindola, 'Cuba: Centre of Peace or Conflict', *South*, Aug. 1982, p. 20.

standing concerning the tasks and obstacles at hand: it implied nothing less than unity in action in opposition to US imperialism.

The commitment manifested itself in several ways. Adopting a self-appointed role as Third World spokesman, Castro called many times after 1973 for the OPEC countries to unite with the less developed world in order to ease dependence and swing the global balance against imperialism. Within the Non-Aligned Movement, Cuba spent some considerable effort trying to isolate and force out of the movement those countries not considered 'progressive'. Within Latin America, too, Cuba played a more active diplomatic role, establishing close relations in the early and mid-1970s with the governments of Mexico and Venezuela, two more 'progressive' administrations. Indeed, at that time Cuba was willing to extend military and economic assistance to such regimes all over the world – in Africa and the Middle East as well as Latin America – in an attempt to promote Third World solidarity.

Rather surprisingly, given the absence of previous connections, the closest inter-governmental links established by the Cuban regime in this period were with some of the Commonwealth Caribbean countries. Yet these were slow to emerge; even in the early 1970s, when the Cuban government began its diplomatic offensive in the western hemisphere following the bitter arguments of the previous decade, the Commonwealth Caribbean states were not included.[4] The initiative was taken, first of all, within the Commonwealth Caribbean itself when, in October 1972, well before the OAS could bring itself to lift its ban on such relations, the region's four independent states – Jamaica, Trinidad and Tobago, Guyana and Barbados – issued a joint declaration affirming their intention to work towards the rapid establishment of relations with Cuba, 'be they economic, political or both'.[5] Castro hailed this 'challenge to imperialism', which he said indicated that 'the English-speaking nations of the Caribbean did not acquire the bad habit – as did the Latin American governments – of being dreadfully afraid of Yankee Imperialism',[6] and moved promptly to establish ties.

This initiated a period of close co-operation between Cuba and the Commonwealth Caribbean, particularly Jamaica. The Manley government was ideally suited to the broad thrust of Cuban policy towards the Third World in the 1970s. As Castro himself put it, 'in a nutshell, we like the government of Jamaica because we believe it is a

4. See R.E. Jones, 'Cuba and the English-speaking Caribbean' in C. Blasier and C. Mesa-Lago (eds), *Cuba in the World* (Pittsburgh, 1979), p. 131.
5. *Trinidad Express*, 15 Oct. 1972.
6. *Granma Weekly Review*, 20 April 1975.

progressive government'.[7] In 1973 Manley was invited by Castro to travel in his plane to the Non-Aligned conference in Algiers and subsequently paid a highly publicised visit to Cuba, where he was awarded the prestigious José Marti National Order established 'for heads of state and government and leaders of political parties and movements who have distinguished themselves for their international solidarity with the struggle against imperialism, colonialism and neo-colonialism and for their friendship with the Socialist Revolution of Cuba'.[8] Supplementing these personal ties was the structure of bilateral relations. Cuban aid to Jamaica was not only considerable, but highly visible, widely publicised and aimed directly at the problems of the poor. The construction of a secondary school in Spanish Town by a joint Cuban-Jamaican workforce, the assignment of Cuban doctors to the Jamaican health service, and the provision of condensed milk from Cuba for sale in Jamaica to low-income groups are just a few examples of assistance given by the end of 1975. There also developed collaboration in the fields of fisheries, agriculture, tourism, transportation and public health, to name some of the more prominent areas; wider commercial relations were established between the two countries; there were exchanges of personnel, including the training of young Jamaicans in Cuba in aspects of the construction business; and there was a considerable degree of co-operation in foreign policy, especially in connection with North-South issues.

By the middle of the decade Cuba had started to reap rewards for its pragmatic diplomacy. In July 1975 a motion was introduced at the OAS to allow each member to resume relations with Cuba if it so wished. The matter had been raised previously but on this occasion was passed by a large majority.[9] Sanctions, it must be stressed, were not officially lifted, but their effectiveness had been eroded throughout the early 1970s, and the extent to which Cuba was now accepted as a full member of the Latin American economic community was underlined by its endorsement of the Latin American Economic System, a body established in 1975 to negotiate a common Latin American front on economic matters, which specifically – and significantly – excluded the United States. Cuba's position in the Caribbean Basin at the end of 1975 was thus greatly enhanced by comparison with that of five years earlier. The change had been

7. Ibid., 30 July 1975.
8. Ibid., 20 April 1975 and 29 June 1975.
9. See C. Mesa-Lago, *Cuba in the 1970s: Pragmatism and Institutionalisation* (Albuquerque, 1978).

brought about almost exclusively by Cuban and Caribbean initiatives, thereby demonstrating the plausibility in this period of an autonomy of development in the region outside the control of either the United States or the Soviet Union.

Militant anti-imperialism. The substantial achievement noted above laid the basis for the marked turn towards the wider world and even greater self-confidence which characterised Cuban foreign policy in the third identifiable phase which lasted until the end of 1979. In the Cuban view this period was marked by a shift in the international 'correlation of forces'. The US defeat in Vietnam, the increased strategic influence of the Soviet Union, the new international cohesion of the Third World, symbolised by the success of OPEC – all these factors were interpreted as signs that the balance of world power was tipping in favour of socialism and national liberation and against imperialism. It meant that Cuba was less constrained in its actions than previously and could undertake diplomatic and even military initiatives more directly and with a greater expectation of success. Although Angola and Ethiopia stand out in this connection, they were not the only examples of Cuba's more pronounced international profile in these years. Within the Non-Aligned Movement Cuba's leading position was formally recognised by Castro's election to the chairmanship at the 1979 Havana summit, while within Latin America the policy of making joint cause with any government that sought to resist US domination of the area was both extended and deepened.

In the Caribbean this required above all a policy of continued support for the Manley regime. Castro paid a long-expected visit to Jamaica in November 1977 and was followed by the Cuban Minister of Foreign Affairs in February 1978. Manley and his foreign minister reciprocated in due course. More technical and commercial agreements resulted from these exchanges and, more importantly for Cuba, several areas of common political concern were identified. They included support for Cuba's call for the independence of Puerto Rico – a cause of particular irritation to the United States – as well as approval of the revolutions in Nicaragua and Grenada. Further afield, and by no means coincidentally, Manley sought to establish closer relations with the Soviet Union and Eastern Europe. He visited the Soviet Union and had talks which led to the signing of agreements on trade and technical and economic co-operation. A close relationship between Jamaica and the Soviet Union was never fully consummated, but at no stage, even in the declining days of the Manley administration, did the bond between his government and the Cuban regime weaken.

Cuba was in any case joyfully coming to terms with the fact that it no longer represented the sole bastion of revolutionary change in the Caribbean Basin. The Grenada revolution in March 1979 and that in Nicaragua in July the same year had given it new allies and revived the concept of revolutionary militancy as the path to power. 'There is only one road to liberation: that of Cuba, that of Grenada, that of Nicaragua. There is no other formula'[10] was how Castro put it in a speech to the Cuban people made shortly after a visit to Nicaragua. At the same time he recognised that a cautious approach based upon carefully measured assistance was the most judicious policy. Aid to Nicaragua in the first year after the revolution was thus almost exclusively medical and educational in character, not military, and corresponded to the 'low key' approach taken by Cuba during the insurrectionary struggle against the Somoza dictatorship.[11] Likewise, in respect of Grenada, Cuba was initially more wooed than wooing.

In short, Cuba recognised that if 1979 had seen a significant shift in its favour in the Caribbean Basin, further gains elsewhere should not be jeopardised by making too much of this fact. This was made explicit in the 'Resolution on International Policy' adopted in 1980 by the Cuban Communist Party. While welcoming 'the resounding people's victories in Nicaragua and Grenada', it also considered 'other situations in Latin America and the Caribbean to be very important'. Accordingly, it declared:

> In the coming years, Cuba will express its continuing solidarity with all patriotic, anti-imperialist governments that have decided to oppose Washington's domination with dignity. Cuba will maintain its strategic guideline of seeking the broadest possible unity for national independence, progress and democracy in the region. Our party encourages and supports all sovereign actions and attitudes by Latin American and Caribbean governments and political forces protecting their legitimate national interests and promoting more just and equitable economic relations.[12]

Declining prestige. The irony was that no sooner had Cuban influence in the region peaked than it began unexpectedly to decline. A fourth phase – one of declining prestige in Latin America and the Third World – started in 1980 and has yet to be arrested. Several factors explain this. The first reflected the beginnings of a reaction against Cuba's close alliance with the Soviet Union. Whereas intervention in Angola had generated widespread admiration among

10. F. Castro, 'There is only one road to Liberation: that of Cuba, that of Grenada, that of Nicaragua', speech given on 26 July 1980 in vol. 1 of M. Taber (ed.), *Fidel Castro Speeches* (New York, 1981), p. 326.
11. See W. Leo Grande, 'Cuba and Nicaragua', *Caribbean Review*, IX, 1 (1980).
12. 'Resolution on International Policy' in Taber, *Fidel Castro*, Appendix B.

Third World governments, Cuba's Ethiopian involvement was less well received. It looked rather too much like a favour dutifully performed for a powerful patron. Indeed, within the Non-Aligned Movement as a whole Cuba's argument that there existed a 'natural alliance' between the underdeveloped world and the socialist camp was increasingly unacceptable to those members of the movement who still favoured the tradition of neutrality between the power blocs of East and West.

Critical to this debate was the Soviet invasion of Afghanistan. The UN General Assembly resolution calling for the withdrawal of Soviet troops was supported by almost all Caribbean Basin countries, including Jamaica and Nicaragua; only Cuba and Grenada voted against it. Cuba tried to minimise its loss of face in the Third World by making no effort to defend the Soviet intervention, but the damage was done. Proof came with the withdrawal of support for Cuba, and the subsequent selection of Mexico, as Latin America's representative on the UN Security Council later in 1980. For Cuba, the incident revealed that it had yet to devise effective means for managing the tension inherent in its dual identity as a member of the Third World and a close ally of the Soviet Union. Forced to choose between these two roles in the case of Afghanistan, it could not avoid losing respect with one of its two constituencies - in this case, the states of the non-aligned Third World - many of which, including some in the Caribbean, had genuinely looked to Cuba for leadership in the previous decade.

The second factor which brought about a decline in Cuba's standing, especially in the Caribbean, was the election of Ronald Reagan to the US Presidency. Reagan's views about Cuba's role in the politics of the hemisphere were well advertised before he won office, and the many US government measures introduced from the beginning of 1981 with a view to damaging Cuba's economic and political position came as no surprise to those in power in Havana. What was less predictable was the willingness of former allies in Latin America and the Caribbean to fall in line with Washington's hostility. Under US pressure, relations between Cuba and countries such as Venezuela, Panama and Peru soon deteriorated, and diplomatic ties with Colombia and Costa Rica were broken off in 1981. Cuba's relations with Jamaica eventually met the same fate, but more as a consequence of Manley's electoral defeat just a month before Reagan's own victory. As we have seen, the Seaga government asked the Cuban government to recall its ambassador within days of taking office, and a year later it severed diplomatic ties completely.

The final factor contributing to the fall in Cuban prestige concerned events in Cuba itself. An incident at the Peruvian embassy in Havana in April 1980 opened up a means whereby disaffected Cubans could flee the island to the United States and, to the delight of opponents of the Cuban regime, revealed a massive number of people who wanted to do precisely that. Many of the refugees complained of food rationing, shortages of consumer goods and high prices. Their disaffection underlined the difficulties which had afflicted the Cuban economy since the beginning of the 1980s. Declining foreign exchange earnings forced the government to seek the rescheduling of part of its foreign debt, the price of which was the promise of tight financial management, involving a considerable degree of austerity, for a period of two or three years at least. This further intensified Cuba's economic dependence on the Soviet Union and meant that resources were no longer available, even if they were desired, to finance subversion or military activity in the Caribbean or elsewhere.

Cuba was thus in no position to match the new aggressive thrust of US policy under Reagan towards the Caribbean Basin; it could only condemn it. And in Central America its profile remained relatively low, making it difficult for the US government to pin-point any firm evidence of significant military assistance to the insurgents in El Salvador. Cuba remained committed to Nicaragua and has been generous in its supply of largely non-military assistance to the Sandinista government, but elsewhere, especially in the Commonwealth Caribbean, it has found itself increasingly isolated. After the defeat of the Manley regime Cuba retained the support of just one government, that of Grenada, and when the Grenadian revolution was finally brought to an end in October 1983 by a combination of implosion and invasion, the blow to Cuba was severe. The affair shook Castro and brought home to him the extent of US military power in the Caribbean. Asked shortly afterwards to what extent Cuba would be able to support Nicaragua in the face of a similar US attack, he warned strongly against any such action, but indicated that there was little he could do since Cuba lacked the naval and air power to send direct assistance to Nicaragua or any other beleaguered Caribbean territory.[13] In general, the Cuban response to the invasion was one of perplexed and then resigned anger, expressed in terms of heightened revolutionary vigilance at home and the continued pursuit of measured diplomacy abroad. The latter has certainly been difficult to accomplish: Cuba is not the force in the

13. *Granma*, 6 Nov. 1983.

world it once was, and it has no close allies in government in the Caribbean. In fact, the Cuban connection has come to have negative associations. Governments like the Seaga administration have found that castigating Havana is now one of the more successful means of squeezing money out of the United States.

The Jamaican perspective

Jamaican foreign policy since 1962 has also been characterised by sharp discontinuities. It too can be described as a blend of pragmatism and idealism, of nationalism and socialism, the combinations of which have varied over time more or less in keeping with the four phases detected in the case of Cuba: But there the similarity ends: the substance of Jamaican foreign policy over the last twenty or so years reveals a very different outlook on the world.

Conformity to the West. Far from being preoccupied with notions of revolutionary subversion, Jamaica's policies in the international economic and political sphere in the 1960s have been accurately designated as ones of 'relative acquiescence and conformity to the American-dominated Western international arena'.[14] The assumption of political independence in 1962 was not regarded as an opportunity to shape a foreign policy in accordance with a national view of appropriate external links and priorities. Instead, a remarkably deferential set of guidelines was enunciated by the new JLP administration. The government would

1. not follow doctrinaire lines of policy but tend to look to the practical lines of policy;
2. take an anti-socialist line and support people everywhere seeking freedom and democracy;
3. support the policy of the Western powers with regard to conflicts with the Soviet Union and Soviet supporters;
4. oppose the communist way of life and communist imperialism;
5. support any demand in the United Nations for the destruction of racial and colour prejudice wherever it existed;
6. seek to encourage the United Nations to create conditions that would give more force to the Declaration of Human Rights;
7. seek through the United Nations to encourage the settlement of international disputes;

14. Vaughan Lewis, 'Issues and Trends in Jamaican Foreign Policy 1972–1977' in Carl Stone and Aggrey Brown (eds), *Perspectives on Jamaica in the Seventies* (Kingston, 1981), p. 43.

8. support the United Nations and abide by the principles of the charter.[15]

Although at one level these guidelines indicated a lack of confidence on the part of a new state coming to terms with international affairs, they also reflected a realistic awareness of the foreign policy implications of the dependent model of development favoured by the JLP in the 1960s.

The creation and maintenance of a favourable climate for investment was deemed to require an image of political reliability which, in turn, demanded a close identification with western political and economic interests. JLP policy was never very active in pursuit of these goals, but the appropriate signals were given. For example, Jamaica voted against the expulsion of Nationalist China (Taiwan) from the United Nations and for a long while afterwards refused to sever diplomatic relations with it. It condemned the Soviet invasion of Czechoslovakia in 1968 while remaining silent on the intervention of the United States in the Dominican Republic, a neighbouring Caribbean state. It is true that in the latter part of the 1960s the JLP demonstrated a more lively interest in issues relating to apartheid and decolonisation in Southern Africa and even took Jamaica into the Non-Aligned Movement as an observer. However, these shifts in policy, though significant, were so tentative as not to damage Jamaica's overall standing as a loyal friend of the West, especially on matters relating to the fight against communism.

Because of the extreme hostility of the United States to Castro's communist revolution, Cuba offered an obvious opportunity to demonstrate ideological affinity with the West, and the JLP government did not miss the chance. It spoke critically of Castro's regime at all times, joined the trade embargo against Cuba, restricted its nationals from visiting the island, and even seized the passports of those, including academics, who nonetheless found their way there. Yet in 1962 it established consular relations with Cuba and resisted considerable OAS pressure to sever them, mainly on the grounds that a large number of Jamaicans and their descendants lived and worked in Cuba, many of them at the US military base at Guantanamo. The activities of Cuba's consular representatives in Jamaica were certainly severely restricted in this period, but that does not alter the fact that a diplomatic link, albeit of a wholly pragmatic nature, did exist throughout the 1960s.

In this era the PNP accepted that, as far as possible, foreign policy

15. These points were outlined by Senator H. Wynter in the *Daily Gleaner*, 17 Dec. 1962.

should be conducted on a bi-partisan basis. It did not openly challenge the broad thrust of Jamaican foreign policy as pursued by the JLP, but it is clear that different views were beginning to develop in its ranks. In particular, it was felt that too close an alignment with the United States might inhibit the diversification of Jamaica's trading links. The then PNP leader, Norman Manley, put the point as follows:

> . . . England is prepared to trade with Cuba. So is Canada. We do not have to trade with Cuba. Cuba has nothing to sell to us and I doubt if we have anything to sell to Cuba. But so long as we are aligned to the West we would not dare to trade with Cuba no matter what the advantage of that trade might be. I speak from knowledge. The United States would put, has put, the utmost pressure on every country in the Western Hemisphere not to have trade with any country of that sort.[16]

Indeed, he argued that attachment to any single power-bloc limited Jamaica's manoeuvrability in the international arena and he proposed, as an alternative, identification with other Third World countries, something which the JLP regime had tried to avoid out of a self-important belief that Jamaica was somewhat above the level of economic development of most of the Third World.

Third Worldism. These themes laid the basis for the second phase of post-independence Jamaican foreign policy which began in 1972 with the election of the PNP and lasted approximately till mid-1975. It was characterised by precisely this new identification with Third World interests. Almost as soon as he took office, Michael Manley explained his government's thinking to the Jamaican House of Representatives:

> I say quite bluntly . . . that Jamaica is part of the Third World . . . and to me and to us, the Third World is not a matter of political ideology but of economic survival . . . because all the developing countries, whatever their political system, face the same difficulties in their dealings with the mighty metropolitan countries up north. . . . To the extent that the Third World can be led away from its distraction with political matters into the exploration and the recognition of a common economic interest, to that extent it is our own strength in the Third World that is promoted . . . We will go boldly into the Third World . . .[17]

Although reference was made to the demands of economic reality, it was clear that Manley's approach to foreign policy derived from the same philosophical commitment to egalitarian values which underpinned his domestic programme. He envisioned the creation of a

16. *Jamaica Hansard. Proceedings of House of Representatives*, 1, 1 (1965–6), p. 419.
17. Ibid., 1, 1 (1972–3), p. 313.

new international economic order characterised by a more equitable relationship between the core industrialised countries of the Western world and the peripheral commodity-producing countries of the Third World. Only collective action by the latter group could bring about such a goal, hence the emphasis on Third World solidarity.

The continuation of JLP policies in areas such as anti-colonialism and anti-racism should not therefore disguise the fact that a new dynamic underlay Jamaican foreign policy after 1972. The PNP government quickly assumed a prominent position in the Non-Aligned Movement, reactivated its membership of the Socialist International, took an active role in the promotion of international economic reform and, not least, established full diplomatic relations with Cuba. This last decision was taken jointly by all the independent governments within the Caribbean Community, but it owed a good deal to Manley's personal enthusiasm. Thereafter cordial relations between Jamaica and Cuba were developed. As has been noted, in September 1973 Manley flew in Castro's jet to the Non-Aligned summit in Algiers, a number of economic and technical exchanges were inaugurated between the two countries, and in May 1975 a group of Jamaican youths went to Cuba for a year-long course in construction technology as part of what became known as the '*brigadista*' programme.

These moves generated considerable domestic political controversy. The JLP used the opening of diplomatic relations with Cuba to revive old allegations about the PNP's secret predilection for socialism and communism. For example, Hugh Shearer claimed that this 'extension of foreign policy into the Communist area was going to involve Jamaica in ideological warfare in which its traditional friends would come in for direct or indirect attack'.[18] The PNP's 'rediscovery' of its commitment to democratic socialism in 1974 rekindled these accusations and allowed the regime's opponents to link the country's evolving domestic political orientation with the development of increasingly close relations with Cuba. In this context the dispatch of groups of largely unemployed youths to Cuba could not but give rise to the fear of political indoctrination.

Even so, the domestic reaction at this time was less important than the attitude of the US government. Official US concern about Jamaica's relations with Cuba was first expressed in January 1974 in the form of a warning that Jamaica might fall foul of certain US government regulations designed to give effect to the OAS trade embargo against Cuba. As Vaughan Lewis has argued in his commentary on Jamaican foreign relations in this period, the

18. *Daily Gleaner*, 4 Dec. 1972.

government's reply, given through its then Minister of Industry and Commerce, P.J. Patterson, was highly revealing:

> In the course of this review the opportunity was taken to clarify at diplomatic level whether or not in the light of existing US legislation a limited trade [with Cuba] could be conducted without incurring a penalty provided there was no conflict with United States laws and regulations.[19]

In short, the government had no illusions as to the reality of Jamaica's dependence on US trade and aid and, for the moment, it was careful not to challenge US domination of the hemispheric system.

Militant anti-imperialism. This relatively measured pursuit of Third Worldism, and all that it meant in respect of relations with countries like Cuba, came to an end with Manley's visit to Havana in July 1975. This journey initiated a third phase in post-independence Jamaican foreign policy, which was to last till the defeat of the PNP government in 1980. This phase was marked by a heightened use of rhetoric and a more intensely ideological commitment to change on the part of the Manley administration. In the speeches he made during his visit, and increasingly afterwards, Manley identified 'capitalism' and 'imperialism' as the forces which were blocking his government's aspirations at every point. It was within this context that the theme of 'destabilisation' of the Jamaican polity and economy by external forces began to be asserted by the government. Domestically, the strategy worked to the extent that the PNP won the elections of 1976, albeit at the cost of destroying the coalition of social forces which it had previously represented. Externally, the consequences were highly damaging.

Manley reacted to the threat from imperialism by seeking to promote a deeper Third World solidarity. For him the critical test came not long after his return from Havana, when the Cubans sent troops to Angola. As we have seen, Manley insisted in spite of US warnings on declaring Jamaica's support for Cuba's action. Manley has himself argued that it was Jamaica's position on this question which was the decisive turning-point in the Ford administration's attitude towards his government.[20] State Department officials, by contrast, have contended that it was the tenor of the whole Jamaican–Cuban relationship which resulted in US hostility to Jamaica. Whatever the truth of the matter, the subsequent negative

19. Cited in Lewis, 'Issues and Trends' in Stone and Brown, op. cit., p. 73.
20. Michael Manley, *Jamaica: Struggle in the Periphery* (London, 1982), pp. 115–17.

reports on Jamaica in the North American press, the economic antagonism which led to reduced US aid, the possible covert funding of the opposition, and ultimately the strictures of the IMF were the principal factors which brought the Manley government down.

The striking feature of Jamaican foreign policy in this period is that it was not used to ameliorate these threats. In fact, its radical hue deepened. It was as if the government, depressed by its domestic economic problems, thought it could use an expansive foreign policy to offset these difficulties. The result was inconsistency and the pursuit of a foreign policy which, in the words of one analyst, 'increasingly became devoid of content or local implication and was merely political symbolism'.[21] In particular, Jamaica continued to identify itself with a number of socialist governments, including that of Cuba. Exchanges between the two countries were actually strengthened, a new recruitment drive for the '*brigadista*' programme was held, and Castro made his long-awaited visit to Jamaica. For his part, the Cuban leader handled the situation with impeccable diplomacy: he vowed not to interfere in Jamaican internal affairs and expressed his gratitude that the previous JLP government had at least maintained consular relations with Cuba. The Jamaican government awarded Castro the Order of Jamaica, the highest Jamaican honour given to non-Jamaicans, designating him 'a giant in the struggle against imperialist intervention and aggression'.[22]

The Manley government defended its efforts to establish relations with socialist and communist countries as part of its short-term need to seek financial resources for the Jamaican economy and its long-term strategy of effecting a reorganisation of international economic relations. However, the evidence suggests that the gains attained were massively outweighed by the consequential loss of support from traditional sources. Nowhere was this more true than in the case of Cuba. Whatever tangible benefits to Jamaica resulted from Cuban aid, there can be no doubt about the negative net effect of the close ties that were established. In US government circles Cuba's relationship with Jamaica was perceived as part of a conscious Cuban design to spread the influence of communism within the Caribbean. Alternative explanations, couched in the language of an honourable solidarity between underdeveloped countries, were

21. P.W. Ashley, 'Jamaican Foreign Policy in Transition: From Manley to Seaga', Caribbean Institute and Study Centre for Latin America Working Paper No. 5, Inter-American University of Puerto Rico, San Germán, 1984, p. 7.
22. *Daily Gleaner*, 14 Oct. 1977.

regarded as naive at best and a deliberate deception at the worst reckoning.

This even applied during the relatively liberal phase of policy which marked the first two years of the Carter administration. However, the presence in the US administration of friends of Jamaica like Andrew Young gave the Manley government one last chance to repair its relations with the United States. Again, it was Manley's penchant for the dramatic in international relations which prevented this. In September 1979 he travelled to Havana to deliver an address to the Non-Aligned summit. His reference to the significance of Lenin's contribution to world history, his general praise of Cuba, and his specific call for Puerto Rico to enjoy self-determination were all unfavourably received in Washington, so eliminating the final possibility that a rescue package for Jamaica's beleagured economy might be mounted by the United States.

In addition, there was the continuing domestic political impact of the Cuban connection to consider. The JLP had boycotted Castro's visit in 1978 and used the occasion to renew its allegation of a secret PNP commitment to a communist agenda. In the deteriorating economic circumstances of the time, this message had greater political importance than ever before. The JLP took the hint and under Seaga's leadership made the link with Cuba the main plank of its campaign against the government. It called for the withdrawal of the Cuban ambassador to Jamaica on the grounds that he had been a member of the Cuban secret service; accused the PNP of planning to introduce a one-party state in Jamaica along Cuban lines; and bitterly denounced the mood and content of Manley's speech to the Non-Aligned Movement. Opinion polls testified to the effectiveness of this propaganda, which must be regarded as part of the explanation of the PNP's crushing defeat in 1980.

Fighting communism. The tenor of the JLP's politics in opposition left no doubt as to what its policy towards Cuba would be when it came to office: the relationship would be swiftly and decisively dismantled. Indeed, Seaga announced at his swearing-in ceremony as prime minister that, even 'at this moment', a message was being delivered to the government of Cuba calling for the withdrawal of its ambassador, Ulises Estrada.[23] The haste with which the decision was taken ensured Seaga extra publicity and set the tone for the conduct of foreign policy by the new administration. It marks the beginning of the fourth, and current, phase in the post-independence history of

23. 'A New Beginning', Prime Minister Seaga's speech at his swearing-in, Agency for Public Information pamphlet, Nov. 1980.

Jamaica's external relations. What Seaga promised was the pursuit of a 'balanced' foreign policy similar to that followed by the JLP administration before 1972. In that context the cooling of relations with Cuba and even Estrada's expulsion were only to be expected. A year later, however, the government took the unprecedented step of breaking off relations completely. According to the official statement, tapes found in the possession of the chairman of the PNP Youth Organisation indicated that several men on Jamaica's 'most wanted' list had been given safe refuge in Cuba. This was deemed an action not befitting a 'friendly government'. The Cubans were given twenty-four hours to return the criminals and, failing that, forty-eight hours to close their embassy in Kingston and withdraw all their personnel. The argument was highly dubious, and was widely regarded as being so throughout Jamaica.

The Seaga government's rabidly anti-Cuban posture cannot be understood without grasping the broader thinking which underlies it. This is to demonstrate to the US government the sincerity and extent of its commitment to the fight against communism in the Caribbean. The *quid pro quo* was to be the provision of sufficient US economic assistance to prevent the re-emergence of socialist politics in Jamaica or any other part of the region. While still in opposition, Seaga called several times for the development of a greater US interest in the Caribbean, and in government he has devoted the major part of his diplomatic efforts to the nurturing of this link. Travelling regularly to the United States he has talked to businessmen, bankers and travel agents, as well as government officials and politicians. Such 'balance' as has been achieved in Jamaican foreign policy has resulted from the endeavours of Shearer, as deputy prime minister and Minister of Foreign Affairs, to maintain some Jamaican contact with Third World organisations and other Third World governments. Jamaica thus retains its membership of the Non-Aligned Movement, continues to oppose apartheid and still calls for the pursuit of the North-South dialogue. In none of these areas of policy, however, does it carry conviction or display leadership. It is clear to all that the global range of Jamaican foreign policy, which attracted such attention in the 1970s, has been replaced by a narrow concentration on traditional ties.

Conclusion

Where does this leave Jamaica and Cuba? The answer at the time of writing is 'as far apart as ever'. The two states have danced to four different tunes over the course of more than twenty years, but only rarely have they been in step. Their relationship as two independent states began on proper, if distant, terms. Consular relations were established and maintained. This was followed by the discovery that they had common social and economic problems, and that there was scope for political cooperation, mediated initially through formal ambassadorial channels and latterly by means of exchange visits of ministers. Co-operation grew into an anti-imperialist alliance, which was eventually pushed to breaking-point by the conflicting demands of the rival geopolitical systems to which the two states primarily belong. Breakdown led to divorce, and the present situation of two close neighbours which do not recognise each other diplomatically.

It is a sad story, but one which contains a lesson: Jamaica and Cuba need to develop a consistent relationship. This they can do if certain rules are observed. Its basis must inevitably be common hemispheric membership and common Third World solidarity - a sharing of problems so obvious as not to require argument. Its conduct, however, must take note of the dual reality of a dominant US interest in the entire Caribbean, alongside the Soviet Union's long-standing interest in Cuba in particular. This means that in present geopolitical conditions it is not likely that Jamaica and Cuba will be allies - but they do not necessarily have to be enemies.

10
JAMAICA AND CARIBBEAN INTEGRATION

Relations between the territories of the Commonwealth Caribbean have always been governed by the underlying paradox of the region's geography. It must never be forgotten that the West Indies are a chain of islands, stretching from Jamaica on the western tip of the northern Antillean range, through the Leeward and Windward Islands, to Barbados and Trinidad at the south-eastern point of the archipelago, and embracing the two mainland territories of Belize and Guyana at either end. The distances involved are considerable - Jamaica is fully 1,000 miles from the eastern Caribbean, and Belize is some 700 miles west of Jamaica. Moreover, water undeniably separates peoples more effectively than land. As one writer has testified, 'Polynesians and Melanesians, more at home with the ocean, make it a highway instead of a barrier, but the Caribbean Sea more often constrains and attenuates the social network'.[1] Yet the facts of geography do, paradoxically, impose a unity: separated by sea though they may be, the territories of the West Indies clearly constitute a 'region' in the geographic sense, being more or less contiguous in location; the Leewards and Windwards, in fact, are close enough together for them to be within sight of their nearest neighbours. In other words, the frame of reference for the Commonwealth Caribbean is at one and the same time the island *and* the region. Historically, this dualism has been internalised within the minds of those native to or concerned with the area, and has engendered persistent doubts as to whether the island or the region is the appropriate political and economic unit. Hence the history of intra-regional relations in the Commonwealth Caribbean has come to acquire a schizophrenic character, exhibiting simultaneously the stamp of integration and fragmentation.

The federation

Although 'closer union' and functional co-operation had long been familiar themes of political discussion in the region, the first major drama of that history in the modern era concerned the establishment of a federation as the means to political decolonisation. In this

1. D. Lowenthal, *West Indian Societies* (London, 1972), p. 8.

respect, the breakthrough came with the despatch which the then Secretary of State for the Colonies in the British government, Oliver Stanley, sent to representatives of all the British West Indian colonies in March 1945, inviting them to meet with him at Montego Bay in Jamaica to discuss a positive advance towards federation. The initiative was long overdue. By the end of the war the idea of federation had come to be taken for granted by the new generation of elected leaders in the eastern Caribbean. Even in Jamaica (where the federal notion was embraced much later and in a less emotional way), leaders like Norman Manley had been impressed by their experience of the various inter-island links which had evolved over the preceding two decades. There also existed considerable common ground between the West Indian leadership and the British government. According to the British official view at the time, it was 'clearly impossible in the modern world for the present separate communities, small and isolated as most of them are, to achieve and maintain full self-government on their own'.[2] The reasoning here was that certain minimum criteria of size (economic resources, population and territorial area), which countries as small as Jamaica and Trinidad, and, much less, Barbados, did not fulfil, were necessary for a colony to be 'viable' and thus to be able to claim and sustain sovereign status. From this point of view, federation was a means of increasing the effective size of the West Indian territories to a point where they became eligible for self-government as a single unit.

Within these limits, the attitude of the British government towards the West Indies was benevolent, and regional leaders endorsed without question the prevailing assessment of the implications of small size. At Montego Bay, for example, Norman Manley argued in very similar terms to the British government that it was 'impossible to suppose that every single one of these territories, or perhaps even the largest of us, can achieve alone the basic services which it is the whole aim of politics to create and make possible for the common man.'[3] At times there seemed almost to be a unity of spirit between British policy and West Indian thinking. The Fabian background of Manley and other leading figures of the federation period and their confidence in the British Labour Party prevented them from renouncing the 'values of empire' and, indeed, attracted them to the

2. *Memorandum on the Closer Association of the British West Indian Colonies*, Cmd. 7120 (London, 1947), Part II, paragraph 11.
3. *Proceedings of the Conference on the Closer Association of the British West Indian Colonies, Montego Bay, Jamaica, 11–19 September 1947*, Col. no. 218 (London, 1948), submission of Mr N.W. Manley.

ideal of Dominion status for the future West Indian federation. There was certainly no need for them to bang on the door of the Colonial Office, demanding federation and independence from an intransigent British government. The consequence of this broad consensus of purpose was that the West Indian leaders found themselves engaged in negotiation, not with the Colonial Office over the *principle* of federation, but with each other over the *details* of the structure of the proposed federal constitution. It was a task which proved to be much more fraught with problems than anyone had anticipated, and it gradually took its toll of the participants. When the planning stage was at last completed - eleven long years later - in January 1958, the West Indian spirit, as Springer observed, 'was at a very low ebb and only momentum carried forward the unifying process'.[4]

Since 1947 circumstances had changed radically in two ways. First, all the territories of the region had advanced constitutionally under the British policy of granting measures of self-government to individual islands throughout the very period in which they were supposed to be hammering out a common political fate within a federation. The seeds of dissension over this question were sown at Montego Bay, when the delegates declared that the political development of the 'several units of the British Caribbean territories . . . must be pursued as an aim in itself, without prejudice and *in no way subordinate* to progress towards the federation'.[5] Bustamante, who was the leader of the Jamaican delegation, gave the conference full warning that unless federation and self-government came together, those territories which were more advanced constitutionally would be held back, and that this would be unacceptable. He was not heeded. Universal adult suffrage, which had already been granted to Jamaica in 1944 and Trinidad in 1946, was extended to Barbados in 1949 and to the Leeward and Windward Islands in 1951. As if that were not a sufficient indication of the prizes to come, ministerial government was established in Jamaica in 1952, then in Trinidad and Barbados, and was even granted to the Leewards and Windwards in 1956.

Secondly, both Jamaica and Trinidad, the other leading West Indian territory, had experienced vast economic improvements in the years after 1947, chiefly because both countries appeared to have

4. H.W. Springer, *Reflections on the Failure of the First West Indian Federation* (Harvard, 1962), p 42.
5. *Report of the Conference on the Closer Association of the British West Indian Colonies, Montego Bay, Jamaica, 11-19 September 1947*, Cmd. 7291 (London, 1948), Resolution 2. My emphasis.

succeeded in initiating policies of industrialisation. Their governments had erected the institutional and legal apparatus necessary to attract an inflow of foreign capital, and subsequently enjoyed the resultant growth of manufacturing enterprises. In addition, bauxite production began in Jamaica in 1952 and expanded swiftly, while in Trinidad the volume of oil production more than doubled over the years 1947–58. Indeed, in terms of their overall gross domestic product, Jamaica and Trinidad were among the fastest-growing economies in the world in the decade after 1947.[6]

The combined effect of these changing circumstances undermined the political basis of the federation. As Sir John Mordecai put it, 'the desire for self-government now began to work against Federation, instead of in its favour.'[7] It did so largely because the idea that federation was an indispensable prelude to the attainment of West Indian self-government gradually lost relevance as the region's leaders came to perceive that the world-wide process of decolonisation had drifted so far past its original conception of what constituted a feasible new state that it was beginning to incorporate territories as small as their own. They also increasingly realized that the planned federation, so far from being in the vanguard of the region's march towards self-government, was actually not a very convincing vehicle in which to make the journey.[8] In the economic sphere, too, the changes described raised doubts about the necessity for joint regional action in order to be able to secure economic development. Springer has testified that, whereas in 1947 the economic position of Jamaica

> had been such that it was natural to believe that union with the Eastern Caribbean territories, including oil-rich Trinidad, was the best if not the only avenue to economic improvement, by 1958, the position had changed; it was possible to hope with some confidence that Jamaica would achieve on her own the self-sustaining economic growth that would lead her eventually into the ranks of the 'modernised' and developed countries.[9]

6. For a fuller account of the economic history of Jamaica and Trinidad in these years, see O. Jefferson, *The Post-War Economic Development of Jamaica* (Kingston, 1972), and S.D. Ryan, *Race and Nationalism in Trinidad and Tobago: A Study of Decolonization in a Multiracial Society* (Toronto, 1972), pp. 384–428.
7. J.S. Mordecai, *The West Indies: The Federal Negotiations* (London, 1968), p. 33.
8. The federal constitution finally agreed upon still did not add up in constitutional terms to full internal self-government, a status which was granted to Jamaica just a year after the federation had been inaugurated, and to Trinidad and Barbados before it was conceded to the federation itself.
9. Springer, op. cit., pp. 18–19.

Some Jamaican industrialists even felt that this could be facilitated by withdrawing altogether from the federal venture and openly seeking association with the United States and Canada.

These were important changes of perception. Just as the region's sense of common destiny was eroded under pressure from what Etzioni has called 'uneven internalisation',[10] so the governments of the larger territories grew in self-confidence. In Trinidad, for a time, this new assertiveness was channelled into a demand for a strong, centrally directed federal system. In Jamaica it developed into a virulent localism. With the benefit of hindsight, some have seen the various inter-unit struggles of the federal period as evidence of a principled confrontation between a powerful Hamiltonian vision of federation, as advocated by Trinidad, and a looser Jeffersonian notion of federation, as favoured by Jamaica. In reality the conflict was a baser, less high-minded affair, which could more aptly be called 'Jamaica versus the Rest'.[11]

The history of the period 1947–62 is very much the story of the limitation of the planned and actual powers of the federal government – whether over taxation, customs duties or other matters – in successive attempts to make the resulting balance of responsibility between centre and units acceptable to Jamaican opinion, and its most sceptical voice, Bustamante. It was Bustamante's opportunistic resistance to the federation which at a very early stage forced Norman Manley to go on the defensive in his espousal of the federal cause, discouraged him subsequently from assuming the prime ministership of the federation, which was his for the taking in 1958, and finally turned this most convinced federalist into a narrowly insular negotiator in all his dealings with his regional colleagues. At the end of the final inter-governmental conference of 1961, it was clear that Jamaican pressure – which reached its peak with the proposal to submit to a binding referendum of the Jamaican people the question of membership of whatever federal structure was finally decided by the conference – had won a complete victory. The majority of Manley's demands had been conceded, including the exclusion of the federal government from any responsibility for the collection of income tax or the promotion of the region's industrial development. By this stage, too, Trinidad's earlier magnanimity had faded and had been replaced by a Jamaican-like determination not to allow its own entrenched economic interests to

10. A. Etzioni, *Political Unification: A Comparative Study of Leaders and Forces* (New York, 1965), p. 149.

11. For an excellent discussion of these themes, see G.K. Lewis, *The Growth of the Modern West Indies* (New York, 1968), pp. 377–83.

be prejudiced by handing over too much power to the federal centre.

From the federalist point of view the unfortunate truth was that in the last resort neither the government of Jamaica nor the government of Trinidad was prepared to endanger in any way the economic growth which each was presiding over. Indeed, as economic units, the members of the federation competed more than they collaborated, a situation well illustrated by Jamaica's attempts to set up its own oil refinery in direct competition with Trinidad's position as the leading oil refiner in the Commonwealth Caribbean. In the face of these sorts of policies, the federal government was unable to make any headway in the direction of the economic integration of the region. It failed even to establish a customs union, without which, as every report on the question emphasised, a federation becomes an absurdity.[12] In the end, all that was left to represent the hopes and aspirations of federationists throughout the West Indies was a weak and powerless central Cabinet – in one dismissive phrase, 'just a lot of Federal Ministers running about Port of Spain spreading joy'.[13]

In sum, then, the fate of the federation was settled by its inability to become anything more for the larger islands than a forum for the expression of regional rivalries. It had always been seen in the West Indies as a means to an end, latterly as the gateway to independence, and never as an end and an ideal in its own right. When this argument was finally invalidated by Britain's intimation to Norman Manley in January 1960 that Jamaica was eligible for independence on its own, the little remaining substance to the federation was removed and only the formal structure remained. The negative vote of the Jamaican people in the referendum of September 1961 merely applied the *coup de grâce*.

The establishment of CARIFTA

The formal dissolution of the federation in June 1962 undoubtedly marked the end of an important phase in the history of Caribbean

12. See *Report of the Commission on the Establishment of a Customs Union in the British Caribbean Area* (McLagan Commission), Col. no. 268 (London, 1950); *The Plan for a British Caribbean Federation. Report of the Fiscal Commissioners* (Caine Report), Cmd. 9618 (London, 1955); and *Report of the Trade and Tariffs Commission* (Croft Report), West Indies Federal Government Port of Spain (1958). For a commentary on these reports and a discussion of the politics of a customs union during the federation period, see Mordecai, op. cit., esp. pp. 42–3, 48–50, 55–6, 59–60, 163–4, 214–6, and 264–7.
13. E. Williams, 'Speech to PNM Special Convention, 27 January 1962', *The Nation*, 2 Feb. 1962.

integration, but it did not in the event bring the curtain down, as many feared it would. Gradually it came to be perceived that federation was but one manifestation of the regional idea and that forms of regional *economic* integration were perhaps more appropriate to the needs of the mid-to-late 1960s. Both Jamaica and Trinidad had become independent in 1962, Guyana and Barbados following in 1966. Even the small Leeward and Windward Islands were granted Associated Status in 1967, an arrangement which conceded full internal self-government but kept responsibility for defence and foreign affairs in the hands of the British government. In other words, the region was for the first time beginning to feel the cold draught of self-government.

The various governments felt themselves to be under pressure on several fronts. They were concerned about the region's lack of economic development - as opposed to growth which was in any case starting to come up against the limitations of small market size. They were anxious too about the future prospects of their vital exports of primary products in the light of Britain's application to join the European Economic Community and its possible abandonment of the Commonwealth preference policy; and they were alarmed by the way that opportunities for migration to Britain, the United States and Canada were being steadily whittled away. In these circumstances, 'unity in adversity' seemed to most Commonwealth Caribbean governments to be a slogan worth supporting.

It was thus primarily as a means of economic salvation that the case for regional integration was reconsidered. The first move was made by the governments of Barbados and Guyana when they announced in July 1965 that a free trade area would be established between their territories not later than January 1966. It was stated that participation by other states in this proleptically named 'Caribbean Free Trade Association' (CARIFTA) would be welcomed, and that the ultimate objective was the creation of a viable economic community and common market for all Commonwealth Caribbean territories which desired them.[14] Reactions were mixed, and the pace of advance was slower than anticipated, but eventually it was agreed that a regional conference of officials would meet in Guyana in August 1967 with a view to preparing a plan for the implementation of regional economic integration to be put to a summit meeting of heads of government in Barbados two months later. This was the fourth in a periodic series of inter-governmental conferences which had been taking place since

14. See *Agreement establishing the Caribbean Free Trade Association*, Dickenson Bay, Antigua, 15 Dec. 1965.

the middle of 1963, and was the first to be attended by the leaders of all the Commonwealth Caribbean territories. It was, in consequence, the largest and most prestigious gathering of West Indian leaders since the days of the federation and, to their credit, the leaders seized the opportunity. A deal was clinched – the adoption of the CARIFTA agreement by the region as a whole, thereby providing the prospect of trading benefits for the more industrialised states; the establishment of a secretariat in Guyana to preside over the agreement; and the promise of the simultaneous creation of a regional development bank to channel development finance on favourable terms to the smallest and poorest states in the area.

However, the deal did not hold for long in the face of the hard-nosed attitude of the government of Jamaica. Throughout its history Jamaica has maintained an aloof attitude towards the eastern Caribbean. Jamaicans were widely viewed by other West Indians as aggressive and assertive, while the prevailing Jamaican image of the 'small' islands of the eastern Caribbean was one of poverty, parochialism and a desire to exploit Jamaica's greater prosperity. The experience of the federation had served only to reinforce these stereotyped attitudes and to widen the psychological gulf between the two ends of the Caribbean. In the intervening years such disrespectful feelings had been cloaked by the formal politeness of intergovernmental diplomacy, but they had never been extinguished, least of all within the ranks of the JLP, the party that led the fight against the federation and had since formed the government. Jamaica played its part in the widening embrace of regional economic integration during the mid-1960s, and it was obviously one of the countries with the most to gain from freer trade. Yet it had done so with obvious reluctance, and although its delegation went along with the broad sweep of the decisions made at the October 1967 Heads of Government Conference, the Jamaican government's commitment to the integration movement was demonstrably less wholehearted than that of its eastern Caribbean partners. By the same token, its interest in extra-regional economic links with North America and with the EEC – including the possibility of being granted Associated Overseas Territory status by the latter – was somewhat greater than that of its neighbours. In consequence, in all its dealings with the other governments of the region the Jamaican government was calculating and cautious in outlook, alert to the balance of advantage, and constantly looking for signs that the eastern

Caribbean states were really striving to revitalise the idea of federation.

In a sense, the domestic political environment in Jamaica gave the government no alternative. The response the government delegation received on its return from the Barbados conference was far removed from the warm congratulations proffered in the region's other capitals. It was summed up by two pieces in the *Gleaner*: an editorial intimating that, as a result of the conference decisions, Jamaica would have to forgo some industrialisation,[15] and an article by the 'Political Reporter' questioning whether, in the light of the events of September 1961, 'any Government in Jamaica has the moral or constitutional right to place us in any relationship with the rest of the West Indies whatsoever which would to any great extent affect our sovereignty without putting the matter for decision by a Referendum to the voters of Jamaica'.[16] In response to this, the government's Ministry Paper, reporting on the conference, drew special attention to Jamaica's willingness to co-operate with the other countries of the Caribbean, 'so long as it is clearly understood that the operative words are "economic cooperation" and NOT "political integration" '.[17]

The issue on which the JLP government decided to demonstrate its independence of its eastern Caribbean partners was the location of the proposed Caribbean Development Bank (CDB). Although nothing had been decided in Barbados, the suggestion had been made that the Bank should be sited in St Vincent, one of the least developed of the West Indian islands, precisely in order to symbolise its function as an instrument of integration designed to benefit such countries most of all. The Jamaican delegation had argued at the time that the decision should be taken not on sentimental grounds but on sound banking criteria, a theme which its representatives continued to develop in subsequent meetings of officials. Disaffection with the arrangements for the location of the Bank spilled over into other areas, and Jamaica failed to send a ministerial representative to an important Trade Ministers' conference in Guyana in February 1968, thereby provoking the rumour that it was about to renege on its commitment to CARIFTA.

Such doubts were not assuaged by the explanatory statement issued by the country's High Commissioner to Trinidad, one of the

15. Editorial, *Daily Gleaner*, 4 Nov. 1967.
16. The Political Reporter, *Daily Gleaner*, 5 Nov. 1967.
17. Government of Jamaica, *Ministry Paper No. 57. Report on the Fourth Heads of Government Conference* (Kingston, 1967). Paper's emphasis.

only two Jamaican officials to appear at the conference. 'Jamaica', he declared,

> does not believe in the principle of marrying in haste and repenting at leisure. The suggestion has been made that other Commonwealth Caribbean countries contemplate going beyond a Free Trade Area and are looking towards the establishment of a common market with a common external tariff. The decisions of the recent Barbados Heads of Government Conference contain no commitment by the Caribbean countries to this immediate end. Certainly the CARIFTA document which was accepted as the basis of our economic co-operation does not contemplate a common market at this stage.[18]

Despite this reiteration of interest in free trade, the statement revealed a major difference of approach. The Jamaican government conceived of regional free trade merely as an exercise in economic *co-operation*, and declined to discuss economic *integration*, the term always used by the other West Indian territories. The distinction was much more than semantic, although it revealed itself less in the immediate preoccupation with planning free trade than in regard to the subsequent strategy of market integration. The Jamaican government feared that questions such as the uniformity of external tariffs and the free movement of persons and capital, apart from nudging just a shade too close to the great taboo of political integration, might prejudice the negotiation of an Association agreement with the EEC (which it considered to be the more important goal). Thus Jamaica's policy towards the Caribbean region took the form of participation in the economic integration movement, tempered by a concern to restrain it at all costs from reaching a point where it closed off other economic options.

Moreover, with regard to the establishment of CARIFTA itself, there is no doubt that, in addition to its reservations over the siting of the Bank, the Jamaican government was being urged by its own manufacturing interests to think again. These argued that unless they were allowed to import raw materials duty-free, as was generally the case in the rest of the region, free trade would place them at a competitive disadvantage with their eastern Caribbean rivals.[19] They would be unable to compete effectively in both the

18. Statement by A. Wright, Jamaican High Commissioner to Trinidad, *Trinidad Guardian*, 21 Feb. 1968.
19. Brewster and Thomas provide empirical confirmation of the Jamaican manufacturers' argument that, in terms of labour productivity, they were at an absolute cost disadvantage in comparison with Trinidad. See H. Brewster and C.Y. Thomas, *The Dynamics of West Indian Economic Integration* (Kingston, 1967), pp. 10–11.

enlarged regional market and in the domestic Jamaican market, with obvious and damaging consequences for existing industries and the prevailing level of employment in the island. The Jamaican government perhaps thought, as many commentators certainly did,[20] that the apprehensions of the business sector were also due to loss of nerve after so many years of being sheltered behind the protection of high tariff barriers. But, given the structure of the Jamaican political economy, it could not afford to ignore their views.

The Cabinet was far from united on the issue. Pro- and anti-CARIFTA factions emerged behind the respective figures of the Trade Minister, Robert Lightbourne, and the Finance Minister, Edward Seaga. Their particular offices naturally gave them a different perspective on regional integration – the one seeing the trade advantages at first hand, the other having to handle the Bank negotiations – but, more than this, the two were engaged in a personal battle for ascendancy within the Cabinet, a struggle with which the integration issue became entangled. In the short term, it was resolved in favour of the regional connection, for soon after the Trade Ministers' meeting, Shearer (newly installed as Prime Minister) cabled all the other heads of government to reaffirm his country's readiness to participate fully in CARIFTA as from 1 May 1968, as originally agreed.[21]

Yet this move did not presage any softening of the Jamaican position on the location of the Bank. Indeed, the row was almost immediately propelled into the open. The cause was the continued lobbying by a number of eastern Caribbean delegations in favour of St Vincent as the most suitable site. On behalf of the Jamaican government, Seaga reminded his fellow Finance Ministers of the criteria agreed to, and witheringly demonstrated that St Vincent failed to meet them in every respect. He was also at pains to point out that:

> . . . The Caribbean region does not consist of the eastern region alone. Regional members extend from Belize in the west to Barbados in the east to the Bahamas in the north to Guyana in the south. The region is not the eastern Caribbean, . . . and when I look at my map, which might be different from the maps of others, I see St Vincent located in the eastern Caribbean well distant from a section of it and, at the same time, if I am to

20. See, for example, The Industrial Reporter, *Daily Gleaner*, 9 July 1968.
21. The cable noted Jamaica's acceptance of the principles and provisions of the CARIFTA agreement and promised appropriate steps to implement this acceptance in the Jamaican legislature. It was reprinted in full in the *Daily Gleaner*, 23 March 1968.

look at Jamaica, I see it lying on an east-to-west axis almost midway between Belize and the eastern Caribbean and a north-to-south axis almost midway between the Bahamas and Guyana.[22]

Seaga's speech gave full voice to Jamaica's contempt for the eastern Caribbean and dramatically exemplified a favourite Jamaican thesis that the rest of the region depended upon the relative strength of its economy. Jamaica, he observed, was to be the largest subscriber of equity to the Bank, its contribution being 43 per cent of the regional total; he therefore felt justified in rejecting Guyana's proposal that the headquarters of the Bank be located in St Vincent and a branch in Jamaica. Jamaica would support the motion if it was put the other way round, but would otherwise have no alternative but to 'withdraw from membership in the Bank'.[23]

Objectively, the Jamaican case was strong. The Bank's initial capitalisation was such that it needed, from the outset, to attract investment from commercial and governmental sources outside the Caribbean, a task in which the greater wealth of Jamaican contacts with the international economic system would perhaps have proved useful; it also required the presence of a central bank in which to deposit its funds. Yet to give undue emphasis to the rationality of the Jamaican argument would be to misunderstand the highly-charged atmosphere of the negotiations. 'Horse-trading' was very much in evidence, and Jamaica did not have that much to trade. Because of its 'minimalist' commitment to the integration movement and its general reluctance to associate fully with the West Indian region, the other territories were prepared, on balance, to risk Jamaica's complete withdrawal rather than give in to its aggressive bargaining tactics. At a subsequent meeting, Barbados was put forward as a compromise site; Jamaica again objected, demanded a vote, and lost, at which point its delegation dramatically walked out and flew home. Such a reaction obviously revived doubts about Jamaica's participation in the whole integration process and led to further delay. Nevertheless, despite the boost that the Bank decision had given to the belief that the rest of the region was 'ganging up' on Jamaica to force it into a regional association, the implications of which had not been fully spelled out, the supporters of CARIFTA within Shearer's government were still able to point to the benefits potentially attainable from free trade and to the consequences of not joining; for then Jamaican goods would have had to compete with

22. E. Seaga, 'Speech to the Conference of Ministers of Finance on the Caribbean Development Bank, Georgetown, 25–26 March 1968', mimeo.
23. Ibid.

tariff-free products in the Caribbean market while facing a duty barrier themselves. In the end they won the day: on 18 June 1968 the Jamaican House of Representatives approved a motion authorising the Jamaican government to seek membership of CARIFTA, and on 26 June the first CARIFTA Council – which at that stage consisted only of representatives from Antigua, Barbados, Guyana and Trinidad – approved an application from Jamaica to join. Regional integration was again afloat. Jamaica was on board, but only just.

The first four years

During the first few years of its existence, CARIFTA lived constantly in the same politically charged atmosphere that had surrounded its birth. Fragility was always its most striking characteristic, and disintegration an ever-present possibility. From the very start, problems arose. Jamaica's belated accession to the agreement had done nothing to bridge the gap separating her from the rest of the West Indies, and in the last few months of 1968 disaffection with Jamaica grew in strength. It annoyed eastern Caribbean opinion that the Jamaican government showed no sign of relenting over the question of its non-participation in the Bank. On the contrary, it worked assiduously, if in secret, to fashion a 'Western Caribbean Bank' with headquarters in Nassau, comprising Jamaica, the Bahamas and British Honduras (now Belize). The gulf was further widened by the 'Rodney incident' in October 1968, when Shearer publicly blamed the violent demonstrations at the Mona campus on the subversive activity of students and staff who were predominantly (he said) West Indians from the other islands.[24] Shortly afterwards, Seaga spoke of the effect the non-Jamaicans at Mona were having in 'emasculating Jamaican nationalism', and revealed that the government had 'given thought' to the establishment of a Jamaican university.[25] The University of the West Indies was the longest-standing symbol of West Indian integration, and this threat to its existence immediately set off moves to call an emergency summit of the region's leaders not only to discuss the future of the University but to try and reach a *modus vivendi* on the Bank issue. Shearer did not formally object, but he demonstrated his lack of concern for regional issues – to the anger of his colleagues – by three times finding proposed dates for the conference inconvenient.

24. *Daily Gleaner*, 19 Oct. 1968.
25. Ibid., 3 Nov. 1968.

When, finally, the Fifth Heads of Government Conference opened in Trinidad in February 1969, the issue at stake was not just UWI, or the Bank, but once more the future of Caribbean integration itself. The smaller, less developed countries felt that Jamaica was being allowed to dictate the pace and direction of the integration movement in a way detrimental to their well being, and only postponed a planned meeting to review their position in CARIFTA when at last dates for a full summit conference were agreed. Their intention to take a hard-headed look at their role in Caribbean integration was not concealed. In the event, agreement was reached with surprising ease. It was decided to establish the Bank at the earliest possible date in 1969 and to proceed immediately with the recruitment of staff. Jamaica's 'special problems' were diplomatically recognised and, having refrained from reopening the debate about the Bank's siting, the Jamaican government was allowed to reserve its final decision on whether or not to take part till 31 May 1969.[26] The dispute over the future of UWI was allowed to dissipate of its own accord. In the end, the Jamaican government had been represented by neither Shearer nor Seaga, but by Lightbourne, whose conciliatory manner and personal commitment to the concept of regional free trade did much to improve the atmosphere. On his way to Trinidad he visited some of the Leeward and Windward Islands and managed throughout the conference to give the impression that, whatever the Jamaican government's position might be on particular subjects, it was not rigidly opposed to the interests of the eastern Caribbean.

What really contributed to the preservation of the integration movement was the fact that the more developed countries began to garner some of the benefits promised by the advent of regional free trade. While the heads of government were engaged in crisis diplomacy, CARIFTA itself was working quite efficiently. There were 'growing pains', such as an early dispute over the entry into Guyana of paper bags produced in Jamaica and a clash over alleged Jamaican discrimination against Trinidadian textiles, and in keeping with the tension inherent in intra-regional relations, the wrangling was conducted in a declamatory fashion. Yet they were exceptional incidents which belied the efforts made by the CARIFTA Council and the Secretariat to ensure that the agreement functioned smoothly.

Jamaica, for example, achieved a number of early successes by

26. See *Final Communiqué of the Fifth Heads of Government Conference* (Port of Spain, 1969).

winning export orders in the eastern Caribbean market, especially for its manufactured goods – items like chemicals and paints, footwear and fabrics, matches, stoves and metal products generally. In fact, the extent of the rise in Jamaican exports to the rest of the region seemed to come as a pleasant surprise to most Jamaicans. In March 1969 the *Gleaner*'s 'Trade Reporter' wrote:

> There is no doubt that, in spite of what appeared at first to be apathy or even distrust of closer economic association with the rest of the Commonwealth Caribbean, the Jamaican businessman – manufacturer as well as exporter – has become fully alive to the fact that there is everything to be gained, and nothing whatsoever to lose, from trading with these neighbours of ours.[27]

CARIFTA, he concluded, 'has been a good thing for Jamaica'.[28] This change in Jamaican public opinion also fostered a more conciliatory attitude towards the Bank. Given the initial success of CARIFTA and growing awareness of the widespread feeling in the less developed countries that Jamaica should not be allowed to reap the benefits of CARIFTA without paying the costs involved in the Bank, the view began to develop that the government might, after all, be wise to have second thoughts over its refusal to join the Bank. It would be senseless, the argument ran, to provoke the other islands and unnecessarily risk the disintegration of the free trade arrangements by giving the impression that Jamaica had joined CARIFTA purely from selfish motives. Perhaps the contribution to the Bank's funds required of Jamaica should simply be regarded as an investment which would pay off in the form of increased trade benefits in the future? With this change of mood in Jamaica, the JLP government's view of the regional experiment gradually changed too. If it never came to enthuse over economic co-operation, it grew at least to tolerate it. Accordingly, on 28 May 1969 – only a day or so before the deadline set by the Fifth Heads of Government Conference – Shearer sent a telegram to his colleagues around the region, announcing Jamaica's willingness to participate in the Bank, 'subject to review of some aspects and provision of certain safeguards to be discussed'.[29] These were resolved, with the consequence that in February 1970, some twenty-one months after CARIFTA's inauguration, the Caribbean Development Bank was able to begin work.

The final establishment of the Bank could not, however, dispel the

27. *Daily Gleaner*, 9 March 1969.
28. Ibid.
29. Quoted in ibid., 30 May 1969.

reality that little else had been done to advance the integration process in the ways that had been planned. As part of the CARIFTA agreement, an annex had been signed envisaging various other steps such as the erection of a common external tariff, the harmonisation of fiscal incentives to industry, and the initiation of joint industrial development projects in the area. In the jargon adopted, this was to constitute the 'deepening' phase of the integration movement. Guyana, Trinidad and Barbados were broadly in favour of embarking on this road, albeit perceiving the need to do so with differing degrees of urgency. The countries in doubt were the less developed islands, which already felt excluded from the benefits of integration, and once again Jamaica. The JLP government insisted, quite correctly, that it was only formally committed to regional free trade - economic *co-operation* - and that it had never hidden its disinclination to advance to a set of arrangements which would be construed throughout Jamaica as fully embracing economic *integration*. There was inevitably a certain loss of autonomy in the harmonisation of fiscal incentives, which in the eyes of the Jamaican government was a negative point; and since Jamaica's tariffs were already high, there was arguably no economic advantage to be gained from the adoption of a common tariff code throughout the region. It was felt that free trade alone would bring, and indeed had already brought, such trading benefits as were to be had from the regional connection. In short, there appeared to the Jamaican government to be no good reason for altering its well-tried policy of keeping the eastern Caribbean at arm's length. Very much the opposite, in fact: some of the island leaders in the eastern Caribbean were beginning to flirt again with the notion of political integration, while the increasingly radical economic policies of the Guyanese government under Forbes Burnham were anathema to the conservative philosophy which characterised Jamaican élite opinion.

Hence, for all these reasons the 'deepening' approach met with resistance from Jamaica, which favoured instead the idea of simply 'widening' the scope of the free trade area to embrace countries in the wider Caribbean with a Spanish, French or Dutch heritage. When one adds to these conflicting views the simultaneous failure of regional governments to reach agreement on a common policy towards the European Economic Community following the re-opening of negotiations about British entry, it is easy to appreciate the stress which the integration movement was experiencing at the end of 1971.

From crisis to CARICOM

In the event, disintegration was averted. The necessary reinvigoration of the integration movement came just in time, and from the most unlikely source. Although the reasons for the JLP's loss of office in Jamaica in February 1972 had little to do with regional integration – the issue itself played no part in the campaign – the election of the PNP government under Michael Manley did significantly alter the environment in which CARIFTA had to survive. Historically the PNP's record on the question of Caribbean integration was very different from that of the JLP. It was the party which had supported the federation and which campaigned to stay in during the referendum in 1961. Although it had formally opposed entry into CARIFTA when the issue came to a vote in the Jamaican House of Representatives in 1968, it did so on the grounds that free trade was a weak form of economic integration – 'neither fish nor fowl nor red herring', as its spokesman put it at the time.[30] It has been suggested too that the phenomenon of 'opposition politics' was instrumental in dictating PNP tactics on that occasion.[31] In other words, the PNP had remained broadly true to its early regional ideals. The problem was that it had tended to be afraid of espousing regional integration too enthusiastically, because its own loss of power in 1962 in the elections immediately following the referendum had been almost universally attributed to its support for the federation.

Michael Manley understood the dilemma into which the PNP seemed to have been driven, and was determined to lead his party away from it. In an article entitled 'Overcoming Insularity in Jamaica', which appeared in the American journal *Foreign Affairs* at the end of 1970, he expressed his commitment to CARIFTA in particular and to regional economic integration in general:

> Although many counsel caution – and indeed, this may be the price of ultimate success – one wishes that a greater sense of urgency attached to the whole exercise. . . . Clearly, regional economic development provides a more ample prospect in a situation where peaceful progress cannot be more than a marginal possibility. Yet, although the aisle is clearly marked, we seem to come to the altar of history like a reluctant bride with faltering step and lowered gaze.[32]

30. *Jamaica Hansard. Proceedings of House of Representatives,* 1,1 (1968-9), p. 251.
31. By the phenomenon of 'opposition politics' is meant 'the dictum that Opposition parties oppose'. R.E. Wiltshire, 'Regional Integration and Conflict in the Commonwealth Caribbean', unpublished Ph.D. thesis (University of Michigan, 1974), p. 131.
32. M. Manley, 'Overcoming Insularity in Jamaica', *Foreign Affairs*, 49, 1 (1970), p. 106.

What was needed, he suggested, and what indeed he appeared to possess was 'a tough-minded recognition that national survival, like business survival, is a matter of margins, and that regionalism can provide the framework in which internal markets are increased, external bargaining power enhanced and international recognition maximised'.[33] For the benefit of those who still doubted, he outlined four specific advantages which, in his view, Jamaica stood to gain from regional integration: first, the potential fulfilment of what he saw as an urgent need for all the countries of the region to 'develop techniques for handling trade and other relations with the outside world on the basis of a common policy';[34] secondly, the increased negotiating strength which could be achieved by handling major foreign capital interests, like the bauxite companies, on a common basis; thirdly, the provision of a base from which to enter the mainstream of Third World politics; and fourthly, and less tangibly, the psychological boost which regional integration would give to the security and dignity of the West Indies. In Manley's estimation the choice lay between 'a low road of self-imposed, insular impotence and a high road of adventure into Caribbean regionalism leading on to the wider possibilities of Third World strength'.[35] The rhetoric may have been dramatic, but it was not wholly misplaced, and if the coming to power of a PNP government in Jamaica in 1972 had less adventurous consequences for integration than Manley's peroration might have led one to expect, it certainly denoted a marked change of strategy in Jamaica's policy towards the development of CARIFTA.

The integration movement immediately took on new life. In a number of post-election interviews, widely reported throughout the region, Manley spoke eloquently of Jamaica's new interest in economic integration and of his government's continuing and unqualified support for the regional character of the University of the West Indies.[36] At the time the University was embroiled in a dispute over a Jamaican proposal to reduce the level of entry qualifications and institute a preliminary year of study in a number of departments. The suggestion had been fiercely opposed by the Trinidadian Prime Minister, Dr Eric Williams, partly out of a characteristically Oxonian desire to maintain 'academic standards'

33. Ibid.
34. Ibid., p. 107.
35. Ibid., p. 110.
36. See *Trinidad Guardian*, 16 and 19 March 1972.

of entry, and partly out of a reluctance to subsidise (in effect) the education system in islands which, unlike Trinidad, had inadequate secondary schools. Under questioning, Manley at least showed signs of flexibility on this point. A more concrete indication of the new government's attitude came over a row which had broken out between Trinidad and Jamaica over the imposition in Jamaica of new controls on the import of textiles from Trinidad. Soon after taking office, the new Jamaican Minister of Trade and Industry took action to defuse the tension by announcing that Jamaica, without further ado, would revert to the import licensing arrangements that had been in force previously. It was a move clearly meant to be seen as a gesture of intent.

For their part, the technocrats of the Secretariat responded eagerly to the opening that was being offered them. They had long tried to secure Jamaica's agreement to the 'deepening' programme, and become increasingly frustrated at their inability to do so. They now quickly organised the preparation of a booklet designed to give publicity to the various issues confronting the regional movement: *From CARIFTA to Caribbean Community*. Published in July 1972, this set out the further steps which the Secretariat thought were needed to achieve what it referred to as 'meaningful economic integration'.[37] The programme embraced most of the issues over which the regional governments had been deliberating since 1967: a common external tariff and protection policy; the harmonisation of fiscal incentives; a common policy on foreign investment; rationalisation of regional agriculture; the development of a regional industrial policy; co-operation in tourism and in fiscal and monetary affairs; agreement on external commercial policy, especially towards the European Economic Community; the adoption of further measures to enable the less developed countries in the region to benefit from economic integration; and the extension of functional co-operation into new areas. However, it also contained some items which were yet to be discussed, like the co-ordination of foreign policy.[38] The significant factor was that for the first time all these diverse ideas and proposals were brought together and conceived as a package. For, as the Secretariat admitted, what was really being proposed was more than just an injection of new life into CARIFTA; it was that the time had come

> to take the decisions necessary to convert CARIFTA into a Caribbean

37. Commonwealth Caribbean Regional Secretariat, *From CARIFTA to Caribbean Community* (Georgetown, 1972), p. 5.
38. Ibid., pp. 57–112.

> Common Market. At the same time, as common services and areas of functional co-operation generally are extended, a certain amount of tidying up is required. These two processes . . . point to the need to give a formal juridical basis to the entire complex of regional co-operative arrangements, including the Heads of Government Conference, which is the apex of the entire regional movement.[39]

Thus was born the idea of CARICOM - the Caribbean Community and Common Market.

The actual process of negotiation of the new Community was long and difficult. The less developed countries - led by Montserrat, the smallest of them - battled hard for concessions in their favour, but the Jamaican government's new enthusiasm for regional integration was unwavering. The governments of the other larger territories - Trinidad, Barbados and Guyana - supported the change, and the bargaining eventually came to a successful conclusion with the signing of the Treaty of Chaguaramas in July 1973. It expressed agreement on the establishment of CARICOM, and laid out three broad areas of co-operation which, taken together, extended far beyond the limited commitment to free trade represented by CARIFTA. The first was the furtherance of regional integration by the creation of a common market; the second was the expansion of functional co-operation in such fields as health, education, transport and meteorology; and the third was the co-ordination of foreign policy among the fully independent states of the Community. On paper, therefore, CARICOM was a distinctly ambitious venture.

Divisions and difficulties

Yet almost as soon as the Treaty of Chaguaramas was signed, the Caribbean Community ran into problems. Its inauguration coincided with the period - late 1973 to early 1974 - when the world economy was entering the severe crisis from which it has still fully to recover. As a petroleum-exporting country - the only one in the region - Trinidad was partly insulated from the problem, and indeed benefited to the extent that substantial sums of money accrued to its exchequer as a result of the new high price of oil. However, the other territories all suffered serious budgetary and balance of payments deficits and experienced significant increases in the cost of living, to which they responded with a variety of stern

39. Ibid., p. 125.

measures, including higher levels of taxation, the intensification of import restrictions and exchange controls, and the imposition of subsidies on vital consumer goods. Barbados was temporarily helped by the high price of sugar on the world market in 1974, and Jamaica and Guyana were able to increase the revenue yield from their bauxite and alumina industries by imposing extra levies and taking into public ownership recalcitrant foreign companies. But in all these cases only palliatives were provided. Before long, Jamaica and Guyana turned to the IMF and, as we have seen, the PNP regime in Jamaica was forced to undertake a series of devaluations, public expenditure cuts and generally restrictive measures in a vain attempt to regenerate the country's economy. It was, in short, an unpropitious time for the launching of a renewed programme of regional economic integration, for the effects of these difficult economic circumstances unavoidably took their toll of CARICOM's prospects. The then Secretary-General of the Community, Dr Kurleigh King, commented: 'The ink was hardly dry on the signatures of the Treaty when the full force of the international economic crisis struck the bottom out of everything we had hoped to accomplish.'[40]

The first breach in the unity achieved when the Community was established came to light in 1975. In a speech in April that year, Dr Eric Williams complained that the recent advances in Caribbean integration were being prejudiced by the way in which many of the member-states of CARICOM were making bilateral economic arrangements on supplicant terms with wealthy Latin American countries.[41] He was particularly concerned by the growing economic penetration of the region by Venezuelan 'petro-dollars', and in a subsequent speech he contemptuously denounced the visits of several of his regional colleagues to Venezuela as 'pilgrimages to Caracas'.[42] What angered Williams most in this connection was the economic co-operation agreement signed with Jamaica in mid-1975, whereby Jamaica agreed to supply Venezuela with considerable quantities of bauxite and alumina for a planned new aluminium smelter, and Venezuela agreed to contribute part of the cost of a new alumina processing plant to be built in Jamaica. In his view, it was 'simply not possible' to regard this treaty 'as anything but a calculated attack'[43] upon the proposal, announced a year earlier, to build two CARICOM aluminium smelters to be owned jointly by the

40. K. King, 'Statement by the Secretary General of the Caribbean Community Secretariat to the 9th Annual Meeting of the Board of Governors of the Caribbean Development Bank, Barbados, 25–6 April 1979', mimeo., p. 7.
41. See *Trinidad Guardian*, 27 April 1975.
42. Ibid., 16 June 1975.
43. Ibid.

governments of Trinidad, Jamaica and Guyana. That project had been widely regarded as a major step forward in Caribbean integration since it was the first time that an attempt had been made within CARICOM to establish a joint production programme between member-states. However, as a consequence of the row over Venezuela, the scheme was cancelled, and Williams informed a special convention of his party: 'One can only take so much, and I have had enough. To smelt or not to smelt, no big thing'.[44] Manley responded by insisting that the CARICOM smelter had not been deprived of its viability by Jamaica's other deals, and he succeeded in isolating Williams within the region on this issue.

Nevertheless, the row had grave implications for the co-ordination of foreign policy within the Commonwealth Caribbean. By this criterion it was unquestionably a major lapse - for two reasons. First, it showed that nearly all the countries of the region (with the exception of Trinidad) were seeking bilateral deals with Venezuela instead of trying to formulate a common regional front on the matter. Jamaica was particularly culpable because the nature of its particular deal with Venezuela - concerned, as it was, with the bauxite-alumina industry - clearly affected CARICOM policy in the same sphere. (One can be absolutely sure from the vehemence of Williams's reaction that Manley had not consulted the Trinidad government before agreeing to the deal.) Mention should also be made of the fact that one of the other equity contributors to the new Jamaican alumina plant was to be the Mexican government, which agreed to put up no less than 29 per cent of the cost in return for Jamaica contributing 29 per cent of the equity of a new aluminium smelter to be built in Mexico. This deal did not arouse Williams's anger in the same way that the Venezuelan agreement had done, but it irritated the technocrats in the Secretariat, since the Caribbean Community states, as a group, had signed a trade and co-operation agreement with the Mexican government in July 1974. It illustrated, again, the tendency to bilateralism in Jamaican foreign policy and highlighted the diverse interests that were beginning to appear in the external trade policies of the various Community states in direct contravention of the commitment they had given in the CARICOM Treaty to seek the co-ordination of policy in such matters.[45]

Secondly, the row highlighted the existence of two different and

44. Ibid.
45. Andrew Axline suggests that an early draft of the CARICOM Treaty in fact included an article which went a long way towards a commitment to a co-ordinated external economic policy, but that Jamaica, among others, objected to it so strongly that a much watered-down version eventually appeared as Article 34 of the Annex to the Treaty. W.A. Axline, *Caribbean Integration: The Politics of Regionalism* (London, 1979), p. 203.

conflicting concepts of the countries that comprise the Caribbean – what might be termed the 'Williams Latin American doctrine' and the 'Manley Latin American doctrine'. The main ingredients of the Williams doctrine were a deep suspicion of the motives of certain Latin American states in relation to the Commonwealth Caribbean and the consequent avoidance of relations with them. It was founded upon a definition of the Caribbean which firmly excluded the Central and Latin American states except, of course, for what had once been the three Guianas. Williams was accordingly contemptuous of a Venezuelan plan to call a conference of 'the Caribbean basin' – 'whatever that may be', as he put it[46] – and saw it as his mission to preserve 'the Caribbean personality' and not allow it to be lost in a wider Latin American identity. In May 1975 he succeeded in getting the United Nations Economic Commission for Latin America, at its sixteenth session, to create within its structure a Caribbean Development and Co-operation Committee, designed to perform just that function. By contrast, the hallmarks of the 'Manley Latin American doctrine' were friendship, co-operation and closer ties with Latin American states in the battle to create a 'new world economic order' in favour of developing countries. It, in turn, was obviously based upon a strong sense of the Caribbean's geopolitical affinity with Latin America. Faced with this clash, the other states of the region tried to remain agnostic. They were manifestly prepared to look upon Venezuela as a friend for as long as resources were being proffered in their direction; on the other hand, they had all had much longer than Jamaica to become attuned to the idea of West Indian unity, and remained emotionally more committed to that goal. In this respect, at least, the greater global range of the foreign policy pursued by Michael Manley in Jamaica worked against the narrower interests of Caribbean regional integration.

After the angry exchanges of mid-1975, tension within the integration movement lessened for a time, but was renewed in 1977 when Guyana and Jamaica came under attack for restricting their imports even from CARICOM partners as a means of alleviating their financial situation. This produced a real crisis in the Community, to the point where fears were expressed about the future of the whole integration movement. Notwithstanding the fact that the Treaty permitted the imposition of quantitative restrictions on regional goods in the face of serious balance of payments difficulties, the plight of Jamaica and Guyana aroused little sympathy, and some

46. *Trinidad Guardian*, 16 May 1975.

form of retaliation seemed likely. Trinidad, in fact, announced its intention of instituting its own system of quantitative controls on the import of regional goods. Some twenty-three products were identified as requiring protection.[47] In the event no action was taken, and the immediate crisis passed when both the Jamaican and Guyanese governments signalled their intention to restore the value of their imports from the rest of the region to at least 1975 levels as soon as possible.

Nevertheless, by exposing the fragility of the free trade regime, which was as much the mainstay of CARICOM in its early days as it had been of CARIFTA, the quarrel constituted another setback in the progress of Caribbean integration, and clouded the atmosphere within the Community. For part of 1978, the Secretariat found it hard to persuade the governments even to convene CARICOM meetings. The morale of the staff began to suffer, especially since the post of Secretary-General was left vacant for fifteen months during 1977 and 1978. All these factors meant that CARICOM was failing to develop into the deeper form of integration to which the Treaty aspired. An attempt to reach agreement on the terms on which foreign investment could enter the region failed; virtually no regional industrial programming had been achieved; and although a Regional Food Corporation was set up in an effort to organise joint schemes of agricultural production, it took a long time to become operational.[48] Even the Community's long-standing attempt to redesign the so-called 'origin rules', which determined the products which were eligible for free trade treatment, had not been brought to completion by the end of 1979.

In short, CARICOM survived the trauma of the international economic crisis of the 1970s, but at the cost of stagnation. However, the crisis did more than just temporarily disrupt the movement. In retrospect, it can be seen to have changed the nature of the circumstances in which Caribbean integration had to be pursued in several crucial ways. First, the approximate balance of power which had previously existed between the larger constituent states of CARICOM was fundamentally changed. An enormous gap opened up between Trinidad, which became unequivocally the dominant economy and pivotal state within the region, and Jamaica and Guyana, which were both experiencing severe economic and political difficulties. Secondly, the high degree of ideological consensus in the region was shattered by Guyana's adoption of

47. Government of Trinidad and Tobago, *White Paper on CARICOM* (Port of Spain, 1979), p. 35.
48. See Axline, *Caribbean Integration*, pp. 136–57.

'co-operative socialism' in 1973, Jamaica's proclamation of 'democratic socialism' in 1974 and the emergence of the revolutionary government in Grenada in 1979. Admittedly, the extent of the left-right split in the area was often exaggerated by commentators, but it was nonetheless a further source of real problems. Thirdly, the rapport between the heads of government of Commonwealth Caribbean territories which had contributed so much to the transformation of CARIFTA into CARICOM disintegrated as personal relations between Eric Williams, Michael Manley and others cooled. Finally, there was the fact that the Caribbean was increasingly being opened up to international competition as several major powers began to vie for influence in the region's affairs. This had dangerous implications for regional unity, since it contained the possibility that the region might again become, as it had been historically, a battleground for the rivalries of outside powers.

Cold War politics

This tendency was greatly exacerbated by the result of the 1980 presidential election in the United States. Ronald Reagan was determined to 'win back' the Commonwealth Caribbean for the West, and cared little whether in the process the chances for deeper regional integration were damaged. Reagan's main weapon was the Caribbean Basin Initiative, the programme of assistance for the Caribbean and Central America which eventually emerged from the original call for the installation of a 'Mini-Marshall Plan' for the region made by Edward Seaga on his post-election visit to Washington early in 1981.

Even before the CBI was formally announced, the thinking behind it was plain. In June 1981, CARICOM's Foreign Ministers tried to fire a shot across the bows of the Reagan ship of state by officially noting their concern at the economic pressure being exerted by the United States on the government of Grenada. They were particularly alarmed by US attempts to stipulate that a grant to the Caribbean Development Bank to help the least developed countries in CARICOM should not be disbursed to that island. The Bank's directors had voted unanimously to reject this grant on the grounds that it would contravene that aspect of the Bank's charter which prohibited it from interfering in the political affairs of any member-country. Whatever they felt about the particular merits of Grenada's revolution, and many were very critical, the region's governments were not prepared to see one of their number isolated by an external power. As the Foreign Ministers put it in their communiqué, they condemned any effort 'to subvert Caribbean regional institutions built up over long years of struggle'.[49]

With the need to defend their own interests in the forefront of their minds, the ministers soon met again to formulate a set of common principles as the basis for negotiation with the United States over the CBI. They insisted that the programme be open to all territories in the region, that it should respect the sovereignty and integrity of states, reflect national priorities for development and, finally, 'be directed towards strengthening ongoing regional integration and cooperation'.[50] Yet when the details of the CBI were unveiled by President Reagan in a speech to the Organisation of American States in St Lucia in February 1982, it was immediately apparent that these points had not been met. As many had feared from the outset, the CBI divided the Commonwealth Caribbean, rather than uniting it. Following Reagan's flattering reference in his speech to Jamaica as a country which, since the change of government in October 1980, was 'making freedom work',[51] Seaga was quick to applaud the proposals. The plan, he said, was 'bold, historic and far-reaching in concept'.[52] He also indicated that he would not object to Grenada's exclusion, since other countries would be taking care of its needs. In the rest of the region, however, the reaction varied from disappointment to bitter condemnation.

Criticism came from a variety of angles. One strand of opinion expressed concern at the emphasis placed on investment and trade, rather than on direct development aid capable of building up the region's inadequate infrastructure. Another viewpoint, held especially strongly in the eastern Caribbean, felt that Jamaica had been excessively favoured in the proposed allocation of supplemental assistance under the CBI. There was also, as expected, considerable disquiet over the Reagan administration's preoccupation with the communist threat and its insistence on excluding Grenada and Nicaragua, as well as Cuba, as possible beneficiaries of

49. 'Sixth Meeting of the Standing Committee of Ministers of CARICOM Responsible for Foreign Affairs', Caribbean Community Secretariat, press release 46/1981.
50. 'Memorandum by the Caribbean Community (CARICOM) Secretariat' (86/81-82/FM) in *Fifth Report of the Foreign Affairs Committee of the House of Commons: Caribbean and Central America*, together with an Appendix; part of the proceedings of the Committee relating to the report; and the minutes of evidence taken before the Committee with appendices (London, 1982), p. 304.
51. 'The US Caribbean Basin Initiative', speech to the Organisation of American States, Washington, DC, 24 Feb. 1982, p. 8.
52. *Latin America Regional Report: Caribbean*, RC-82-03, 26 March 1982.

the CBI. With these different positions being taken up, all CARICOM could do as a body was equivocate. The divisions could be seen clearly in the March 1982 statement of the Standing Committee of Foreign Ministers. It carefully observed that 'while the US proposal did not adequately address all of the issues or fulfil expectations for a comprehensive plan for the development of the economies of Caribbean states, it nonetheless would make a positive contribution'.[53] The group's former unity could be salvaged only with respect to the governments' collective disappointment that 'there were no specific elements of supporting their own intergovernmental institutions such as CARICOM and the Caribbean Development Bank'[54] and their complaints about the information-sharing proposal which a recipient-country under the CBI was required to enter into as part of a bilateral executive agreement with the United States. The principle that participation in the CBI should be open to all CARICOM countries was also reaffirmed, although everyone knew that Seaga's Jamaica was not going to forgo the benefits of the programme for this cause. The whole saga was a vivid illustration of what happens when external definitions and perceptions interfere with regional aspirations. On the most important test of foreign policy co-ordination yet faced by CARICOM, its ranks had been split and the integration movement further weakened.

That was not all. The region's growing involvement in Cold War politics was also very nearly the cause of CARICOM's complete disintegration, with Grenada once more the main issue at stake. As we have already seen, the heads of government conference held in Ocho Rios in November 1982 – which, as the first such meeting to have been held in seven years, was conceived as a 'relaunch' of Caribbean integration – was dominated by an attempt to expel Grenada from the organisation. Seaga was at the centre of the attempt and remained bitterly opposed to the whole revolutionary experiment being conducted in Grenada. When the Grenadian government collapsed in bloody disarray in October 1983 and an invasion was mounted, he was quick to involve Jamaica and subsequently to reap his electoral reward. From his point of view, and that of the United States, the prize was a victory in the battle against communism. For CARICOM, by contrast, the damage was enormous. It was not just that the region disagreed about what to do in Grenada once the coup had taken place, but that the 'invading

53. 'Seventh Meeting of the Standing Committee of Ministers of CARICOM Responsible for Foreign Affairs', Caribbean Community Secretariat, press release 16/1982.
54. Ibid.

states' deliberately connived to conceal their intentions from their remaining CARICOM partners – Trinidad, Guyana, Belize and the Bahamas. As accounts of the events show, several participants in the crisis meeting of CARICOM heads of government which took place in Port of Spain during the weekend after Bishop's murder already knew of, and had contributed to, the decision to invade.[55] No mention was made of such a commitment during the CARICOM discussions, which focused exclusively upon the sanctions that could be brought to bear on the military regime in Grenada.

Understandably in the circumstances, the other leaders – especially George Chambers, the Prime Minister of Trinidad, and Forbes Burnham, then President of Guyana – felt that they had been made to look foolish. Chambers's statement to the Trinidad parliament after being told of the invasion made no attempt to conceal how offended he felt. Subsequent off-the-record remarks by other Trinidadian ministers also suggested that they would be very reluctant to work again with Seaga, whom they saw as mainly responsible for the deception. Seaga, for his part, launched an equally fierce attack on unnamed regional leaders whom he accused of treachery for having leaked to the Grenadians some of the details of the invasion plan. 'In days to come', he told a party rally, 'you may know of whom I speak because it will be very hard for me to sit around a table with them'.[56]

In such a recriminatory atmosphere it is hardly surprising that many commentators should have wondered whether CARICOM would finally fall apart. The critical factor was whether anyone would actually work to destroy it, and for this reason the debate tended to revolve around the role of Seaga. Other Commonwealth Caribbean leaders had known for some time that Seaga wanted to include in CARICOM other generally pro-U S countries in the wider Caribbean region, such as Haiti and the Dominican Republic. In the few weeks after the invasion of Grenada, a number of them came increasingly to suspect that his real aim was the replacement of CARICOM with a looser organisation embracing non-Commonwealth Caribbean countries and excluding any existing member-state that was not willing to accept US leadership in regional affairs. He fuelled these fears by speaking of the possible creation of a CARICOM Mark II,[57] arousing the suspicion in Trinidad and Guyana that he was making a threat directed mainly at them.

55. See Anthony Payne, Paul Sutton and Tony Thorndike, *Grenada: Revolution and Invasion* (London, 1984), pp. 151–3.
56. *Jamaican Weekly Gleaner*, 9 Nov. 1983.
57. *Latin America Regional Report: Caribbean*, RC-83-10, 9 Dec. 1983.

Nothing more has been heard of this idea since then, and it is doubtful whether it would be to Seaga's advantage to seek to break up CARICOM. More probably, he is attracted by the idea of widening the membership and thus of turning the organisation into a strategic and economic alliance representing United States interests in the wider Caribbean. There is no doubt that, under the JLP, CARICOM matters are a low priority in Kingston compared with the question of Jamaica's and the region's dealings with Washington. Should the two come into conflict, the former must not only be subordinated to the latter, but if possible brought into a position of support for it.

On these terms CARICOM survives, albeit in emasculated form when the original ambitions of some of its architects are remembered. Indeed, meetings of heads of government, ministers and technocrats continued automatically in the period after the Grenada invasion in a kind of collective pretence that nothing important had happened. The work of the organisation in the economic and functional areas continues and is not to be disparaged, but it is not the same as asserting an independent regional voice in respect of the major international issues besetting the Caribbean – the goal to which CARICOM aspired when it was first established in 1973. Jamaica, under Seaga's leadership, accepts US leadership, and that restricts the rest of the region. As throughout its modern history, Caribbean integration can only prosper when it is enthusiastically espoused by the government in power in Jamaica.

EPILOGUE
POLITICAL PROSPECTS

At the end of this survey of modern Jamaican politics it is appropriate to examine the country's immediate political prospects. Contemporary politics revolve around the next general election, and have done so ever since the 'non-election' of December 1983. The campaign began immediately that contest ended, has ebbed and flowed in the interim, and may not be brought to a conclusion until the end of 1988 - the latest moment at which Seaga can go to the country within the terms of the constitution. The controversial events of 1983 also shaped the parameters of the subsequent party battle. The JLP knew that it could not pull off the same trick a second time, and has had to manage the economy with a constant eye on the need to create a favourable electoral opening in the not too distant future. The PNP has presented itself as the defender of the country's democracy, and has tried as much as possible to avoid re-defining the nature of its commitment to socialism. The WPJ has had to cope with the burden of its support for the Grenadian revolution in a period when, as a result of the collapse of that experiment, the political centre of gravity of the whole Caribbean region has moved to the right. In other words, since 1983 each of the parties, for different reasons, has had some cause to be uneasy about its immediate prospects. This final chapter thus looks at 'the politics of non-confrontation' which has characterised Jamaica in the years following the 1983 election, and considers how long it is likely to continue.

The JLP's political strategy since 1983 is not difficult to describe: it has been to hang on - long enough for some economic improvement to turn up to justify the 'suffering', as the present austerity is popularly referred to among the people. By stages, the government was forced to acknowledge that its policy of structural adjustment was causing widespread hardship and to accept that from time to time some tactical amelioration of the worst aspects was necessary. In spite of bargaining with the IMF on terms, the broad thrust of the adjustment policy was adhered to, and the promise that recovery was just around the corner was maintained through the gas price protests and the 'general strike'. After securing the latest IMF agreement in February 1987 Seaga claimed that 'overall structural adjustment' had been achieved and the time was now right to move into phase two of the programme, with the emphasis on growth rather than austerity. This growth still needs to be securely generated, but it cannot be denied that extra time has been won for its achievement by the tactic of repeatedly holding out the prospect.

While waiting for its economic policies to bear fruit, the JLP has striven to keep political life at a low ebb. In particular, it has sought to avoid challenges which might have demonstrated the true extent of its mid-term unpopularity, and thus damaged long-term confidence in its ability to deliver the economic goods. The biggest problem it faced in this connection was local elections. Due originally in June 1984, they were first postponed a year by agreement of the parties while new voter registration was completed. In April 1985, however, Seaga suddenly announced a plan to abolish more than half the number of parish council seats and transfer their functions to government departments. Protests were fierce, and the scheme was ultimately withdrawn – but only when it was too late to organise elections, as then scheduled, for June 1985. A further postponement at the end of the year meant that, when the local elections were finally held in July 1986, they were more than two years overdue. The result was still a heavy defeat for the JLP. After a campaign fought wholly on national issues, the PNP took 57 per cent of the vote, compared to 43 per cent for the JLP, and won 126 of the 187 available local authority seats. The WPJ received only a few votes in the handful of divisions it contested. Manley immediately renewed his long-standing demand for an early general election, to which Seaga was predictably unresponsive though admitting that his party would have to look closely at 'its organisation, its candidates, its MPs, its policies and . . . its leadership'.[1]

Signs of internal dissension had been visible within the JLP for some time. Some senior figures had long disliked the extent of Seaga's pre-eminence within the party's leadership. His repudiation of the agreement with the PNP over the voting register at the time of the 1983 election made them uneasy, and they felt increasingly concerned over the future of their party as opinion polls during 1984 and 1985 consistently showed a large PNP lead. In October 1985, for example, the JLP chairman, Bruce Golding, also Minister of Construction, called for fresh ideas on economic policy, saying that he feared a majority of the Jamaican people believed that a change of government would end their economic difficulties. The veteran JLP politician, Robert Lightbourne, also came out of retirement to accuse the government of 'abdicating' its responsibilities to the electorate.[2]

1. *Caribbean Insight*, Aug. 1986, p. 1.
2. See ibid., Nov. 1985.

As might have been expected, the local election results considerably exacerbated these internal conflicts. In October 1986 Seaga tried to assert his authority over the party by threatening to resign – first as JLP leader, and in the following year as Prime Minister. Although widely regarded as a bluff, the manoeuvre enabled him to reshuffle his cabinet, dismissing or moving ineffectual ministers and bringing in to the government several loyalists whom he appointed to junior positions, often in the ministries of critics and potential rivals. However, the strains in the party were not brought to an end: in January 1987, just as the IMF agreement was being finalised, Douglas Vaz – who had been demoted from his position as Minister of Industry and Commerce in the reshuffle – resigned, saying that the agreement would have further detrimental effects on manufacturing industry. The fact is that the political difficulties of the JLP remain. The campaigning machinery, which it built up in opposition in the late 1970s, was neglected for a long time once office was achieved, and the party did not find it easy to revive support – on demand, as it were – when the going again got tough. Despite occasional private talk about the possibility of Shearer returning to the leadership, the JLP's fortunes are inextricably tied to Seaga, notwithstanding the reservations still felt about his character and policies by older-style JLP politicians who have maintained closer ties with the party's traditional trade union base.

In these circumstances, in a competitive party democracy, one would expect the main opposition party to enjoy the ascendancy. The PNP is no exception: it has had a substantial lead in most opinion polls taken in the mid-1980s and, as the July 1986 local election results amply revealed, it has the ability to turn the preferences expressed in replies to polls into votes. The distribution of the vote in those elections was in exactly the same proportion as that which gave the PNP its huge victory in the 1976 general election. Nevertheless, the PNP's performance as an opposition party has aroused criticism, mainly on the grounds that it has displayed a lack of vigour and campaigning zeal. As indicated previously, the charge is substantially true; it has often given the impression since 1980, and even since 1983, that it is uncertain whether it really wants to resume office.

What is the explanation? For understandable reasons, the party deliberately took time to consider its position after the crushing defeat of 1980. There was an emotional need for soul-searching, and for left and right to argue out their interpretations of the party's failure in government. In February 1981 Manley offered his resignation as leader to the national executive committee, only to have it rejected by a massive majority, thus re-establishing his command of the party, as intended. He immediately insisted upon the ending of all ties, formal and informal, with the WPJ but continued to try to hold together the two mainstream wings of the party. By the end of the year, the PNP was ready to begin 'rebuilding for the future', as the theme of the 1981 party conference put it. The most important decision taken was to proceed with a political education programme for constituency leaders aimed at raising the level of ideological understanding in the party. All PNP officers and candidates were required to attend a specified number of these political education sessions. Two party schools were set up, and much progress was made, but it should be noted that the sector of the party where the political education programme made least headway was the parliamentary group.[3]

The main problem which came to light in the reappraisal undertaken at the 1981 party conference was the desperate situation of the PNP's finances. Up till 1972 it had relied on its allies among the local business class; between 1972 and 1980 it was able to utilize the resources of the state; but after 1980 it depended almost entirely on the small amount of money which could be provided by its union affiliate. This was the main reason for Dr Duncan's removal, once again, as general secretary in January 1983; PNP-oriented businessmen made his replacement the condition for considering their renewal of financial support for the party. His successor, Paul Robertson, was also more associated with the left than with the right, but that did not matter: the point was that Duncan had become the symbol of what businessmen saw as the 'dangerous' wing of the PNP. But even in Duncan's absence, the money did not begin to flow freely and the party has remained in financial difficulty throughout the 1980s. This has inevitably constrained its activities.

For all that, the PNP spent little time in the early 1980s working on its policy and programme. In his address to the 1981 conference, Manley enunciated the party's continuing belief in 'democratic socialism' and declared that in future economic, rather than social, policy would be given priority. At that time another PNP government seemed a long way off, and little serious attention was given to policy development or revision. The party's capture of the lead in the opinion polls in October 1982 took the leadership by surprise and led the 1983 conference to reconstitute the economic commission

3. For a valuable discussion of this programme, see E.H. and J.D. Stephens, *Democratic Socialism in Jamaica* (London, 1986), pp. 265–6.

(first established after the Manley government's break with the IMF in 1980) and charge it with the task of developing a comprehensive economic development plan. That, in effect, was all that had been done when Seaga called the December 1983 election. From that moment, the party's energies turned to focus on the issue of democracy: repeated calls were made for the holding of elections to repair the damage done to the country's political system, especially after what the PNP regarded as Seaga's 'proper' mandate had run out in October 1985.

As this campaign proceeded, the more difficult task of shaping a workable socialist economic policy was given less importance. Part of the explanation for this can be found in Manley's virtual absence from the political scene during much of 1985 due to a serious illness. The left, which is smaller and weaker following the break with the WPJ and the decline in Duncan's influence, was in no position to seize the initiative. Only when Manley's health recovered in time for the annual conference at the end of 1985 did the framework of a new economic policy begin to emerge. According to his speech and other interviews given at the time, a future PNP government would continue to deal with the IMF but on a negotiated rather than a suppliant basis; it would fix and maintain a value for the Jamaican dollar, reverse many of the JLP's policies of economic deregulation, undertake a major exercise in debt re-scheduling, and set up a national planning council, including the trade unions, producer associations and business organisations, to join with the political directorate in preparing a production-based solution to the country's economic crisis. What was not mentioned was equally important, namely any talk of a 'break' with the IMF or the re-nationalisation of privatised concerns. On foreign affairs, Manley spoke of Jamaica's natural friendship with the United States and indicated that he had no wish to alienate a US administration. At the same time, closer relations with Western Europe would be pursued as a potential counter-weight to US pressure. As Manley put it, 'we will also go to Europe because . . . Jamaica stands high in all the great forces of social democracy in Europe'.[4] There was a marked absence of discussion of Cuba and the Soviet Union, although the latter was referred to as a potential market for increased sales of bauxite, something which the Seaga government has itself pursued.

What did the programme add up to? In an interview, Manley condemned the suggestion that the PNP had moved to the right since 1980 as 'a cliché of analysis'.[5] He went on:

4. *Caribbean Insight*, Oct. 1985, p. 1.
5. *Latin America Weekly Report*, WR-85-37, 20 Sept. 1985, p. 6.

> Where the policies of the party are concerned, there is no change. If we are less strident, that's no bad thing: one hopes to God that we've learned something about diplomacy and methodology, especially methodology. Some of the left have become less active . . . but the difference in the party is more of style than substance.[6]

His remarks were fair comment. The party had, in effect, gone back to 1974. It remained committed to a programme which it chose to call 'democratic socialism', but it meant by this the pursuit of a more favourable national relationship with the international economy, improvement of the collective lot of the Jamaican people, and the creative use of the state machine to bring about these changes. That its links with the local capitalist class are closer than for many years is epitomised by the appointment of Claude Clarke, the President of the Jamaica Exporters' Association, to the PNP shadow cabinet in mid-1986. Many 'old guard' ministers from 1972–5, men such as David Coore and Ken McNeil who are known to be on the right of the party, have also come back into leadership positions from time spent working overseas. Under their influence, and with Manley's full agreement, the PNP came to accept that policies such as the former close relationship with Cuba and the 'strident' espousal of the language of class confrontation were politically damaging, and were not essential to its basic programme.

This is where the argument about elections and democracy, as mounted since 1983, fits in. The party leadership believes that it alone is sufficient to mobilise the people in its support. There are, of course, cynical explanations of the PNP's playing down of the socialist question, from the point of view of both those on the right who fear the PNP's hidden agenda and those on the left who regard the party as no more than a front for bourgeois policies. Equally, however, there is the view that it expects to win a future election on its democratic credentials and the JLP's manifest failure to manage the economy. From this perspective, nothing is to be gained by rousing the people to a fervour of socialist expectation which cannot be delivered or which unnecessarily provokes the wrath of the United States, especially with a rather short time to go before President Reagan's term of office comes to an end. Manley's strategy has been to lower expectations and not, as in the past, to raise them to unattainable heights. As he told the party in his 1985 address to the conference, 'no path is easy. What we may finally do or may not do is not a thing I can tell you now. I know I am going to find problems and that I am going to share those problems with you.'[7] To this

6. Ibid.
7. *Caribbean Insight*, Oct. 1985, p. 2.

extent the PNP, though still angrily demanding early elections, actually appears ready to wait for the moment of decision, as chosen by Seaga, in the normal course of a five-year term dating from December 1983.

Mention should finally be made of the WPJ. Although a minor actor in Jamaican politics by comparison with the JLP and the PNP, its role has not been unimportant on a number of occasions since the late 1970s. In particular, its activities have often been used to give substance to JLP charges of communist infiltration of the PNP. However, the WPJ also had to adapt to the post-1983 political situation in the country and adjust its tactics accordingly. The main problem it faced after December 1983 was the reaction to the internecine killings in Grenada. Although it was the PNP which was most widely associated with the Grenadian revolution in the minds of the Jamaican people, the WPJ's politics were in fact closer than the PNP's to the programme of the People's Revolutionary Government in St George's. The party's leader, Trevor Munroe, was invited to Grenada in the midst of the internal conflict to advise on its resolution,[8] and he remained close to events up till the last few days of the regime. What is more, his immediate reaction to the conflict revealed that he was firmly behind the challenge to Maurice Bishop's leadership, regarding it as a necessary step on the way to a deepening of the revolutionary process. Munroe's analysis also gave credence to the view that Bishop's supporters were the aggressors in the shooting which led to his death, in marked contrast to the immediate condemnation of his *execution* offered by both Seaga and Manley.[9] Given the revulsion felt in Jamaica at the Grenada murders, the WPJ lost much of its support by taking this stance.

Its efforts after this event have largely been devoted to recovering that ground. They have been described as the adoption of 'a new line of moderation in Jamaican oppositional politics', calculated in part to capture support from an 'inert' PNP.[10] The evidence adduced for this view was that from mid-1984 onwards the party tried to befriend the churches and, more important, that it began to espouse an alternative programme for the country which 'read very much like a PNP election manifesto: radical nationalism, progressive social

8. Anthony Payne, Paul Sutton and Tony Thorndike, *Grenada: Revolution and Invasion* (London, 1984), p. 128.
9. See Trevor Munroe, *Grenada: Revolution, Counter-Revolution* (Kingston, 1984), pp. 72–4.
10. Harry Goulbourne, 'Oppositional Politics in Jamaica since the Invasion of Grenada', unpublished paper presented to the Centre for Caribbean Studies, University of Warwick, 1985, p. 19.

policies, concessions to the bourgeoisie'.[11] But the comparison is misleading. According to its occasional journal *Struggle*, the party still envisages the formation of a People's Government with WPJ cadres in a vital role, which would unite all patriotic social classes – including progressive elements of the national bourgeoisie – in a battle against the common enemy, defined as imperialism. It is no 'middle-of-the-road' proposal but the classic programme of a Soviet-inspired non-capitalist development path, as pursued in a Caribbean context in Grenada and Cuba. Although in its early phase it accepts a mixed economy and relies on a multi-class political alliance, these are conceived only as steps along the road to the ultimate elimination of bourgeois representation and the creation of a dominant state operated wholly in the interests of workers and peasants. The WPJ cannot openly articulate the theory of non-capitalist development in the context of contemporary Jamaican politics, especially in view of what happened in Grenada, but it would be a mistake to suppose that it is no longer committed to such a path.

Where the party has recently changed tactics is over the matter of fighting elections. In the days of PNP government it preferred to give support to PNP candidates, more or less regardless of whether or not this was welcomed. After the PNP dissociated itself from its former 'ally' in 1981, the WPJ had to decide whether to face the voters openly or concentrate on changing the climate of ideas by operating as a non-electoral party. The serious case for the former option was that it asserted a commitment to the democratic rules of the game at a time when revolutionary methods were discredited in the region. The expedient case was that the party was receiving relatively favourable levels of support in opinion polls in mid-1985. For example, in a Stone poll published in April 1985 but taken in February, shortly after the gas price protests, 10 per cent of respondents said that they liked the WPJ, mainly because they thought it defended the small man and spoke out strongly against injustice and oppression; 1 per cent had no strong positive or negative feelings towards the party; 20 per cent were 'don't knows'; and 58 per cent expressed hostility.[12] Given the traditionally strong anti-communist flavour of Jamaican political culture, the last figure was surprisingly low. It encouraged WPJ leaders to believe that sympathy for the party was growing, and contributed to the decision to contest some wards in the local elections whenever they were held.

11. Ibid., p. 20.
12. *Latin America Regional Report: Caribbean*, RC-85-04, 10 May 1985.

As already indicated, expectations had been falsely raised, and the support gained by the party in July 1986 was very limited. In the aftermath of this disappointment and in the face of declining membership the subsequent party congress decided to try to build the WPJ into a mass party and to suspend electoral participation until this restructuring was completed. It was a decision born of weakness rather than strength, and will be immensely difficult to accomplish. In the meantime the WPJ is not to be regarded as a significant force in Jamaican politics.

The country's political prospects for the near future nevertheless remain uncertain. An election will be called by Seaga at a time of his choosing before December 1988, probably later rather than sooner, with September and October the most likely months. Although JLP ministers tried for a while to create a 'window of opportunity' out of some extraneous issue, they did not succeed. At the end of 1986 it was alleged that PNP leaders had links with the '*ganja* barons'; by April 1987 it was claimed that a senior PNP official had been trying to establish a Libyan terrorist presence in Jamaica; a month later the old tactic of the 1970s was once more revived – the accusation that the PNP was sending young party supporters to Cuba for military training.[13] However, the anti-communist scare will be harder to run than before, given the distance which the PNP has placed between itself and the WPJ, and Manley's frequent and apparently friendly talks with various US State Department officials. Even the right-wing Heritage Foundation has admitted that it is now convinced that Manley is not a communist! This means that ultimately the JLP government's electoral fortunes will be decided by the state of the economy. In this respect it can claim with some justification that economic growth is once again under way, that the bauxite market is improving and that the economy has so far passed the performance tests required under the terms of the current IMF agreement. Indeed, the successful completion of this agreement at the end of March 1988 will prove critical to the JLP's prospects of electoral recovery. A further humiliation involving an IMF imposition of renewed deflation and another currency devaluation would be politically fatal for Seaga. Yet, even assuming that this does not occur (and the Fund is far from being politically illiterate), it is difficult to see how the improvement in the economy could be on a scale sufficient to be of more than marginal electoral benefit to the government. A massive campaign of optimistic official propaganda will be needed to offset the popular memory of the 'suffering' with which the Seaga regime is associated.

In these circumstances it still remains in the PNP's interests to

13. *Caribbean Insight*, Dec. 1986, May 1987 and June 1987.

maintain a low-key style and to hope to inherit power without too much of a struggle. It would be especially propitious for the PNP if this coincided with the election of a Democrat to the US presidency. However, it faces two problems in making this strategy work. The first relates to the health of Michael Manley. The PNP leader was again forced to absent himself from politics for four months between April and July 1987 while undergoing another major operation. He returned to make a powerful speech at the party's September conference and was said, even by the *Gleaner*, to look fit and strong. Nevertheless, the issue of the succession to the leadership of the PNP has been unavoidably placed on the Jamaican political agenda. Manley remains a vital figure in the party's popular appeal and will want to lead the party into the election campaign. Nevertheless, the JLP is bound to raise the question of whether he would be fit enough to sustain the gruelling demands of the prime minister's job throughout a whole parliament and to cast doubt on the qualities and experience of any putative successor. The second problem concerns the increase in political violence, which had already reached a serious level by the autumn of 1987. Many of the worst incidents can be attributed to crime, especially insofar as they relate to drug trafficking between South and North America, in which Jamaica is increasingly involved. But as Seaga nears the end of his term, especially if opinion still seems to be against the JLP, political tension will inevitably increase, since a change of regime in Jamaica's clientelist political system always involves the transfer of jobs and homes between party supporters. The PNP has more to lose from a violent election campaign than the JLP and will therefore need to do all it can, preferably by agreeing a code of conduct with the JLP leadership, to curb the excesses of its more excitable supporters.

To conclude, then, who can be expected to win the 1988 election? Any prediction is a hostage to fortune, and certainly a new element of doubt was generated in August 1987 when an opinion poll gave the PNP 40 per cent of the vote and the JLP 31 per cent. This was a significantly narrower gap between the parties than shown in the latest of the regular Stone polls a month or so earlier, for which the equivalent figures for the two parties were 49 per cent and 34 per cent, and was interpreted by some media commentators as evidence that the JLP was catching up fast. However, Stone demonstrated in a newspaper article that the two polls used a different definition of the uncommitted voter and that, adjusted for this discrepancy, the two surveys were not that far apart.[14] In short, although the PNP's popular support has not increased from its high point reached

14. *Daily Gleaner*, 21 Sept. 1987.

in 1985, and the JLP's following has recovered slightly since its nadir in 1984, the opposition is still well ahead, at least as far as opinion polls are concerned. The time left for the Seaga government to regain its former support is short and the likelihood must be that the PNP will win the election and that Michael Manley will be given another chance to lead his country. The JLP will almost certainly accept the result out of respect for Jamaica's electoral tradition, but may be tempted again while in opposition in the early 1990s, as in the late 1970s, to make the country more or less ungovernable. As for the WPJ, it will again have been the victim of Jamaica's well-entrenched attachment to democratic, capitalist politics.

SELECT BIBLIOGRAPHY

Ambursley, F., 'Jamaica: The Demise of "Democratic Socialism" ', *New Left Review*, 128: 1981, pp. 76–87.

——, 'Jamaica: From Michael Manley to Edward Seaga' in F. Ambursley and R. Cohen (eds), *Crisis in the Caribbean* (London: Heinemann, 1983).

Beckford, G., *Persistent Poverty* (New York: Oxford University Press, 1972).

——, and M. Witter, *Small Garden, Bitter Weed* (Morant Bay: Maroon Publishing House, 1980).

Bell, W., *Jamaican Leaders* (Berkeley and Los Angeles: University of California Press, 1964).

——, 'Independent Jamaica Enters World Politics: The Start of Foreign Policy in a New State', *Political Science Quarterly*, 92: 1977–8, pp. 683–703.

Bradley, P., 'Mass Parties in Jamaica: Structure and Organization', *Social and Economic Studies*, 9, 1960, pp. 375–416.

Brown, A., 'The Mass Media of Communications and Social Change in the Caribbean: A Case Study of Jamaica', *Caribbean Quarterly*, 22(4), 1976, pp. 43–9.

——, and H. McBain, 'The Public Sector in Jamaica' in *Studies in Caribbean Public Enterprise* (Mona, Jamaica: Institute of Social and Economic Research, University of the West Indies, 1983).

Cargill, M., *Jamaica Farewell* (Secaucus, New Jersey: Cinnamon Books, 1979).

Davies, O., 'Economic Transformation in Jamaica: Some Policy Issues', *Journal of International Development Studies*, 19(3): 1984.

Eaton, G.E., *Alexander Bustamante and Modern Jamaica* (Kingston: Kingston Publishers Ltd, 1975).

Feuer, C., *Jamaica and Sugar Workers' Co-operatives: The Politics of Reform* (Boulder, Colorado: Westview Press, 1984).

Girvan, N., 'After Rodney – The Politics of Student Protest in Jamaica', *New World Quarterly*, 4(3): 1968.

——, *The Caribbean Bauxite Industry* (Mona, Jamaica: Institute of Social and Economic Research, University of the West Indies, 1967).

——, *Foreign Capital and Economic Underdevelopment in Jamaica* (Mona, Jamaica: Institute of Social and Economic Research, University of the West Indies, 1971).

——, R. Bernal and W. Hughes, 'The IMF and the Third World:

The Case of Jamaica', *Development Dialogue*, 2: 1980, pp. 113–55.

——, and O. Jefferson (eds), *Readings in the Political Economy of the Caribbean* (Kingston: New World Group, 1971).

Jefferson, O., *The Post-War Economic Development of Jamaica* (Mona, Jamaica: Institute of Social and Economic Research, University of the West Indies, 1972).

Jones, E., 'The Role of Statutory Boards in the Political Process in Jamaica', *Social and Economic Studies*, 19(1): 1970, pp. 114–34.

Kaufman, M., *Jamaica under Manley: Dilemmas of Socialism and Democracy* (London: Zed Books, 1985).

Lacey, T., *Violence and Politics in Jamaica 1960–1970* (Manchester: Manchester University Press, 1977).

Lewin, A., 'The Fall of Michael Manley: A Case Study of the Failure of Reform Socialism', *Monthly Review*, Feb. 1982.

Manley, M., 'Overcoming Insularity in Jamaica', *Foreign Affairs*, Oct. 1970.

——, *A Voice at the Workplace* (London: André Deutsch, 1975).

——, *The Politics of Change: A Jamaican Testament* (London: André Deutsch, 1974).

——, *Jamaica: Struggle in the Periphery* (London: Third World Media Ltd, 1982).

Mills, G.E., 'Electoral Reform in Jamaica', *The Parliamentarian*, 62(2): 1981, pp. 97–104.

——, and P.D. Robertson, 'The Attitudes and Behaviour of the Senior Civil Service in Jamaica', *Social and Economic Studies*, 23(2): 1974, pp. 311–43.

Munroe, T., *The Politics of Constitutional Decolonization: Jamaica 1944–1962* (Mona, Jamaica: Institute of Social and Economic Research, University of the West Indies, 1972).

Nettleford, R. (ed.), *Manley and the New Jamaica* (London: Longman Caribbean Ltd, 1971).

——, *Mirror, Mirror: Identity, Race and Protest in Jamaica* (Kingston: Collins & Sangster, 1970).

O'Flaherty, J.D., 'Finding Jamaica's Way', *Foreign Policy*, 31: 1978, pp. 137–59.

Post, K., *Arise ye Starvelings* (The Hague: Martinus Nijhoff, 1978).

——, *Strike the Iron* (The Hague: Martinus Nijhoff, 1981).

Robertson, P.D., 'Party "Organization" in Jamaica', *Social and Economic Studies*, 21(1): 1972, pp. 30–43.

Robinson, R.V., and W. Bell, 'Attitudes Towards Political Independence in Jamaica After Twelve Years of Nationhood', *British Journal of Sociology*, 29(2): 1978, pp. 208–33.

Stephens, E.H., and J.D., 'Democratic Socialism in Dependent Capitalism: An Analysis of the Manley Government in Jamaica', *Politics and Society*, 12(3): 1983, pp. 373–411.

—, *Democratic Socialism in Jamaica* (London: Macmillan, 1986).

Stone, C., *Class, Race and Political Behaviour in Urban Jamaica* (Mona, Jamaica: Institute of Social and Economic Research, University of the West Indies, 1973).

—, *Electoral Behaviour and Public Opinion in Jamaica* (Mona, Jamaica: Institute of Social and Economic Research, University of the West Indies, 1974).

—, *Democracy and Clientelism in Jamaica* (New Brunswick, NJ: Transaction Books, 1980).

—, 'Jamaica's 1980 Elections: What Did Manley Do; What Seaga Need Do', *Caribbean Review*, 10(2): 1981, pp. 4–7, 40–3.

—, *The Political Opinions of the Jamaican People* (Kingston: Jamaica Publishing House, 1982).

—, and A. Brown (eds), *Perspectives on Jamaica in the Seventies* (Kingston: Jamaica Publishing House, 1981).

—, *Essays on Power and Change in Jamaica* (Kingston: Jamaica Publishing House, 1977).

Swaby, R., 'The Rationale for State Ownership of Public Utilities in Jamaica', *Social and Economic Studies*, 30(1): 1981, pp. 75–107.

Waters, A., *Race, Class and Political Symbols: Rastafari and Reggae in Jamaican Politics* (New Brunswick, NJ: Transaction Books, 1985).

INDEX